POLITICAL INTEGRATION IN
FRENCH-SPEAKING AFRICA

Political Integration in French-Speaking Africa

ABDUL A. JALLOH

Institute of International Studies
University of California, Berkeley

Standard Book Number 0-87725-120-7
Library of Congress Catalog Card Number 73-620178
©1973 by the Regents of the University of California

Dedicated to my father

PREFACE

Independence came to most of the African territories in the late 1950's and early 1960's. It was hoped that independence would lead to the formation of political entities grouping several (or all) of the independent African states.

This hope was based on several factors. One was that the ideology of Pan-Africanism, which is built on the assumption of the political unification of the independent African states, had been adopted by several nationalist movements in Africa. Even in areas in which the Pan-African ideology was not strongly rooted, such as French-speaking West and Equatorial Africa, there were political movements advocating regional political unification. Further, in areas such as French West Africa, French Equatorial Africa, and East Africa, institutional inter-territorial links had been created by the colonial powers. Finally, there was the assumption that many small and underdeveloped African territories committed to rapid economic development would see regional political integration as an attractive solution to the problems stemming from their size and lack of development.

Numerous attempts at regional political integration have been made in Africa since the late 1950's. In this study we shall examine one such effort in detail. This effort was formalized in September 1961 with the adoption of the treaty creating the Union Africaine et Malgache. We shall be concerned with three basic questions: What level of political integration has been attained? What factors have determined the degree of political integration achieved? What direction is the movement toward political integration likely to take in the future? It is our hope that this study not only will shed light on efforts at regional political integration in Africa, but will also prove useful in refining general theories of regional political integration.

ACKNOWLEDGMENTS

This study was begun in 1966 as part of the "Studies in Regional Political Integration" of the Institute of International Studies, University of California, Berkeley. A grant from the Institute enabled me to conduct field work in Europe and Africa during parts of 1966 and 1967. Subsequently, the Institute provided both secretarial assistance and office space, without which the process of completing this study would have been considerably longer and more difficult. Grants from the Carnegie Endowment for International Peace and the International Concilium at Yale University enabled me to do further research in Africa during 1970.

Many individuals have contributed to this study. To the many persons in Europe and Africa who tolerated my questions and furnished me with documents, I want to express my gratitude. Many thanks go to Bojana Ristich for supervising the typing of the manuscript. Paul Gilchrist did an excellent job in correcting my grammar, improving my style, and helping me express my meaning more effectively. It was my good fortune to be associated with a colloquium on regional political integration at the Institute of International Studies for several years. My intellectual obligations to its participants are great. Most of all, I am greatly indebted to Ernst B. Haas for his never-ending stimulation, encouragement, and guidance. Despite all this help, responsibility for the shortcomings of this study must rest with the author.

A.A.J.

Dar es Salaam
June 1973

CONTENTS

LIST OF TABLES

Chapter 1

THE COLONIAL LEGACY

Patterns of Constitutional Change

The African colonies acquired by France in the late nineteenth century were grouped into two administrative units--the Federation of West Africa, which became a legal reality in 1904, and the Federation of Equatorial Africa, which was constituted in 1910. These two federations were to endure until the "de Gaulle" constitution of 1958, which eliminated all direct constitutional links among France's territories in West and Equatorial Africa. Except for the very early phase of French rule in tropical Africa, there were never any direct constitutional links between the Federations of West and Equatorial Africa. Similarly, the Trust Territories of Cameroun and Togo, acquired by France after World War I, were individually administered. In this chapter we shall discuss the various forms of political and economic integration achieved in French colonial Africa up to 1958, the effects of these different types of integration, and the reactions of the relevant political elites--particularly the emerging African political elites--to this integration.

It is perhaps best to begin with a consideration of the motives that led France to create the Federations of West and Equatorial Africa. In neither instance was the federation based on the pre-colonial unity of the area. To be sure, large empires and kingdoms existed in West and Equatorial Africa prior to French rule; these empires and kingdoms never embraced more than a limited part of the areas included in the federations, and control of the periphery by the center was weak. In addition, prior to or as a result of French conquest, much of the unity existing in West and Equatorial Africa was destroyed.[1] The motives underlying France's decision to create federations must be sought elsewhere.

With respect to the Federation of West Africa, one author has offered the following explanation:

---

[1] For discussions of pre-colonial unity in West and Equatorial Africa, see William J. Foltz, From French West Africa to the Mali Federation (New Haven: Yale University Press, 1965), chapter 1, and Abdul A. Jalloh, "The Politics and Economics of Regional Political Integration in Equatorial Africa" (unpublished dissertation, University of California, Berkeley, 1969), chapter 11.

1

For the French the creation of the Federation was in part an administrative convenience. It enabled them to run general overhead coordinating services more cheaply, and it satisfied the French penchant for centralized government. But it was something else too. It was a financial necessity, a pooling device aimed at relieving the French Treasury of the charge of administering the poorer territories of the area. . . . Its essential purpose was to centralize much of the revenue and expenditure of the territories. Senegal, Dahomey and Guinea would henceforth replace the French Treasury as the source of support of the Soudan (presently the Republic of Mali), Niger and other areas of the interior.[2]

Similar considerations, combined with an inclination on the part of France to pursue uniform policies with respect to her colonies in tropical Africa, led to the creation of the Federation of Equatorial Africa.[3]

The constitutional forms under which the two federations were administered during the French Third Republic were virtually identical. At the head was a governor-general residing in the federal capital (Dakar for West Africa and Brazzaville for Equatorial Africa). He was the "repository of the Republic's powers" and controlled all local civilian, judicial, and military services. Only the governor-general was empowered to correspond with the French Minister of Colonies, and with respect to the territories under his jurisdiction, he could intervene at any level. In the exercise of his functions, he was assisted by a purely advisory Council. The Council was made up of federal officials, French citizens selected by the Chamber of Commerce, and French-speaking Africans--all of whom were named by the governor-general. Each territory was headed by a lieutenant governor (the title was later changed to governor) who was "under the high authority of the Governor-General." Except for Senegal, which had a Colonial Council with quasi-legislative powers in financial matters, the lieutenant governors--like the governor-general--were assisted by purely advisory councils.

With minor modifications, this constitutional form endured until 1946. It was a highly centralized system of government which (as we shall see) was one of its main shortcomings. Another unfortunate feature was its almost complete exclusion of Africans

---

[2]Elliot J. Berg, "The Economic Basis of Political Choice in French West Africa," American Political Science Review, Vol. LIV, No. 2 (June 1960), p. 402.

[3]See Henri Ziéglé, Afrique Equatoriale Francaise (Paris: Editions Berger-Levrault, 1952), p. 174.

from the governmental process. It has been said of Equatorial
Africa during this period that "there was no democracy or representative assemblies, but a hierarchical administrative regime
supported by traditional feudalism."[4] With very minor modifications, this judgment is equally applicable to West Africa.

This governmental form was changed by the constitution
of 1946. Each territory was provided with an Assembly, the members of whom were elected in a two-college system (except for
Senegal, in which elections were based on a single college system).
Members of the first college were mostly Europeans, while most
Africans belonged to the second college. The numbers of assembly
members elected by each of the two colleges in each territory were
as follows:

French West Africa

	First College	Second College
Mauritania	6	14
Soudan	20	30
Niger	10	20
Guinea	16	24
Dahomey	12	18
Upper Volta	10	40
Ivory Coast	18	27
Senegal	50 [One college]	

French Equatorial Africa

	First College	Second College
Gabon	12	18
Moyen-Congo	12	18
Oubangui-Chari	10	15
Chad	10	20

These assemblies had legislative powers over certain matters, most
notably the territorial budgets, and had to be consulted on certain other subjects, such as loans, the organization of the territorial administrations, and public works. They could make
recommendations to their governors in some areas, but were forbidden to discuss political matters that were the exclusive province
of the administration. Executive power remained in the hands of
the territorial governor.

---

[4] Michèle Dévezé, La France d'outre-mer, de l'empire colonial à
l'Union Française 1938-1948 (Paris: Hachette, 1948), p. 72. For
a similar conclusion with respect to French West Africa, see
Foltz, pp. 19-20.

At the interterritorial level, legislative bodies--the Grand Councils--were created for each of the federations. The Grand Council in West Africa had 40 members (five from each territory), while the Grand Council in Equatorial Africa had 20 members (also five from each territory). The members of these two bodies were elected by the territorial assemblies. The Grand Councils exercised, at the federal level, all the powers exercised by the territorial assemblies at the territorial level, but they also had additional powers: they determined the subsidies to be given to the territories from the federal budget, they established fiscal duties on imports and exports, and they had to be consulted on matters affecting two or more states. As was the case at the territorial level, executive power remained in the hands of the governors-general.

The 1946 constitution also provided for representation from West and Equatorial Africa in French parliamentary bodies. The voters in West Africa elected 17 members to the French National Assembly, and indirectly elected 19 members to the Council of the Republic and 27 members to the Assembly of the French Union. The comparable figures for Equatorial Africa were 6, 8, and 7 respectively. The French parliament retained final legislative powers, of course, and the French executive had the power to legislate by decree.[5]

Two detrimental consequences for regional integration resulted from the 1946 constitution. One was that indirect election of members of the Grand Councils "put a premium on control of the territorial assembly, which in turn meant that political parties organized along territorial lines and oriented their propaganda to a specific territorial audience."[6] The other was that, given the large representation in Paris and the importance of decisions taken at the Paris level, "the most prestigious of the Grand Councillors were preoccupied with affairs on the Parisian level while the others (who were not members of French parliamentary bodies) were too few to offset the territorial legislator's drive for political influence."[7]

The next major constitutional change in French tropical Africa was introduced by the Loi Cadre of 1956.[8] It empowered

---

[5]For more details on the 1946 constitution, see Kenneth E. Robinson, "The Public Law of Overseas France since the War," Journal of Comparative Legislation, Vol. XXXII (1950).

[6]Foltz, p. 25.   [7]Ibid.

[8]For the causes and events leading to the Loi Cadre, see Ruth Schachter Morgenthau, Political Parties in French-Speaking West Africa (Oxford: Oxford University Press, 1964), pp. 61-66.

the French government to implement measures which would lead to decentralization in the territories so that the populations would be more closely involved in the management of their own affairs. The federal structures were to be transformed into "coordinating bodies." The decrees implementing the Loi Cadre granted the territorial assemblies genuine legislative powers over a wide range of significant issues, while the authority of the Grand Councils was restricted to relatively unimportant matters. Previously interterritorial services were transformed into state services, to be administered by the High Commissioner of each federation. Provision was made for executive councils at the territorial levels, but not at the federal levels. Members of the territorial assemblies were elected by universal adult suffrage, in single electoral colleges, while members of the Grand Councils continued to be elected by the territorial assemblies. Each territory was headed by a governor, subordinate to the High Commissioner, who retained great (though diminished) powers. The High Commissioner was given all executive powers. Supreme legislative power remained in the hands of the French parliament, in which the territories continued to be represented. Thus the 1956-57 constitutional reforms increased the disintegrative effects of the 1946 constitution. Political power continued to reside at the territorial level, and prestige as well as authority remained greater at the territorial and Parisian levels than at the interterritorial level.

The next stage in the process of constitutional reform--the de Gaulle constitution of 1958--led to the abolition of the Federations of West and Equatorial Africa. Each territory was to be directly linked to France in the French Community (although Article 76 provided that members of the Community could form larger groupings). No right to independence for members of the Community was included in the 1958 constitution. Control over foreign policy, defense, currency, common economic and fiscal matters, and policy on strategic raw materials was in the hands of the Community. The Community institutions were a President, who was to be the President of France, a Senate, an Executive Committee made up of the Prime Ministers of the Community, and several other lesser bodies.[9]

Like the Loi Cadre of 1956, the 1958 constitution was rapidly overtaken by events, and the French Community never amounted to much. All the territories of French West and Equatorial Africa became independent in 1960, with members of the Conseil de l'Entente refusing to remain in the Community. Only

---

[9]For details concerning the French Community, see Frédéric Dumon, La Communauté Franco-Afro-Malgache (Brussels: Université Libre de Bruxelles, 1960).

Senegal and Soudan made use of Article 76, forming the short-lived Mali Federation. The constitutional links between France and her colonies in West and Equatorial Africa were replaced by the contractual Accords de Coopération which each signed with France at the time of independence. In essence, these agreements provided for cooperation in matters of foreign policy, defense, economics, finance, and education.[10]

Thus by the end of the 1950's, France had completely reversed the policies of centralization introduced in West and Equatorial Africa around the turn of the century. In what follows, we will examine the attitudes of the relevant actors in order to show the climate of political opinion which prevailed with respect to post-independence efforts at political integration.

Independence and Unity

From the earliest days, the Federation of West Africa met with opposition, largely from European traders. It will be recalled that a main consideration for setting up the federation was to centralize revenues and expenditures and enable the richer territories to financially subsidize the poorer ones. Most of the revenue of the federal budget came from taxes on exports and imports, and thus the burden of financial support fell on the colonies with the largest exports and imports. In West Africa these were Senegal, Dahomey, and, to a lesser extent, Guinea. The creation of the federation resulted in violent anti-federal reactions in Senegal and significant unrest in Dahomey and Guinea.[11] In Equatorial Africa, on the other hand, there were no such reactions, largely because of the extreme poverty of the area. It is estimated, for example, that the total trade for Equatorial Africa in 1920 was 146 million francs, compared with 1.2 billion francs for French West Africa.[12] This meant that local revenues were very limited, and up to World War

---

[10]See Maurice Ligot, Les Accords de Coopération entre la France et les états africains et malgache d'expression française (Paris: La Documentation Francaise, 1964).

[11]Raymond D. Buell, The Native Problem in Africa (New York: Macmillan, 1928), Vol. I, p. 933.

[12]Catherine Coquery-Vidrovitch, "French Colonization in Africa to 1920: Administration and Economic Development" in L.H. Gann and Peter Duignan, eds., Colonialism in Africa, 1870-1960 (Cambridge: Cambridge University Press, 1969), Vol. I, p. 190.

II, France was forced to provide heavy financial subsidies.[13]
Thus during the initial phase, there were no <u>financial</u> grounds
for opposing the Federation of Equatorial Africa, but the high
degree of centralization and the need to refer even minor matters
to the federal government in Brazzaville led to dissatisfaction
and a call for devolution of authority in favor of the territories.

During the French Fourth Republic, objections continued
to be raised with respect to the two federations. In Equatorial
Africa, resentment against the centralization of power in Brazzaville continued--in particular, increasing resentment by the
Gabonese of the federal government's dominant position in budgetary matters on grounds identical to those raised earlier by
Senegal, Dahomey, and Guinea with respect to the Federation of
West Africa.[14] Meanwhile, the Ivory Coast had emerged as the
main provider of federal revenues in West Africa, with the result
that opposition to the Federation of West Africa had shifted
there. With respect to the ties between the territories and
France, the major preoccupation of African political leaders
between 1946 and the Loi Cadre reforms of 1956 was "to secure a
more complete identity of political rights and social benefits
with those of metropolitan France."[15] There was virtually no
call for independence from France prior to 1958. The two questions of the relations among the territories of West and Equatorial Africa and the ties between these territories and France
were the major political issues during the 1950's, and were at
the heart of the debate over the Loi Cadre.

It will be recalled that the Loi Cadre left the relations
between France and her colonies in West and Equatorial Africa
unaltered, but greatly strengthened the territorial governments
vis-à-vis the Federations of West and Equatorial Africa. One
reason that the Mollet government, "faced with a strong Communist
group on its left and the unforeseen menace of the Poujadistes
on its right, wanted at all costs to avoid the subject of constitutional reform, lest it lead to collusion of left and right
extremists capable of undermining the shaky structure of the
Fourth Republic."[16] A second reason was a change in attitude of

---

[13]See Virginia Thompson and Richard Adloff, <u>The Emerging States
of French Equatorial Africa</u> (Stanford: Stanford University Press,
1960), pp. 124-126.

[14]See René Paul Sousatte, <u>L'AEF, berceau de l'Union Francaise</u>
(Paris: Chez Brodard et Taupin, 1953), p. 62.

[15]Lord Hailey, <u>An African Survey</u> (London: Oxford University
Press, 1957), p. 214.

[16]Foltz, p. 73.

French political leaders in favor of granting greater autonomy to African political institutions.[17] (The charge was made that France was opposed to reinforcing power at the interterritorial levels for fear this would result in pressures for independence.)[18]

Political leaders in Equatorial Africa were generally greatly pleased with the Loi Cadre, which generated little dissent in the area. They took little part in the debate over the Loi Cadre in the French Assembly, and were more concerned with securing additional financial and economic aid from France and in re-organizing their civil service. Paul Chauvet, the High Commissioner of Equatorial Africa, tried to get Defferre to provide for a federal executive in Brazzaville and greater interterritorial links, but all the territorial leaders, particularly those of Gabon, were opposed to retaining or increasing the powers of the federal government.[19]

The situation was quite different in West Africa, where the Loi Cadre resulted in a great deal of controversy. The reforms were criticized for not granting the territories a more significant measure of autonomy and for weakening the interterritorial governments. This attack was led principally by Léopold Senghor of Senegal, with strong sympathy from the leaders of Soudan and Guinea, in particular. The arch-defender of the Loi Cadre, in whose elaboration he played an important role, was Félix Houphouet-Boigny of the Ivory Coast; he was supported by the leaders of Mauritania, who consistently held the attitude that they must stay away from disputes among Black Africans and avoid membership with them in federal institutions. In the remaining territories of Niger, Dahomey, and Upper Volta, African leaders were divided on the question of federation. This split among African political leaders--between federalists and territorialists, and between the partisans of independence and those who favored retention of the links with France--was to continue into the post-independence period. The latter division was acutely evident at the time of the referendum on the 1958 constitution, which permitted a choice between total independence and internal autonomy within the French Community.

---

[17] For the reasons behind this shift, see ibid., pp. 69-70.

[18] This charge is strongly made in Africanus, L'Afrique Noire devant l'indépendance (Paris: Librairie Plan, 1958). It is supported in part in Foltz, p. 75, but rejected in Edward Mortimer, France and the Africans, 1944-1960 (New York: Walker and Company, 1969), p. 239. For the reasons advanced by the French government, see the speech of Defferre in Journal Officiel, Assemblée Nationale (J.O.A.N.), Débats, March 21, 1956, p. 110.

[19] For further details, see Jalloh, pp. 91-93.

As was the case with the Loi Cadre, the 1958 referendum created few difficulties in Equatorial Africa. No major political figure advocated a "No" vote, and the only political group to campaign for independence was the Parti d'Union Nationale Gabonaise, a small splinter party in Gabon. Barthélémy Boganda, the dominant political figure in Oubangui-Chari (later changed to the Republic of Central Africa), might have advocated a "No" vote, and undoubtedly would have succeeded in carrying his territory. He did not do this because, in private conversations with de Gaulle during the latter's tour of Africa in August 1958, he persuaded de Gaulle to promise that a "Yes" vote did not imply an irreversible renunciation of independence. De Gaulle made this promise in a speech at Brazzaville, and the result was that the territories of Equatorial Africa overwhelmingly voted "Yes," with Gabon casting the largest percentage of "No" votes--8 percent.[20]

The reasons for the rejection of independence in 1958 by the leaders in Equatorial Africa are not hard to find. In part, the decision was based on considerations of domestic political control. With the exception of Boganda, "No other leader was in sufficiently sure control of his territory to risk a 'no' campaign."[21] There was also the factor of economic dependence on France, and the fear that a "No" vote would lead to the withdrawal of French economic support. In addition, there existed "a strong affection for France as an idea, and a respect for the person of General de Gaulle."[22] Finally, as noted above, there was the fact that a "Yes" vote did not close forever the possibility of independence. When independence was granted to the territories of Equatorial Africa in 1960, it was due less to the exertions of the political leaders in Equatorial Africa than to the independence of the Mali Federation and the move toward independence by the other French West African territories.

The situation surrounding the 1958 referendum was more complicated in West Africa. There was never any doubt that Mauritania and the Ivory Coast would vote "Yes" in the referendum. Mauritania, as noted earlier, had remained outside the mainstream of French West African politics, and was dependent on France for military aid against Moroccan-backed rebels. The Ivory Coast, through its leader Houphouet-Boigny, perceived greater economic rewards from direct links with France than from

---

[20]Guy de Lusignan, French-Speaking Africa since Independence (New York: Frederick A. Praeger, 1969), p. 21.

[21]Mortimer, p. 324.

[22]Ibid., p. 325.

independence. Further, Houphouet had a profound respect for and attachment to France and her universalistic ideals, as did most African leaders.[23] On the other hand, for reasons related to domestic political control, Bakary Djibo of Niger advocated a "No" vote even though there was a strong possibility that the campaign for a "No" vote would not succeed, and if it succeeded Niger would face serious economic problems as a result of the termination of French economic aid.[24] The leaders of the other territories were undecided. Guinea had the economic foundation to make a success of independence, and its leader, Sékou Touré, was strongly in favor of it. Given his strong power base, there was no doubt that Guinea would vote in the manner advocated by Touré. Yet Guinea needed French economic aid, and Touré was concerned about the economic consequences of a "No" vote. Touré said he would campaign for a "Yes" vote if the constitution provided for the right to independence, but in the end he advocated a "No" vote. Several factors accounted for this: disillusionment with the constitution and resentment at the consequences threatened by France; anger at the arrogant treatment he received from de Gaulle when the latter visited Conakry; and pressures from students, teachers, and trade unionists in favor of independence combined with the fact that the conservative opposition party advocated independence.[25]

In the remaining territories of West Africa, uncertainty as to which way to vote was even greater. In Senegal, there were strong pressures within the governing party for a "No" vote, and Senghor himself was sufficiently disillusioned with the constitution to have considered advocating such a vote. In the end, economic considerations and concern about domestic political control led to a decision for a "Yes" vote. However, this decision resulted in a split in the ruling party, and the formation of an opposition party which advocated a "No" vote.[26] The circumstances in Soudan were slightly different, in that the Union Soudanaise had a more effective control over the territory. Still, when combined with the fear of French manipulation of the elections, there was enough domestic opposition to create

---

[23]For indications of this feeling, see Houphouet's press conference as reported in West Africa, October 12, 1957.

[24]For details see Morgenthau, pp. 317-18.

[25]See Michael Crowder, "Independence as a Goal in French West African Politics: 1944-60" in William H. Lewis, ed., French-Speaking Africa: The Search for Identity (New York: Walker and Company, 1965), p. 35. [IIS Reprint Series, No. 205]

[26]For details see Foltz, pp. 93-94.

uncertainties as to the possibilities of a successful "No" campaign. Economic dependence on France was also a factor. The
result was that, in the context of a near revolt within the Union
Soudanaise, the party leadership decided for a "Yes" vote. Similar considerations of possible loss of their domestic power base
and negative economic consequences of a "No" vote resulted in
decisions for a "Yes" vote by the major leaders in Upper Volta
and Dahomey.[27]

The outcome of the referendum was a 95 percent "No" vote
in Guinea, while in Niger, in spite of the position taken by
Bakary, there was a 78 percent "Yes" vote. The remaining territories voted "Yes" in overwhelming numbers. Guinea was immediately cast out of the French Community by France, and under
pressure from Houphouet, West African leaders expelled Guinea's
Parti Démocratique de la Guinée (PDG) from the Rassemblement
Démocratique Africain (RDA). Bakary lost control of Niger to
Hamani Diori, a loyal supporter of Houphouet; he was forced to
flee the country, and his party was outlawed. In a little over
a year, however, France agreed to grant independence within the
French Community to the Mali Federation. The remaining territories in West Africa were not long in following the example of
the Mali Federation.

Debate on interterritorial links followed similar lines
as those concerning ties with France. In Equatorial Africa,
Boganda of the Central African Republic was the major advocate
of political unification. He wanted to create a United States
of Latin Africa, with a unitary form of government, consisting
of the territories of Equatorial Africa, Cameroun, Angola, and
the then Belgian Congo. His plan was based on ideological convictions about the desirability of political unity, the expectation that he would be the dominant figure in any political
grouping, and the hope that his country would benefit economically. When Boganda died in March 1959, his successor, David Dacko,
continued advocating political unity in Equatorial Africa as part
of an attempt to wear the mantle of Boganda.

There was little enthusiasm for Boganda's scheme among
the other territories of Equatorial Africa, with Gabon its
strongest opponent. Gabon felt that its riches had been used
to finance the economic development of the other territories,
particularly the Congo, and wanted to halt the practice. A further consideration was that, given its small size, Gabon would
be dominated in any political union. With respect to Chad, the

---

[27]For an excellent detailed treatment of the economic considerations that influenced the decisions of the West African leaders,
see Berg, pp. 391-405.

major political figure at the time was Gabriel Lisette, and he had a relatively free hand in determining Chad's position on the question of federation. Lisette, who was a lieutenant of Houphouet, went along with the latter's opposition to political unity. Many of the leaders who came to power in Chad after the fall of Lisette's government in 1959 were far from enthusiastic about political unification of the area because of resentment over earlier control from Brazzaville and the hope that Chad would do better economically if it was not part of a larger political grouping. However, most of them desired some kind of economic link with the other territories of Equatorial Africa because Chad's geographic position made it dependent on these other territories. The leaders of the Congo were virtually unanimous in favoring close cooperation with the other territories of Equatorial Africa, recognizing that the Congo was economically dependent on them. There were differences among Congolese leaders over acceptance of Boganda's scheme, however. Fulbert Youlou opposed it because he had a scheme of his own which would unite the Bakongo people, and because he himself wanted to be the leader of any political union and was afraid that, given his insecure position in the Congo, his leadership ambitions would not be realized. Jacques Opangault and Jean Félix Tchicaya, Youlou's rivals in the Congo, were sympathetic to Boganda's plan--in part as the result of ideological convictions and in part as a means of weakening the position of Youlou.[28]

Given the varied attitudes toward political federation in Equatorial Africa, it is not surprising that when delegates from these territories met in Paris in December 1959, all they were able to agree upon was the establishment of a customs union and a common administration for common services such as transport and post and telecommunications. When the prospect of independence for the territories of Equatorial Africa arose in December 1959, the issue of political unity in Equatorial Africa emerged once again. Gabon's opposition remained unaltered, but the remaining territories went so far as to sign and ratify a charter creating the Union of Central African Republics.

There were several reasons for the shifts in attitudes. Youlou was now more secure in the Congo, and with the death of Boganda, he felt that his chances of leading the Union were improved. In Chad, Francois Tombalbaye had replaced Lisette as leader; his domestic control was weak, confronted as he was by subversive elements which enjoyed support from the Arab countries, and his hope was that Chad would gain economically from political unification and his domestic position would be strengthened. Dacko maintained his preference for unity.

---

[28] For a more detailed account of the debate over political unity in Equatorial Africa, see Jalloh, Chapter V.

In July 1960, however, the prospects for political unification dimmed with indications that Youlou was going to withdraw the Congo from the Union. Youlou was apparently motivated
by the fact that with the independence of the Democratic Republic
of the Congo, Joseph Kasavubu, as head of an independent state,
would replace him as the potential leader of the Bakongo people.
Further, with Gabon outside the Union, Youlou felt that the economic costs to the Congo would be greater than the rewards. Chad
and Central Africa gave some thought to forming a separate union.
However, the collapse of the Mali Federation in August 1960 convinced the Chad leaders in particular of the instability of
political unions made up of only two states. Further, little
economic advantage was seen as resulting from such a union.
With the failure of the effort to form a union between Chad and
Central Africa, the states of Equatorial Africa acquired their
independence individually and turned their attention to problems
of nation-building and regional economic cooperation.

In French West Africa, for reasons noted earlier, Mauritania and the Ivory Coast continued their opposition to political
unity during the second half of the 1950's. They were now joined
by Niger, under the leadership of Houphouet's ally Hamani Diori.
Senegal under Senghor continued to be a strong advocate of political union, as did Guinea under Touré and Soudan under Keita.
The leaders of these three states were motivated by ideological
convictions about the desirability of African unity, combined
with expectations of economic rewards; the latter played a more
important role for the leaders of Senegal while the former was
of paramount interest for the leaders of Guinea and Soudan.
Dahomey and Upper Volta were divided on the question because of
conflicting political, economic, and cultural pulls from neighboring territories.[29] After a great deal of political maneuver-
ing, Senegal, Soudan, Upper Volta, and Dahomey decided on the
creation of the Mali Federation in January 1959.[30] Guinea, having
been ruled out of the French Community and the French West African
Community, was not invited to participate.

As was the case in Equatorial Africa, this attempt at
political unity in French West Africa ended in failure. A combination of pressures from the Ivory Coast and France caused Dahomey
and Upper Volta to withdraw from the federation, and the remaining
political union between Senegal and Soudan ended in August 1960
when the leaders of Senegal became convinced that its continuation
threatened their domestic political base.

---

[29]For detailed treatment of these tensions, see Morgenthau, pp.
315-321.

[30]See Foltz, pp. 97-102.

POLITICAL INTEGRATION IN FRENCH-SPEAKING AFRICA

If support for the idea of a political union in French West Africa was uncertain, there was widespread interest in and support for the idea of economic cooperation. This was exploited by Houphouet in his effort to draw support from the advocates of political union. In early December 1958, he advocated the creation of a loose Conseil de l'Entente whose task would be the promotion of economic harmonization among its members. Upper Volta, Niger, and Dahomey accepted his invitation, and the Conseil de l'Entente held its first meeting at Abidjan in May 1959. On June 9, 1959, all members of the former Federation of West Africa (again with the exception of Guinea) signed an agreement creating a Customs Union among them. Thus, with the failure of the Mali Federation, the Conseil de l'Entente and the Customs Union became the vehicles for interstate cooperation in French West Africa.

The political debate among the leaders of West and Equatorial Africa on the questions of independence and regional political unification during the second half of the 1950's can be summarized as follows: There was a growing desire for independence, but with the exception of Guinea and Niger (during the time of Bakary), it was outweighed by economic considerations and fear of the possible loss of domestic political control. There was widespread support for loose forms of economic cooperation, but with the exception of a few countries, proposals for interterritorial political unions did not enjoy widespread or enthusiastic support.

Before proceeding to other matters, we should look briefly at French attitudes toward cooperation in West and Equatorial Africa. It will be recalled that France had weakened the interterritorial governments in 1956 and abolished them completely in 1958. Further, France was in part responsible for the withdrawal of Dahomey and Upper Volta from the Mali Federation. There is no evidence that France was responsible for the subsequent failure of the Mali Federation or of the Union of Central African Republics, but it is clear that France made no effort to save either scheme. The situation was different with respect to economic cooperation, however, which was encouraged by France--particularly in Equatorial Africa. Thus, while political unification met with hostility or indifference from France, economic cooperation was encouraged.

Interterritorial Movements

Given the constitutional links among the French West and Equatorial African territories and France, it was inevitable that trans-territorial movements would develop. Prior to World War II and during most of the 1940's, metropolitan parties were active in West and Equatorial Africa. Only under the Fourth Republic did autonomous African political parties develop to a significant degree. The need to coordinate their activities in Paris led to the development of interterritorial links among them. This started during the constitutional conventions of 1945-1946 when the Africans created the Bloc Africain headed by Lamine Gueye of Senegal. The Bloc Africain was closely identified with the French Socialist Party (SFIO), however, because Gueye was head of the Senegalese branch of the SFIO and occupied an important position in the party.

The first truly African interterritorial party was the Rassemblement Démocratique Africain (RDA). The RDA was formed at Bamako in October 1946 to counteract the growing conservative reaction in France. It was to have one branch in each territory, and the territorial branches were to be autonomous within the framework established by the RDA. Interterritorial coordination was the responsibility of a Coordinating Committee meeting in Paris; provision was made for a propaganda office in Dakar, a financial center in Abidjan, and a party newspaper. In its early years, the RDA had links with the French Communist Party, but through the efforts of Houphouet, these were broken in 1950.[31]

The Bamako Congress of 1946 had been called by all the second college representatives from tropical Africa to the French constituent assemblies. Opposition from the French government prevented Gueye and Senghor of Senegal and Yacine Diallo of Guinea from attending, however. Fily Dabo Sissoko of Soudan attended but dissociated himself from the RDA soon after. The withdrawal of such prominent leaders, coupled with administrative repression, made the early years of the RDA very bleak ones. In fact, "prior to 1956, the Ivory Coast section of the RDA was the only solidly implanted party associated with the interterritorial RDA."[32] Until the mid-1950's, Houphouet was the dominant figure within the RDA.

The fortunes of the RDA improved, and by 1957 it had emerged as a truly all-French Black African party. In elections for the territorial assemblies in March of that year, the RDA secured overwhelming majorities in the Ivory Coast, Guinea, Soudan, and Chad, bare majorities in Upper Volta, Gabon, and the Congo, and respectable minorities in Niger and Dahomey. In Senegal, Mauritania, and Oubangui-Chari, the RDA was virtually nonexistent. The electoral victories of the RDA did not increase

---

[31]For details about the RDA-Communist linkage and the reasons for the break, see Virginia Thompson and Richard Adloff, French West Africa (Stanford: Stanford University Press, 1958), pp. 85-92.

[32]Morgenthau, p. 306.

15

its cohesion, however; in fact, the opposite was the case. By the mid-1950's, Ivory Coast domination of the RDA was increasingly challenged by a secondary locus of power made up of Guinea and Soudan.

The split within the RDA was due in large part to differences over the key questions of independence and regional unity, but rivalry for leadership and prestige also played a role. The RDA Coordinating Committee was not called upon to attempt to resolve these conflicts. In fact, from the early 1950's, the functions of the Coordinating Committee were performed for the most part by an informal caucus of RDA members of French parliamentary bodies. The outcome of this was that "the primary instrument of RDA unity functioned less within a purely African context than in the context of French Union politics."[33] An RDA conference was held at Bamako in September 1957 to heal the split in the ranks, and after a great deal of behind-the-scenes fighting, the conference endorsed the Touré position for African unity. Little was to come of this, however, and a subsequent meeting of the RDA Coordinating Committee at Paris in April 1958 merely agreed to leave to the individual territories the problem of deciding on regional political unity. By the end of 1958, the RDA, as an interterritorial party capable of making joint and binding decisions, had ceased to exist.

While the RDA was the most important interterritorial party, it was not the only one. Some of the leaders who had refused membership in the RDA in 1946 formed the Indépendants d'Outre-Mer (IOM) in 1948. Initially, the IOM was strictly a parliamentary group made up of Africans in French assemblies, but there were efforts in 1953 to make it into an extra-parliamentary movement similar to the RDA. The IOM was created largely through the initiative of the French Mouvement Républicain Populaire (MRP), with Senghor's Bloc Démocratique Sénégalais (BDS) as its dominant member: "Only the participation of the BDS leaders in the IOM gave it weight or distinction; for the BDS was the only broadly backed, soundly constructed party associated with the IOM."[34] The fact that the Parti Démocratique de la Côte d'Ivoire (PDCI) was at the time the key group in the RDA meant, therefore, that the IOM-RDA rivalry took on the overtones of a Senegal-Ivory Coast rivalry for leadership. In contrast to the RDA, the early years of the IOM were bright, and in the 1951 elections for the French National Assembly, it emerged a great deal stronger than the RDA. In the elections of 1956 and 1957, however, the IOM suffered considerable losses to the RDA.

---

[33]Foltz, p. 55.

[34]Morgenthau, p. 306.

Meanwhile there was growing interest in a common African political movement on the part of young intellectuals in West Africa, which led to efforts to create a single all-embracing movement. These efforts failed, however, because the RDA wanted to absorb the other groups, while the other groups insisted on amalgamation based on equality. The result of these maneuvers was the formation of the Convention Africaine at Dakar in January 1957. Other than the name, the only difference between the IOM and the Convention Africaine was that the latter was to be an extra-parliamentary party with structures for unified decision-making at the interterritorial level. This did not improve the fortunes of the group, however. In the March 1957 territorial elections, the Convention Africaine did well only in Senegal and Gabon, securing an overwhelming number of seats in the former and about half the seats in the latter. Further efforts at the unification of political parties led to the fusion of the Convention Africaine and the Mouvement Socialiste Africain (MSA) into the Parti du Regroupement Africain (PRA) in February 1958, with the RDA continuing to go it alone. The PRA was split over the issue of the 1958 referendum, with Senegal and Niger--its two dominant sections--adopting opposing policies. Like the RDA, the PRA came to an end in 1958.

Two other interterritorial parties should be noted. One was the MSA, founded in February 1957. It was founded by African members of the SFIO because of grass-roots pressures for a break in the ties to French political parties. Unlike the RDA and the Convention Africaine, the MSA never aspired to centralized interterritorial decision-making. Lamine Gueye (Senegal) was the leading figure in the MSA, but only in Niger was it in control of the government--because of Djibo Bakary's decision to change his affiliation from the RDA to the MSA. In the 1957 elections for the territorial assembly, the MSA won nearly half the seats in the Congo but occupied a minority position in the remaining territories. As noted above, the MSA became part of the PRA in February 1958.

The last of the interterritorial parties was the Mouvement pour l'Evolution Sociale de l'Afrique Noire (MESAN); it was created by Boganda in 1952 after leaving the MRP. As one study has noted, "Since 1952 the political history of Oubangui has been almost wholly that of MESAN, and MESAN meant Boganda."[35] After the March 1957 territorial elections, in an attempt to capture political leadership in Equatorial Africa, Boganda sought to create MESAN branches in Chad and the Congo, but met with little success. There was never any attempt to extend the influence of MESAN into French West Africa, and despite his ambitions, MESAN

---

[35] Thompson and Adloff, French Equatorial Africa, p. 392.

17

remained the personal instrument of one man whose influence was limited to a single territory.

This survey of interterritorial political movements has brought out several points. Except for MESAN, their center was in West Africa, and until the second half of the 1950's, competition between them was essentially a Senegal-Ivory Coast or Senghor-Houphouet competition for leadership. Efforts at creating a single interterritorial movement met with failure, with the competing interterritorial movements becoming increasingly fragmented in the second half of the 1950's and finally disintegrating by the 1960's. This process of disintegration was the result of competition for prestige and ideological differences over basic constitutional issues that arose in large part because of decisions made by France. Given the weak centralized decision-making structures of these movements, the capacity to reconcile these differences was very limited. Thus, as was the case with respect to constitutional links, relations among political parties in French-speaking tropical Africa reveal a shift from a high level of integration in the late 1940's to a low level of integration in the late 1950's. Finally, as was the case in the debates over regional political unification, Mauritania remained aloof from interterritorial political parties.

Interterritorial links among the territories of French tropical Africa extended beyond the political sector and political groups. Prior to 1955, most trade unions were branches of either the French Confédération Générale du Travail (CGT) or the Confédération Française des Travailleurs Chrétiens (CFTC). Efforts by Sékou Touré led to a break with the CGT in 1955 and the formation of the Confédération Générale des Travailleurs Africains (CGTA); and in 1956, the Catholic trade unions in French tropical Africa organized an autonomous Confédération Africaine des Travailleurs Croyants (CATC). A unity conference at Cotonou in January 1957 brought together representatives of the CGTA and the CATC and resulted in the formation of the Union Générale des Travailleurs de l'Afrique Noire (UGTAN), which enjoyed the support of a large majority of the African trade unions. Along similar lines, disaffiliation with French organizations led to unity among youth groups at the Abidjan conference of October 1957 and the creation of the Conseil de la Jeunesse d'Afrique (CJA). Meanwhile, the Fédération des Etudiants d'Afrique Noire en France (FEANF), the Paris-based student organization which was created at the time of the RDA split with the Communist party, remained very active. The main problem in the interterritorial links among trade unions and youth groups was that the structures for regional coordination were very weak. With the move to autonomy and independence, trade unions and youth groups, like political parties, became increasingly territorialized.

We have already had occasion to note that African membership in French parliamentary bodies created a need among the Africans to work out common positions. A consequence of this and the existence of the Grand Councils and interterritorial movements was that leaders in French tropical Africa enjoyed common experiences, got to know each other, and developed personal ties. This tendency was reinforced by attendance at common educational institutions, of which the most important was the Ecole Normale William-Ponty in Senegal: "At Ponty the student body built up connections which transcended territorial or ethnic boundaries. They mastered the French language and learned to evaluate European ideas. They conceived of themselves as Africans rather than as Ivory Coasters or Baulé tribesmen."[36] Other institutions which furthered social integration among the elites of French tropical Africa were educational institutions in France, the federal civil services, the African Corps of the French Army, and the veterans organizations.[37] Thus at the time of independence, there was a high degree of elite integration in French-speaking tropical Africa.

Economic Integration

As indicated above, the decision to vote "Yes" in the 1958 referendum was largely a result of economic dependence on France. A few figures will reveal the extent of this dependence.[38] In 1953, 70 percent of the exports and 68 percent of the imports of French West Africa were to and from France. Comparable figures for 1957 were 69 percent and 62 percent respectively. For Equatorial Africa, the figures for 1953 were 67 percent and 58 percent respectively, while for 1957 they were 61 percent and 60 percent respectively.[39] On the other hand, trade with French West and Equatorial Africa constituted only a small part of French commerce. In 1957, about 5 percent of French exports went to French West Africa and about one percent went to Equatorial Africa. Percentages for imports were about 4 percent and one percent respectively.[40] Finally, the territories of

---

[36] Thomas Hodgkin and Ruth Schachter, "French-Speaking West Africa in Transition," _International Conciliation_, No. 528 (May 1960), p. 385.

[37] See Foltz, p. 21.

[38] For detailed treatment of this point see Berg, pp. 394-399, and de Lusignan, pp. 70-75.

[39] France, Secrétariat Général du Comité Monétaire de la Zone Franc, _La Zone Franc en 1957_, pp. 79-82.

[40] Calculations based on figures in _ibid._, p. 235.

French West and Equatorial Africa consistently experienced large trade deficits with France, financed by the French treasury. For West Africa, this deficit was 10,334 million French francs in 1953 and 11,909 million French francs in 1957. The figures for Equatorial Africa were 3,661 million French francs in 1953 and 12,673 million French francs in 1957.[41]

Another aspect of the economic dependence on France relates to the flow of capital to French West and Equatorial Africa. Official French aid to West and Equatorial Africa is manifold and constitutes a study in itself; only a few indicative figures will be presented here.[42] At the end of World War II, France decided to make a major effort to further the economic development of her colonies. A key agency in accomplishing this goal was the Fonds d'Investissement pour le Développement Economique et Social (FIDES), created in 1946. About 90 percent of FIDES funds came from France, with the territories providing the rest. In fact, the territorial contributions were paid with funds advanced to them by the Caisse Centrale de la France d'Outre-Mer (CCFOM), which had been created during the war. There were two sections to FIDES: the General Section provided grants for projects affecting all or more than one of the territories, while the Overseas Section provided grants or loans (1.5 percent interest repayable in 25 years) for basic territorial expenditures such as transportation, schools, hospitals, housing, and power. FIDES appropriations were made by the Executive Committee, consisting of French parliamentarians and government representatives under the chairmanship of the Minister of Overseas France. Projects were proposed to the Executive Committee by the individual territories, or groups of territories, after approval by the territorial assemblies. From 1947-1958 the General Section made investments of $305 million (U.S. dollars), and it is estimated that about 45 percent of this benefitted French West Africa while about 20 percent benefitted Equatorial Africa.[43] Table 1 provides details on funds from the Overseas Section of FIDES to the individual territories in West and Equatorial Africa.

---

[41]Ibid., pp. 247 and 253.

[42]The most comprehensive work on this subject is Teresa Hayter, French Aid (London: The Overseas Development Institute Ltd., 1966).

[43]The figure of $305 million is in Ambassade de France--Service de Presse et d'Information, New York, French Africa: A Decade of Progress, 1948-1958 (New York, November 1958), p. 7. The estimate was provided by an official in the French Ministère de la Coopération.

Table 1

PUBLIC INVESTMENT THROUGH FIDES: 1947-1957

(in U$S millions)

Country	Amount	Percent
Senegal	140.5	17.8%
Guinea	78.7	9.9
Ivory Coast	109.0	13.8
Niger	25.2	3.1
Mauritania	15.1	1.9
Dahomey	49.9	6.3
Soudan	79.4	10.0
Upper Volta	44.7	5.6
West Africa	(542.5)	(68.4)
Congo	91.0	11.5
Gabon	49.6	6.2
Chad	55.8	7.6
Central Africa	50.4	6.3
Equatorial Africa	(246.8)	(31.6)
TOTAL	789.3	100.0

Source: Ambassade de France--Service de Presse et d'Information, New York, French Africa: A Decade of Progress, 1948-1958 (New York, 1958), p. 7.

If the $198.3 million that is estimated to have been spent by the General Section for the benefit of French West and Equatorial Africa is added to the figures in Table 1, we obtain total expenditures of $987.6 million during a ten-year period. The magnitude of this aid can be better appreciated if it is noted that the current and capital expenditures (including capital expenditures by the federations on behalf of individual territories) for all 12 countries in Table 1 amounted to $226.2 million in 1956.[44]   And FIDES was not the only aid-granting institution.   Substantial loans were made by CCFOM, and civil

[44]Calculations based on ibid., pp. 16-27 and 34-39.

and military administrative expenditures were paid by France. A third aspect of economic dependence on France was heavy subsidies granted to exports from French West and Equatorial Africa in the French market; these subsidies sometimes ran as high as 20 percent.[45]

Further, a large number of French men were employed in the public and private sectors. In 1957, for example, 24,000 of the 487,000 wage earners in the public and private sectors in French West Africa were French. The figures for Equatorial Africa in the same year were 8,000 French in a wage-earning population of 189,000.[46] Only a few of these French men were in genuinely high-level administrative or technical positions, but Africans were for the most part excluded from high-level administrative positions in both the public and the private sectors. Thus as one student has concluded, "Between 1946 and 1958 Africans in French West Africa (and equally so in French Equatorial Africa) secured political power within their territories. But the apparatus of government and the administration of private economic activity remained in the hands of Europeans."[47] Students from the two federations who went overseas for higher education for the most part went to France. In 1957-58, there were 1,612 students from French West Africa and 221 from Equatorial Africa who had scholarships in France.

The final aspect of the links between France and her territories in West and Equatorial Africa that will be noted relates to monetary connections. All twelve countries were part of the franc zone, and their local currencies were the CFA franc issued by the Banque Centrale des Etats de l'Afrique de l'Ouest (BCEAO) and the Banque Centrale des Etats de l'Afrique Equatoriale et du Cameroun (BCEAEC). Prior to independence, half the members of the Board of Directors (including the Managing Director of each bank) were representatives of France; this meant that France effectively controlled the monetary policies of the territories.[48] The payoff for the territories was that the CFA franc enjoyed guarantee of parity with and convertibility to the French franc.

---

[45] See La Zone Franc en 1957, pp. 26-40.

[46] France, Service des Statistiques d'Outre-Mer, Outre-Mer, 1958, pp. 210-211.

[47] Berg, p. 398.

[48] For the evolution and workings of the BCEAO and the BCEAEC, see Michel Leduc, Les Institutions monétaires africaines: Pays francophones (Paris: Editions A. Pedone, 1965).

It is clear that the economies of French West and Equatorial Africa formed an integral part of the economy of France. Given the disparities in levels of economic development, this dependence was asymmetrical. Further, the links with France were of such a nature as to be detrimental to the development of economic interdependence within the Federations of West and Equatorial Africa.[49] In what follows, we will examine the degree of economic interdependence that emerged in these federations.

However, before proceeding with an examination of the degree of economic interdependence among the territories of French West and Equatorial Africa during the colonial period, a brief look at the transportation facilities is necessary. In both federations, transportation links connected the main ports of the coastal states (Dakar in Senegal, Conakry in Guinea, Abidjan in the Ivory Coast, Cotonou in Dahomey, and Pointe Noire in the Congo) with the territories of the interior, but transportation links among the interior states were very few, which was reflected in the economic transactions among them.

Measures of interterritorial trade in French West Africa (FWA) and French Equatorial Africa (FEA) are crude measures, and must be regarded as merely suggestive. Unrecorded frontier trade and fraudulent trade are sources of error, and statistical services are poorly developed. Further, in the case of FEA, interterritorial trade went unrecorded until recently. With these cautionary statements in mind, it is still useful to examine the degrees of economic interdependence indicated by trade figures in FWA and FEA.

On the basis of calculations made by Foltz, in 1956 there were three sets of intensive trading relationships in FWA.[50] These were Senegal, Mauritania, and Soudan; the Ivory Coast and Upper Volta; and Dahomey and Niger. Guinea's trade relationships were almost exclusively with the outside world. A comparison of each country's trade with all of FWA with its trade with third parties for the same year reveals that the trading preferences of Dahomey, Guinea, and the Ivory Coast were with the rest of the world, while the trading preferences of Upper Volta, Soudan, and possibly Niger were with FWA. Senegal was oriented toward FWA with respect to exports but to the outside world with respect to imports. (Mauritania was excluded from this analysis because of its limited trade.) Significantly, with the exception of

---

[49] For this conclusion with respect to West Africa, see Foltz, p. 39. It is clear that this situation was equally true for West Africa.

[50] See Foltz, pp. 42-45; also Berg, pp. 400-401.

Senegal in the case of exports, all the coastal states had weak trade links with FWA, while the opposite was true for the hinterland states. It should be noted that even this degree of trade interdependence is exaggerated, in that trade between coastal and hinterland states was largely transit trade, due to the dependence of the latter on the ports of the former. Trade among the coastal states in 1956 was very small. Less than 10 percent of Senegal's total exports went to the coastal states, and only about 2 percent of its exports came from them. The respective figures for the Ivory Coast are 2 percent and 10 percent, while those for Guinea are less than 2 percent and about 20 percent respectively.[51] Thus it is clear that nothing close to a national economy developed in FWA.

The trade picture in FEA is not much different from that which obtained in FWA. Table 2 provides data on foreign and intra-regional trade in FEA. The figures in Table 2 indicate the following percentages of regional exports to total exports: Congo = 24.4 percent; Gabon = 0.7 percent; Central Africa = 11.5 percent; Chad = 9.0 percent; FEA = 8.9 percent. The percentages for imports are as follows: Congo = 2.5 percent; Gabon = 3.3 percent; Central Africa = 11.7 percent; Chad = 12.7 percent; FEA = 6.4 percent. Clearly, Gabon was hardly a member of the

Table 2

FRENCH EQUATORIAL AFRICA: FOREIGN AND REGIONAL TRADE, 1958

(in million CFA francs)

Country	Exports			Imports		
	FEA	World	Total	FEA	World	Total
Congo	951	2,948	3,899	309	12,137	12,446
Gabon	56	8,370	8,426	245	7,281	7,526
Central Africa	443	3,398	3,841	540	4,058	4,598
Chad	514	5,172	5,686	870	5,983	6,853
TOTAL	1,964	19,888	21,852	1,964	29,459	31,423

Sources: France, Service des Statistiques d'Outre-Mer, Outre-Mer, 1958, and Bureau Central de la Statistique et de la Mécanographie, Etudes Economiques, No. 7 (Brazzaville, 1958).

[51]Berg, p. 401.

economy of FEA, and the Congo was part of the economy of FEA only with respect to its exports. As was the case in FWA, only the interior states of Central Africa and Chad conducted much trade within the region. Thus FEA, like FWA, failed to develop a national economy.

Given the weak trade links within FWA and FEA, it is hardly surprising that trade between the two regions never amounted to much. In 1956, FWA exported goods valued at $343 million, but only $2 million or 0.6 percent went to FEA. In the same year, FWA had a total of $381 million in imports, but only $0.4 million or 0.1 percent came from FEA. Figures for FEA in the same year are as follows: total exports = $79 million; exports to FWA = $0.4 million or 0.5 percent; total imports = $117 million; imports from FWA = $2.0 million or 1.7 percent.[52] Thus trade links between the two regions were far less than those within the regions.

A second feature of economic integration is interterritorial movement of labor. Figures on this subject are even less accurate than those concerning trade. Table 3 provides some "approximate" figures. From the data in Table 3, FEA appears not to have been heavily dependent on foreign African labor, while the Ivory Coast, Mauritania, and Senegal in West Africa appear to have been heavily dependent on foreign African labor. In FEA the coastal states of Gabon and the Congo took in more foreign African labor than the hinterland states; similarly, only the coastal states in FWA were significant importers of African labor.

Unfortunately, it is impossible to determine the precise origins of foreign African labor in FEA and FWA. It is known that in FEA the territories of Gabon and the Congo lacked enough manpower for their mining and forestry industries. Workers for these industries had to be recruited from Nigeria and the hinterland states of Chad and Central Africa. Recruitment from these territories was opposed by the British government and the territorial assemblies of Chad and, particularly, Central Africa. Thus in the early 1950's, a complicated arrangement had to be worked out whereby Chadians would be recruited to work in Central Africa and an equal number of Central Africans would be sent to work in Gabon and the Congo.[53] Thus it seems that the net flow of labor migration within FEA was from Chad to Central Africa

---

[52]United Nations Department of Economic and Social Affairs, Economic Developments in Africa, 1956-1957 (CE/3117/5T/ECA/56), pp. 31 and 48.

[53]Thompson and Adloff, French Equatorial Africa, pp. 258-259.

Table 3

AFRICAN WAGE EARNERS IN THE PUBLIC AND PRIVATE SECTORS: 1957

(in thousands)

Country	Total African	Local African	Other African	
Senegal	89.7	78.5	11.2	(12.5%)
Soudan	34.8	34.8	--	(0%)
Mauritania	4.5	2.8	1.7	(37.8%)
Guinea	106.4	105.2	1.2	(1.1%)
Ivory Coast	164.0	62.4	101.6	(62.0%)
Upper Volta	23.3	23.3	--	(0%)
Dahomey	18.6	18.4	0.2	(1.1%)
Niger	12.2	7.9	4.3	(35.2%)
Gabon	39.4	36.9	2.5	(6.3%)
Congo	60.8	57.4	3.4	(5.6%)
Central Africa	46.8	44.4	2.4	(5.1%)
Chad	33.1	31.8	1.3	(3.9%)

Source: France, Service des Statistiques d'Outre-Mer, Outre-Mer, 1958, pp. 210-211.

and from Central Africa to Gabon and the Congo. Outside of the federation, there was significant labor migration from the Congo to the then Belgian Congo and between Chad and Sudan. There was no outflow of labor from Gabon.

Our knowledge of labor migration in FWA is a little better than that concerning labor migration in FEA. In FWA, most of the labor migrants came from Upper Volta and went to the Ivory Coast and Niger. It is estimated, for example, that around the late 1950's, there were about 300,000 workers from Upper Volta in the Ivory Coast.[54] There was also a substantial amount

---

[54]Aristide R. Zolberg, One-Party Government in the Ivory Coast (Princeton: Princeton University Press, 1969), p. 41. Undoubtedly the figure of 300,000 refers to more than wage earners. The population of the Ivory Coast is estimated at 2.5 million in 1956.

of labor migration from Upper Volta to Niger.[55] The second main
source of labor migration in FWA was Soudan. According to Foltz,
the seasonal migration from Soudan was between 30 and 40 thousand,
two-thirds of whom went to Senegal and most of the others to the
Ivory Coast. There was also some labor movement from Guinea to
Senegal and the Ivory Coast.[56] Finally, though precise figures
are unavailable, there was a movement of government officials
and clerks from Senegal and Dahomey to territories in French-
speaking Africa.

These data on labor migration indicate that, like trade,
labor flowed from the hinterland states to the coastal states,
thus accentuating the imbalance in transaction between the two.
Also, the trade blocs in FWA seem to have been reinforced by patterns of labor migration, making the area even more fragmented.
We will show further in a subsequent chapter that labor migra-
tions in FWA and FEA tended to be disintegrative rather than
integrative.

A third aspect of economic integration that should be examined is the role of the interterritorial governments in centralized economic development planning and the redistribution of
resources. The development role has already been touched upon in
our discussion of FIDES. It will be recalled that between 1947
and 1957, FIDES gave $542.5 million to the individual territories
of FWA and $246.8 million to those of FEA (see Table 1). During
the same period, FIDES made grants estimated at $137.25 million
to FWA as a group and $61.00 million to FEA as a group (see foot-
note 43). These figures make it clear that development planning
was territorial rather than interterritorial in nature. The
secondary role of the interterritorial governments can also be
seen by looking at the investment budgets of the territorial and
interterritorial governments (Table 4). The figures in Table 4
greatly exaggerate the role of the interterritorial governments
in development planning, particularly for FEA, in that most of
the investment funds listed for the interterritorial governments
were in fact FIDES funds. In 1958, this amounted to 2.1 billion
CFA for FWA and 1.3 billion CFA for FEA. On the other hand, only
0.83 billion CFA of the investments made by the FWA territories
came from France, and none for those in FEA.[57]

It will be recalled that FIDES was managed wholly by
France in liaison with individual territories. Projects submitted to FIDES by the interterritorial governments needed the
approval of the territorial assemblies. This, coupled with the

---

[55]See Foltz, p. 46.

[56]Ibid.

[57]La Zone Franc en 1959, pp. 89-91.

Table 4

GROUP REVENUES OF GENERAL AND TERRITORIAL
INVESTMENT BUDGETS

(in million CFA)

	1953	1954	1955	1956	1957	1958
FWA Group	8,800	10,295	7,132	4,371	5,120	2,760
FWA Territories	2,603	2,259	2,540	2,213	2,610	5,049
FEA Group	2,875	2,637	2,671	2,196	2,205	1,547
FEA Territories	111	1.5	144	58.3	145	165

Source: France, Service des Statistiques d'Outre-Mer, Outre-Mer, 1958, pp. 558-559.

financial figures presented in Table 4, indicates that the role of the interterritorial governments in promoting economic develop ment was a minor one. Further, as the figures in Table 4 show, the role of the interterritorial governments in this area became progressively less important, particularly in FWA, as independenc approached.

Another indication of the declining role of the interter- ritorial governments can be seen by comparing the total budgets of the interterritorial governments with those of the territories In 1954, the total budget (investment and working) of the Federa- tion of West Africa was 30,940 million CFA, while for all the territories of FWA, the budget was 22,259 million CFA. The comparable figures for FEA were 7,969 million CFA and 5,084 million CFA. By 1958, the situation had changed radically. In that year, the budget of the Federation of West Africa was 30,708 million CFA while that for the territories was 49,075 million CFA. For Equatorial Africa, the figures were 6,748 million CFA and 8,536 million CFA respectively.[58] Further, the interterri- torial government in FWA returned 11,400 million CFA to the ter- ritories as rebates while the government of FEA returned 2,260 million CFA.[59] Thus as independence approached, the interterri- torial governments lost their abilities to affect the economies of their areas to the individual territories.

---

[58] France, Outre-Mer, 1958, pp. 558-559.

[59] La Zone Franc en 1959, pp. 89-91.

The reason for the change in status of the territorial governments is not hard to find. It will be recalled that the two federations had been created as an economy measure and, in the case of FWA, to get the richer territories to subsidize the poorer territories. This was done by granting the most important revenue receipts to the regional governments. Until the Loi Cadre, the interterritorial governments collected all indirect taxes, the most important of which were import and export duties. This meant that the countries with the largest foreign trade supported those with less foreign trade. In FWA, prior to World War II, this meant Senegal, Dahomey, and Guinea. During the postwar period, the Ivory Coast emerged as one of the leading contributors to the federal budget. In 1954, per capita contribution to the federal budget was as shown in Table 5. Senegal found no cause for resentment in its large contribution. Since Dakar was the seat of the federation, Senegal received substantial economic rewards in return. This was not the case for the Ivory Coast, whose leaders resented having to subsidize the other countries. It was this consideration that led the Ivory Coast to push for greater devolution of power to the territorial governments and the weakening of the interterritorial governments. The demands of the Ivory Coast leaders were satisfied in the Loi Cadre. These reforms weakened the interterritorial governments in the political sector. In the economic sector, these governments were weakened in two ways: (1) their sources of revenue were limited to all import and only half of export taxes, plus royalties on exported minerals and oils; (2) they could spend funds only on federal activities, and had to make the remaining funds available as grants to the territorial governments.

Table 5

PER CAPITA CONTRIBUTIONS TO THE BUDGET OF THE
FEDERATION OF WEST AFRICA: 1954

(in CFA francs)

Senegal	4,590
Mauritania	28
Soudan	15
Guinea	1,773
Ivory Coast	4,560
Upper Volta	11
Dahomey	670
Niger	21

Source: Berg, p. 403.

POLITICAL INTEGRATION IN FRENCH-SPEAKING AFRICA

Unfortunately, figures are not available that will permit us to make precise calculations of the source of federal revenues in FEA. However, by looking at the foreign trade of the territories concerned, we can get some idea of the source of these revenues. Table 6 provides the foreign trade figures of the territories of FEA for 1957, the first year in which these figures were available for the individual territories. On the basis of the figures in Table 6, the percentage contribution of the individual territories to the foreign trade of FEA was as follows: Central Africa = 16 percent; Congo = 31 percent; Gabon = 33 percent; and Chad = 20.5 percent. When we combine these figures with population figures (the 1956 estimates are as follows: Gabon = 0.4 million; Congo = 0.8 million; Central Africa = 1.1 million; Chad = 2.6 million), it seems clear that Gabon was far and away the largest per capita contributor to the budget of the federation. The result was that Gabonese leaders became increasingly hostile to the federation and advocated its elimination.

This discussion of the role of the territorial governments in effecting income redistribution indicates that the interterritorial governments began losing this function in 1956, and lost it completely with the 1958 constitution. It was a function that was resented by the wealthier countries, and became disintegrative rather than integrative.

A final aspect that should be touched upon is the monetary union among the territories of FWA and FEA. As noted earlier, both FWA and FEA were members of the franc zone. Currency for FWA was issued by the BCEAO, while the BCEAEC was the currency-issuing body for FEA. This meant that the territories of FWA had the same currency and there was no problem in capital transfers among them-- although very little capital transfer occurred; the situation was the same in FEA. There were no problems in the exchange of currency or the transfer of capital between FWA and FEA. Thus one could speak of monetary union within FWA and FEA and between FWA and FEA, though this was clearly more a result of common dependence on France than dependence on each other.

Table 6

FOREIGN TRADE OF THE TERRITORIES OF THE
FEDERATION OF EQUATORIAL AFRICA: 1957
(in million French francs)

	Exports	Imports	Total
Central Africa	61.13	69.55	130.68
Congo	48.38	206.23	254.61
Gabon	125.22	146.81	272.03
Chad	69.86	99.77	169.63
TOTAL	304.59	522.36	826.95

From this discussion, it is clear that economic integration in French West and Equatorial Africa during the colonial
period was weak. Dependence on France for trade, capital, education, and manpower was much greater than the dependence of the
colonies on each other in these areas. The pattern of economic
integration in FWA and FEA took the form of dependence by hinterland states on coastal states rather than mutual dependence. Redistribution of income occurred up to the mid-1950's, but declined
around 1956 and ended in 1958. Finally, earlier measures for the
redistribution of income were resented by the states that had to
pay the most, and led to anti-integrationist attitudes on their
part. Thus, in the economic sector, the prospects for political
integration at the time of independence were not very promising.

The Distribution of Capabilities

In the preceding discussion, we have provided data that
indicate that political and economic capabilities were far from
evenly distributed among the territories of FWA and FEA. Table
7 summarizes both data already presented and some new data.

Table 7 shows that in FWA, Senegal and the Ivory Coast
led the other territories in almost all the measures of level of
economic development. Only in the field of education did Senegal
and the Ivory Coast fall behind Dahomey. Mauritania had a high
figure for gross fixed capital formation as a percentage of the
GDP, but this was due to large imports of mining equipment connected with the exploitation of iron and copper deposits in the
early 1960's, and therefore the figure of 67 percent has little
meaning. In 1959, for example, investment as a percentage of
GDP in Mauritania was only 2 percent.[60] In FEA, Gabon was far
ahead of the other territories economically, with the Congo a
distant second. Thus in neither federation did economic resources
come close to being evenly distributed.

A brief statement is necessary on the distribution of
political capabilities--or, more accurately, on the distribution
of prestige among the leaders of FWA and FEA. As noted earlier,
for much of the 1940's and 1950's, political rivalry in FWA was
essentially between Senghor and Houphouet. No other West African
leaders enjoyed as much personal prestige as these men either in
France or in Africa. Houphouet's position in Africa was weakened
around the mid-1950's as a result of the rise to prominence of
Sékou Touré and Modiba Keita, but his influence in France and
among conservative groups in Africa remained strong. Leaders

---

[60]United Nations Economic Commission for Africa (UNECA), Economic Survey of Africa (E/CN/14/370), Vol. 1, 1966, p. 23.

Table 7

DISTRIBUTION OF ECONOMIC CAPABILITIES

Territory	Population in Millions: 1956	Area in 000 sq. km.	Per Capita Exports (CFA 1957 francs)	GDP per Capita: 1956 (CFA francs)	Percent of School-Age Children in School as of 1 January 1957[b]	Annual per Capita Public Expenditures- Working Budget: 1960 (CFA)	Gross Fixed Capital Formation as Percentage of GDP: c. 1960	Secondary Sector as Percentage of GDP
Senegal	2.3	197	10,903[a]	51,000	23.1	7,300	11.6	20
Mauritania	0.6	1,086	--[a]	22,000	6.6	4,900	67.0	6
Soudan	3.7	1,204	--[a]	20,000	7.9	1,800	9.0	12
Guinea	2.5	246	2,048	21,000	10.5	3,300	n.d.	17
Ivory Coast	2.5	322	9,770	34,000	25.8	9,900	13.7	12
Dahomey	1.7	116	1,439	20,000	29.1	3,100	12.6	10
Niger	2.4	1,189	1,084	19,000	4.0	2,200	5.0	3
Upper Volta	3.3	274	272	11,000	6.7	1,500	8.4	10
Gabon	0.4	267	15,653	37,000	66.0	9,000	39.0	33
Congo	0.8	342	3,025	32,000	63.0	5,200	25.0	21
Central Africa	1.1	617	2,778	19,000	24.0	2,500	16.0	12
Chad	2.6	1,284	1,343	15,000	7.2	1,500	10.0	9

[a] Exports from Mauritania and Soudan passed through Dakar. Since no custom barriers existed among them, figures are unavailable for each territory. Most exports come from Senegal.

[b] Number of school-age children estimated at 15 percent of population.

[c] Percentages are for 1958 for the Ivory Coast, the Congo, and Chad; 1959 for Mauritania, Senegal, Dahomey, Mali, Upper Volta, and Niger; 1960 for Gabon; and 1956 for Central Africa and Guinea.

Sources: France, Service des Statistiques d'Outre-Mer, Outre-Mer, 1958; France, Ministère de la Coopération, Planification en Afrique (Vol. IV, January 1963), p. 75; United Nations Economic Commission for Africa, Economic Survey of Africa (E/CN/14/370), Vol. 1, 1966, p. 18; France, Ministère de la Coopération, Republique du Gabon: Economie et Plan de Developpement (March 1962).

with the prestige of Senghor and Houphouet never emerged in FEA, where Boganda and Youlou aspired to regional prestige and influence, with neither of them achieving much success. Thus, to the dominant political and economic position of Senegal and the Ivory Coast should be added the personal prestige of their leaders.

Political Systems

The political systems of the territories of FWA and FEA have been treated in several studies,[61] and only a few words will be said here on the subject. After the 1958 referendum, the territories of FWA and FEA adopted constitutions that were very similar to that of the French Fifth Republic, with power concentrated in the hands of the President. Several of the territories had a single dominant political party, and all were moving toward a single party system. The dominant ideologies of the territories were gradual reformist of the liberal variety, with the exception of Soudan and Guinea, whose dominant ideologies were radical-revolutionary of the Marxist type. Voluntary associations were poorly developed or were integral parts of the dominant political parties. Politics in each territory was essentially a rivalry among personalities, regions, and ethnic groups. Thus the political systems were essentially similar, and the political elites of one country would have had little difficulty in coming to terms with the politics of another country.

The Colonial Legacy: A Summary

Over half a century of French rule left FWA and FEA with an ambiguous legacy for post-independence efforts at regional political integration. The positive aspects of this legacy were: insulation from world conflicts and from contradictory external pulls (high score); similarity in political systems and elite culture and values (moderate score); trans-territorial elite ties, groups, and transactions (moderate). The negative elements were: dissatisfaction with previous cooperation and opposition to political unification combined with relatively widespread support for economic cooperation; low economic capabilities very unevenly distributed; very low degree of pluralism; weak support for political unification by the external elite. All told, the colonial inheritance was not favorable for subsequent political integration. The degree of political integration achieved, and

---

[61] See Thompson and Adloff, French West Africa; Thompson and Adloff, French Equatorial Africa; Morgenthau, Political Parties in French-Speaking West Africa; De Lusignan, French-Speaking Africa Since Independence.

the changes in the background conditions over time, will be our primary concern in the subsequent chapters.

A Note on Cameroun and Madagascar

Both Cameroun and Madagascar were founding members of the Union Africaine et Malgache (UAM), and it is necessary to treat briefly their pre-independence links with FWA and FEA. Neither Madagascar nor Cameroun had direct constitutional links with the territories of FWA and FEA; the former was administered as an overseas French possession and the latter as a UN Trust Territory under France. However, both were represented in French parliamentary bodies, and this made for indirect ties with the territories of FWA and FEA.

Because of geography, racial composition, and the feeling that its inhabitants were not Africans, few links were developed between Madagascar and the other territories. The interterritorial movements in FWA had active branches in Cameroun, and as early as World War II, a limited free trade area existed between Cameroun and FEA. Also, as noted earlier, Cameroun shared the same currency-issuing bank with FEA, and even though its currency was different, it was freely exchanged in FWA and FEA.

The economic structures of Cameroun and Madagascar were not very different from those of the territories of FWA and FEA, as the figures in Table 8 reveal. In most measures of the level of economic development, they fell below the territories of Senegal, the Ivory Coast, and Gabon, and at more or less the same level as the Congo. Politically, Madagascar and Cameroun were also similar to the other territories. Thus the inclusion of Cameroun and Madagascar in the UAM did not introduce any significant new element into the Union.

We now turn our attention to the post-independence efforts at regional political integration in French-speaking Africa.

Table 8

BASIC ECONOMIC AGGREGATES FOR CAMEROUN AND MADAGASCAR

Country	Population in Millions: 1956	Area in 000 sq. km.	Per Capita Exports: 1957 (CFA francs)	GDP per Capita: 1956 (CFA francs)	Percent of School-Age Children in School as of 1 January 1957	FIDES Investment up to 30 June 1958 (in million French francs)	Gross Fixed Capital Formation as Percentage of GDP: c. 1960	Secondary Sector as Percentage of GDP: 1956
Cameroun	3.2	432	4,689	25,000	59%	483	10%	11%
Madagascar	4.9	590	3,313	20,000	46%	385	n.d.	14%

Sources: France, Service des Statistiques d'Outre-Mer, Outre-Mer, 1958; France, Ministère de la Coopération, Planification en Afrique (Vol. IV, January 1963), p. 75; United Nations Economic Commission for Africa, Economic Survey of Africa (E/CN/14/370), Vol. 1, 1966, p. 18; France, Ministère de la Coopération, République du Gabon: Economie et Plan de Développement (March 1962).

Chapter 2

THE UNION AFRICAINE ET MALGACHE (UAM) SYSTEM

The Creation of the UAM: Motives and Expectations

The Union Africaine et Malgache (UAM) system was created
in four conferences of heads of state and one conference of experts between October 1960 and September 1961; it was a result of
the continuation of the 1957-1959 efforts at regional regrouping
in FWA stimulated by the African and world diplomatic situations
of the late 1950's and early 1960's. The context was one of
intense diplomatic activity in West Africa.

Soon after the Mali Federation-Conseil de l'Entente split,
efforts were made to heal the wounds of the earlier conflicts.
Houphouet and Senghor met in Paris in February 1960 to begin the
process of rapprochement, and in March a mission from the Mali
Federation visited the Ivory Coast. Two months later, Houphouet
visited Dakar and called for "a broad union between Mali and the
Conseil de l'Entente." This idea was to remain dormant, however,
until the breakup of the Mali Federation in August 1960.

The breakup of the Mali Federation left both Senegal and
Mali (the name retained by the former Soudan) diplomatically
isolated. It also provided the occasion for Houphouet to play
the role of mediator between Mali and Senegal and to reorganize
FWA under his leadership. Soon after the collapse of the Mali
Federation, Houphouet made an unpublicized visit to Bamako to
assure the leaders of Mali of his support. On his return to
Abidjan, Houphouet paid glowing tribute to Mali and its leader:

> We return from Bamako comforted by everything we saw, by
> everything we heard. This means that the meetings we had
> with the leaders of the Republic of Mali proceeded in an
> atmosphere of frank cordiality, of real friendship and, above
> all, of fraternity. We have faith in the radiant future of
> the Republic of Mali; we have confidence in its leaders,
> and particularly in the one whom we consider not only a
> comrade in arms, a brother whom we have rejoined with joy
> and pride, but who is even more, as you know, the respected
> disciple of our great and wise Mamadou Konate.[1]

---

[1] Le Monde, September 28, 1960.

36

The leaders of Mali were in a mood to respond favorably to the attentions of the Ivory Coast. The split with Senegal had deprived them of the use of the port of Dakar, and Abidjan could serve as an alternate supply port. An arrangement to this effect was negotiated in late September, ending Mali's economic--but not its political--isolation.

Senegal's problems resulting from the breakup of the Mali Federation were more political than economic. To be sure, economic costs were involved: access to the Mali market was lost, and establishments in Senegal that were heavily dependent on the transit of goods to and from Mali were hard hit. For the political leaders, however, the diplomatic isolation of Senegal was more important. For reasons of language, culture, and political temperament, Accra, Lagos, and Conakry were not considered viable alternatives to Mali. Thus only Mauritania and the Conseil de l'Entente states remained.[2]

On August 23, 1960--three days after Senegal had declared its independence from the Mali Federation--Senghor defined the political objectives of Senegal as follows: Keep Senegal in the "Communauté Contractuelle"; reestablish close ties with Mali; create a confederation of the former FWA states; form an "Association of Independent African States." Given Senegal's political isolation, Senghor felt that the initiative in creating a confederation of FWA states and an Association of Independent African States must be taken by Houphouet. On September 21, he wrote to Houphouet suggesting that the time seemed favorable for trying to achieve a regrouping of the former FWA states, and that Houphouet should take the initiative in calling a "round table" conference for this purpose:

No one is in a better position than you to take this initiative. There is first of all your authority and your realism. There is also your situation of being older; there is, finally, the friendship and esteem that all the heads of state have for you.

Thus Senegal was, for the moment at least, willing to play a secondary role to the Ivory Coast. This facilitated the creation of the UAM system by removing the element of rivalry over leadership of the union.

A second important change in the position of Senegal that was favorable to the creation of the UAM system had to do

---

[2]G. Peureux, "La Création de l'Union Africaine et Malgache et les conférences des chefs d'état d'expression francaise," Revue Juridique et Politique d'Outre-Mer, No. 4 (Octobre-Décembre 1961), p. 542.

with the character of the union desired. During the 1957-1959 period, Senegal was the leading advocate of a strong political union to which members would surrender their sovereignty. With the failure of the Mali Federation, its position was revised. The new policy was enunciated by Diop Obeye, Senegal's Minister of Information:

> After the failure of the Mali Federation, we do not hesitate to take inspiration from experiences which have succeeded. The idea of federation is premature. [Mali's] President Modibo Keita himself said it the other day. The more flexible formula of the Conseil de l'Entente, which is that of an association founded on the principles of independence, of equality, and of cooperation among participant nations, could serve as a model for a regrouping of all French-speaking African nations, including Mauritania and Guinea.[3]

By September 1960, then, the Ivory Coast and Senegal had come to a similar position on the nature of the union to be created.

Besides the request of Senghor, Houphouet had reasons of his own for calling a conference of the FWA and FEA states. He had reacted to the creation of the Mali Federation by forming the Conseil de l'Entente, in order to avoid diplomatic isolation. But Upper Volta and Dahomey had been reluctantly pressured into leaving the Mali Federation and joining the Conseil de l'Entente, and they remained uncertain members of the Conseil. In particular, Upper Volta was being assiduously courted by Ghana to provide geographical contiguity for the Ghana-Guinea-Mali union. Upper Volta was motivated to seek closer ties with Ghana because of the more than half a million Voltaic laborers who went to work in Ghana; further, it was dissatisfied with the economic arrangements of the Conseil de l'Entente--particularly the repayment of duties collected at Abidjan on goods destined for Upper Volta. Finally, Maurice Yameogo, President of Upper Volta, saw himself as a peacemaker among diplomatic groups in West Africa. To this end, he refused to sign a defense agreement with France, sought to establish his independence from the Conseil de l'Entente, and engaged in a series of diplomatic contacts with Guinea, Ghana, and Mali. One outcome of the Ghana-Upper Volta flirtation was the symbolic knocking down of a wall specially constructed for the prupose at the border town of Paga by President Kwame Nkrumah of Ghana and Yameogo in June 1961 to signify the establishment of a customs union between the two countries.[4]

---

[3] Le Monde, September 28, 1960.

[4] For details on Ghana-Upper Volta relations during this period, see W. Scott Thompson, Ghana's Foreign Policy, 1957-1966 (Princeton: Princeton University Press, 1969), pp. 204-207.

THE UNION AFRICAINE ET MALGACHE SYSTEM

These diplomatic activities of Upper Volta were, to say the least, not very pleasing to Houphouet, who spent a great deal of time trying to reinforce the Conseil de l'Entente. Between April 1959, when the Conseil de l'Entente was created, and October 1960, when what later became the UAM held its first meeting, the Conseil de l'Entente met eight times. As already indicated, Houphouet was also concerned during this period with establishing close ties with Mali and Senegal. Underlying these diplomatic efforts was what Houphouet perceived as a threat from Ghana.

Soon after independence, Ghana had launched a series of diplomatic initiatives that led to the first Conference of Independent African States at Accra in April 1958, soon to be followed by the first All-African Peoples Conference at Accra in December 1958. To symbolize his Pan-African orientation, Nkrumah had decided that his first state visit as leader of an independent Ghana would be to an African country. The Ivory Coast was selected as ideal for this purpose; it was not only African, but French-speaking African, and a visit there would symbolize the irrelevance of the English-speaking, French-speaking distinction among Africans. Finally, the Ivory Coast and Ghana are contiguous, and it was felt that African unity had to start from close ties among neighbors.

But though Nkrumah had good reasons for seeking amicable ties with the Ivory Coast, the situation was such that conflict between the two countries was a more likely possibility. Ghana and the Ivory Coast were roughly the same in size and resources, with Ghana the more developed of the two. The leaders of both countries were prestigious and ambitious, and neither was likely to accept a position subordinate to the other. Also, the two men held opposite views with respect to independence, domestic reorganization, and African unity. Thus the meeting between the two at Abidjan in April 1957 was filled with tension, and ended in a famous public bet: each country was to follow its own path, without interference from the other, and the results were to be compared ten years later. This challenge was accepted by Nkrumah, who charged Houphouet with having chosen the path of illusion in thinking that he could cooperate with the former colonial powers.

The importance of this encounter between Houphouet and Nkrumah was that it highlighted the opposing choices open to African states with respect to patterns of domestic reorganization, diplomatic orientations, and the nature of the African subsystem. With Nkrumah expending a great deal of effort forming alliances in an attempt to ensure that his views and leadership prevailed, Houphouet was forced to do likewise.[5] Such alliances became even

---

[5] For a discussion of the early diplomatic activities of Ghana, see _ibid._, Part 1.

more necessary when, with the independence of Guinea in October 1958, another pole of attraction for African radicals was created in West Africa. Guinea was hailed as one of the few truly independent African countries, a representative of the new Africa, and its leaders were listened to as the genuine spokesmen of independent Africa. To Houphouet it was time that the moderates spoke out; he was convinced that evolution, not revolution, was the answer to the problems facing Africa. He was to express himself on this matter as follows:

> Neither in the agricultural domain nor in the commercial, industrial, or social domain does revolution respond to our realities. . . . It is the path of evolution that we must follow--evolution of morals and of customary practices, evolution that permits adaptation to the new conditions of life in the country without too great a shock. . . . We do not have factories to nationalize but factories to be created; neither do we have commerce to be brought under state control but commerce to organize better; our problem is not to redistribute land but to exploit it better.[6]

Thus what Houphouet wanted was a new grouping, made up of states subscribing to his views on the best way for Africa to develop, to ensure that the radical path did not become the sole or dominant path.

The need to speak out, to form an alliance of moderate states, was strengthened by the various alliance systems that were then being formed. As already noted, Ghana had convened the first Conference of Independent African States in April 1958, and this body met for a second time at Addis Ababa in June 1960. Further, the All-African Peoples Conference, which had met for the first time at Accra in December 1958, held a second meeting at Tunis in January 1960, and was to meet for a third time at Cairo in March 1961. In November 1958, the Ghana-Guinea Union was formed, and it expanded into the Ghana-Guinea-Mali Union, or Union of African States, in December 1960. The Ghana-Guinea Union had persuaded President Tubman of Liberia to call a conference of the three states at Sanniquellie in Liberia in July 1959 to clarify the problem of African unity. There seem to have been two basic reasons for these diplomatic maneuvers and search for allies: "One was the ideology of unity. . . . The other was the desire to avoid isolation, made particularly sharp in West Africa because of the interdependence and powerlessness of the states."[7]

---

[6] Houphouet-Boigny, "Une Politique d'unité, d'essor et de paix," Communautés et Continents (Avril-Juin 1962), p. 8.

[7] I. William Zartman, International Relations in the New Africa (Englewood Cliffs: Prentice-Hall, 1966), p. 17.

THE UNION AFRICAINE ET MALGACHE SYSTEM

To these motives underlying the process of alliance formation in West Africa in the late 1950's and early 1960's should be added the necessity of speaking out on some very difficult questions that the African states were facing. The most important of these was the Algerian conflict. The relevance of the Algerian conflict to the creation of the UAM has been described as follows by Albert Tevoedjre, Secretary-General of the UAM from 1961-1963:

The formation of the UAM had to do with the position of France in 1960. The worst hour of the Algerian war was at hand. Negotiations were bogged down. Several Afro-Asian, Socialist, and even Western states seriously contemplated a United Nations intervention. The De Gaulle government was resolutely hostile to such a solution. . . . Whether or not the idea was entirely their own, Houphouet-Boigny, Senghor, and their friends wanted to avoid a recourse to the U.N.[8]

Another problem the African leaders had to face was the French intention to conduct atomic tests in the Sahara, which was announced in July 1959.

These issues called for a declaration of position by African leaders, but Houphouet was unhappy at the statements made concerning them by some African statesmen. At the special Conference of Independent African States which met at Monrovia in August 1959, the foreign ministers of Guinea, Ghana, Morocco, Libya, Egypt, Tunisia, Liberia, and the provisional government of Algeria called on France to grant independence to Algeria and refrain from atomic tests in the Sahara. They also recommended recognition of the Algerian provisional government and aid in creating an African Volunteers Corps for Algeria. The next regular meeting of the Conference of Independent African States at Addis Ababa adopted resolutions that were more moderate, but still called for diplomatic and material support for Algeria. To Houphouet these resolutions were unrealistic, and he felt that the conference was an ineffective instrument for African cooperation. He therefore wanted to forge another body which, in his view, would be more realistic and therefore more effective. The main task of this body would be to work out a common position on Algeria and try to mediate the conflict without alienating France.

Another factor that encouraged Houphouet to constitute his own group was concern about externally induced and supported subversion in the Ivory Coast. The most concrete form of this threat was Nkrumah's support of the Sanni dissidents and the

---

[8]Tevoedjre, Pan-Africanism in Action (Cambridge: Harvard Center for International Affairs, Occasional Papers in International Affairs, No. 11, November 1965), p. 11.

National Committee for the Liberation of the Ivory Coast, coupled
with his claims on the southeastern corner of the Ivory Coast.[9]
To be sure, Houphouet was not particularly disturbed by these
activities of Nkrumah's, which he considered futile. Thus in
February 1960 he said: "I am obliged to state plainly to Dr.
Nkrumah that he should stop cherishing illusions. He has neither
the right nor the means to claim or hope to annex the smallest
piece of the Ivory Coast."[10] What worried Houphouet was that
behind these efforts at subversion, he saw the hands of the Communist countries, particularly the People's Republic of China.
A year later, he expressed his anxiety in these words:

> We will not refrain from saying to the Chinese that if their
> ulterior motive is to foist themselves here, they will en-
> counter our opposition. Our wish is for Africa to become a
> large Switzerland, whose neutrality will be guaranteed by
> all. . . . The first African states to gain independence have
> chosen to join the Afro-Asian bloc, that of Bandung, which
> professes positive neutrality. We observe that this is more
> of a veneer, and it is sufficient to scrape it to see what's
> behind--China and the Communist world. If we are naive enough
> to break with the West, we will soon be invaded by the Chinese,
> and Soviet Russia would impose communism in our countries.[11]

Because of the links he perceived between the Communist bloc and
the radical African states, Houphouet took very seriously the
problem of subversion. The UAM, for him, would be a way of coping
with this threat and ensuring that the Communists in general and
the Chinese in particular did not gain a foothold in Africa.

Two other issues played a role in the creation of the
UAM, but they were of greater importance to other leaders than
to Houphouet. One of these was the Morocco-Mauritania dispute.
From the outset, Mauritania's right to independence and separate
existence was questioned by Morocco, on the grounds that Mauritania was part of Morocco. In this matter, Morocco had the support of the Eastern bloc (led by the U.S.S.R.), the U.A.R., Libya,
Ghana, Guinea, Mali, and the provisional government of Algeria.
Thus Mauritania was isolated from the countries of North Africa,
to whom it felt naturally inclined by reasons of race, religion,

---

[9] For details on this point, see Virginia Thompson, "The Ivory
Coast" in Gwendolen Carter, ed., African One-Party Systems (Ithaca:
Cornell University Press, 1962), pp. 297-298.

[10] West Africa, February 13, 1960.

[11] Houphouet-Boigny, "Avant cinq ans," Afrique Nouvelle, March 22,
1961.

and culture, and had to seek allies among her former partners in
FWA. The former territories of FWA (Guinea and Mali excepted)
and FEA supported Mauritania against Morocco, because of past
links and as a means of counteracting the influence of the radical
states. Senegal had additional reasons for supporting Mauritania:
the two countries were contiguous, and Mauritania provided markets
for the industries of Senegal. Further, Senghor saw Mauritania
as an ideal bridge between the Arab world and Black Africa, and
thus felt it vital to cultivate the friendship of Mauritania.

The second of the two additional issues that played a
role in the creation of the UAM was the Congo crisis, which com-
menced in July 1960. This crisis was to have a very important
impact on the second of the five meetings that led to the formation of the UAM--the Brazzaville heads of state conference in
December 1960. On this matter, Tevoedjre in 1965 wrote as follows:

> The UAM to some extent owed its existence and development to
> the Congo crisis, over which African states were and still
> remain sharply divided. It was above all at the Brazzaville
> Conference of December 19, 1960, that the UAM became a real-
> ity. Fulbert Youlou, then President of the former French
> Congo and dreaming of a great and united Congo, opened the
> assembly "in the name of all the Congolese."[12]

Youlou saw the Congo crisis as the occasion for realizing his
ambition (noted in the preceding chapter) of uniting all the
Bakongo people under his leadership. The way to do this, he
felt, was to play a mediatory role in the conflict in the name
of a large group of African states, thereby enhancing his prestige. Other members of what later became the UAM felt that it
was necessary to group together in order to work out common
policies that would be supportive of legal and constitutional
procedures and of President Kasavubu, who was perceived as the
leader of the moderate forces in the Congo--in contrast to what
were considered the interfering, illegal, unconstitutional, and
destabilizing policies of the radical states who were supporting
Patrice Lumumba, Prime Minister of the Congo and leader of the
radical forces. Thus the Congo crisis would become another
battleground between moderate and radical tendencies in Africa.

The need to escape diplomatic isolation, to enhance the
leaders' prestige, to counter radical and subversive policies in
Africa, and to coordinate policies on the major issues of the
day were not the only factors that led to the creation of the
UAM. According to Maurice Ligot and Guy Devernois, "It is

---

[12]Tevoedjre, p. 11.

necessary to add that this Union [UAM], more than a tendency toward African unity, is testimony of the nostalgic regret for this Community [the French Community] and of the wish of French-speaking Africans to substitute for it something similar."[13] Or put differently, "After the colonies were given autonomy and independence, these leaders [of FWA and FEA] missed the forum provided by the Palais Bourbon or the Councils of the AOF and AEF, where they had met together regularly. Several of them, without admitting it, found in the UAM this 'club' that they thought back to nostalgically."[14]

However, something other than mere nostalgia was operating. As we saw in Chapter 1, independence came abruptly, unexpectedly, with nothing of the step-by-step process that characterized British decolonization policies in Africa. The result was physical and psychological unpreparedness for independence on the part of the FWA and FEA states. When we add to this the international environment which prevailed in 1960, it becomes understandable that these new states felt anxious and bewildered, and thought it best to join together for mutual consultation and support.

Finally, there was the climate of opinion in FWA and FEA with respect to regional cooperation. It will be recalled from Chapter 1 that while support for political union was weak, there was widespread support for the idea of economic cooperation during the 1956-1959 period. This remained true in 1960, and was an important factor in the creation of the UAM system. It is interesting to note that while the Abidjan conference of October 1960 and the Brazzaville conference of December 1960 had been occasioned by foreign policy matters, the first new organization created was the Organisation Africaine et Malgache de Coopération Economique (OAMCE), whose tasks were economic in nature. The more strictly political UAM, though part of the same grand design, was created a few months later.

If economic considerations played an important part in the creation of the UAM system, this did not mean that the economic rationale was an elaborate and well-thought-out one. There was a general feeling that "divided, the French-speaking countries would have no hope of industrializing, due to the absence of internal markets that are sufficiently large."[15] Further, the union

---

[13]"L'Union Africaine et Malgache: Une Année d'existence," Revue Juridique et Politique d'Outre-Mer, No. 3 (Juillet-Septembre 1962), p. 317.

[14]Tevoedjre, p. 10.

[15]Gabriel d'Arboussier, "L'UAM," Revue Politique et Parlementaire, Mai 1962, p. 91.

was seen as a means of constituting "a group which will permit us, on the one hand, to retain the best part of our resources and, on the other hand, to receive in the best conditions the foreign aid which we need."[16] Beyond this, economic thinking did not go. Thus the economic motives involved were of a vague and diffuse character.

In summary, external issues relating to avoidance of diplomatic isolation, the desire for international prestige, security considerations, the need to counter the radical offensive in Africa, nostalgia for metropolitan and regional forums, anxieties resulting from the lack of preparation for independence, and the need to adopt positions on the pressing international issues of the day seem to have been the major factors that led to the creation of the UAM system. They occurred in an ideological climate that favored economic cooperation, for economic considerations that were vague and diffuse. On the whole, these motives appear ephemeral and devoid of links with concrete and significant interests. They are, in our view, likely to preserve a union only at a very low level of integration, with disintegration likely to result from significant changes in the international and/or domestic environments, or from an increase in the cost of staying in the union. The level of integration actually achieved by the UAM system will be our concern in the subsequent sections of this chapter.

Building Homogeneity

After deciding to call a conference of FWA and FEA states, Houphouet moved with extreme caution. He took advantage of Nigeria's independence celebrations on October 1, 1960, to sound out interest in such a conference and receive suggestions on the countries to be invited. Senegal's idea, it will be recalled, was that any new group should include all FWA and FEA states, including Guinea. Early in October, Sylvanus Olympio of Togo publicly suggested holding a conference at Lomé of all French-speaking African states, including Guinea and the North African states. The purpose of such a conference was to work out common suggestions to France and the Algerian Front de Libération Nationale (FLN) for the resumption of negotiations between them. Houphouet, however, had different ideas. He felt that any resolution on Algeria that would be supported by Guinea, Morocco, and Tunisia would be unacceptable to France. Thus these three

---

[16] Ahmadou Ahidjo, "Le But ultime de la Conférence de Yaoundé," Communauté France-Eurafrique, Avril 1961, p. 2.

countries were not invited to the Abidjan conference of October 1960. However, Mali was invited, as part of Houphouet's efforts to bring it back to the "Community," and because he felt that the leaders of Mali were more realistic and reasonable than those of Guinea.

After losing the initiative in calling the conference to Houphouet, Olympio developed second thoughts about attending. At a press conference in Abidjan, he congratulated Houphouet on calling the conference, but added that since Algeria was to be discussed, Morocco and Tunisia should be invited because they were the best informed on the subject. Significantly, he added that "Togo belongs to the Afro-Asian group."[17] Reasonable as this position was, it is clear that Olympio had more important reasons for not attending the conference: "He was certainly reluctant to involve Togo, which had heretofore remained aloof from other French African political organizations, in a group whose membership and orientation were both uncertain quantities."[18] More specifically, Olympio felt that Houphouet was still too closely attached to France, while he wanted to reduce French influence in Togo. On these grounds, Togo refused to take part in the conference.

Another individual who had misgivings about the Abidjan conference was Philibert Tsiranana of Malgache. His misgivings had to do with the discussion of Algeria at the Abidjan conference. He said:

> I do not wish to become involved in this affair which relates to the internal politics of France. The Republic of Malgache agrees with the policy of self-rule of General de Gaulle. If someone asks for my mediation or my participation in a mediation, I would certainly not refuse, in spite of my modest abilities. However, to repeat, we are trying to get involved as little as possible in this affair.[19]

Though this was the main consideration behind Tsiranana's absence, the official reason given was that the conference date conflicted with his plans for an official visit to Paris. In order not to rupture his ties with the emerging group, Tsiranana paid a visit to Abidjan immediately after the conference. For reasons similar to those of Tsiranana, neither Léon Mba of Gabon nor Dacko of the Central African Republic attended the conference in person. Both sent representatives to the conference, however.

---

[17]Le Figaro, October 12, 1960.

[18]V. Thompson, "The Ivory Coast," p. 306.

[19]Le Figaro, October 24, 1960.

As noted above, Mali was the only "radical" African state
invited to the conference. It will be recalled that Mali had
responded positively to overtures from the Ivory Coast after the
failure of the Mali Federation. Thus an outright refusal to attend would have been considered an insult to Houphouet. The solution adopted by Mali was to send a low level delegation, headed
by the director of the Center of Islamic Studies at Bamako, to
act as an observer but not a representative. The reason for this
lukewarm response was that even though the Ivory Coast could offer
escape from economic isolation, Mali, given its political orientation, preferred the company of states like Ghana and Guinea.
After Abidjan, Mali was to stay away completely from meetings of
the UAM.

The calling of the Abidjan conference presented special
problems for Cameroun. As noted in Chapter 1, because of its
special status as a UN Trust Territory, Cameroun was not a part
of the French Community. When independence was achieved, the
idea of joining the French Community was rejected on the grounds
that this would only result in a new and worse form of French
domination. On the other hand, it had developed economic links
with FEA and was associated with the interterritorial political
parties of FWA. Like Olympio of Togo, the leaders of Cameroun
felt that the UAM might become too closely identified with France,
and they were anxious to avoid developing "colonial" links with
France--a situation they felt they had escaped because of their
UN Trust Territory status. Thus Cameroun was initially reluctant
to attend the Abidjan conference. Economic, political, and personal leadership ties with the territories of FWA and FEA prevailed in the end, however. The fact that Félix Moumié, a
political opponent of President Ahmadou Ahidjo of Cameroun was
in self-imposed exile in Guinea and receiving support from Guinea,
Ghana, and the U.A.R. in his efforts to overthrow Ahidjo, further
strengthened the case for joining the UAM. Thus, in the end
Cameroun attended the Abidjan conference.

By limiting attendance at the Abidjan conference, Houphouet
tried to ensure that only states with similar political views,
orientations, and close ties would become members of the UAM.
In this he largely succeeded. The early withdrawal of Mali contributed to the homogeneity of the group, as did the lack of
participation by Togo. Of the founding members of the UAM, Mauritania and Madagascar had the weakest ties with the others; the
disintegrative consequences of their membership will be examined
later.

The Preparatory Conferences: Abidjan, Brazzaville, and Yaoundé

The Abidjan conference was held October 25-26, 1960.
Present were the heads of state of Cameroun, Congo-Brazzaville,

the Ivory Coast, Dahomey, Upper Volta, Mauritania, Niger, and
Senegal; representatives of Gabon, the Central African Republic,
and Chad; and an observer from Mali. Discussions centered on
the problems of Algeria, French atomic tests in the Sahara,
Mauritania, tensions in Congo-Leopoldville, and the need for
creating bonds among French-speaking African states. The sessions
were closed to the public (even accompanying ministers were excluded from some sessions), and only with respect to the questions
of Mauritania and closer ties among French-speaking states did
the conference publicly announce the decisions arrived at.

Discussions of the Mauritania problem aroused no dispute.
All were agreed that Mauritania had a right to separate existence
and to membership in the UN. A resolution to this effect was
passed, and it was agreed that Mauritania's application for membership in the UN would be actively supported. Similarly, it
was agreed that subsequent meetings should be held, but the question of whether a permanent organization should be created, as
well as the tasks and membership of such an organization, were
left in abeyance until more thought could be given to them. The
main issue of contention was the size of the union, with Senegal
advocating the inclusion of Guinea and English-speaking African
states, while the Ivory Coast wanted membership limited to those
states that were invited to the Abidjan conference. The final
communique noted merely that "the Conference unanimously agreed
to periodically hold similar conferences, which will be enlarged
by other participants."[20]

On the Congo-Leopoldville issue, it was agreed that the
participants at the Abidjan conference would pursue similar
policies through their representatives at the UN. It was decided
that nothing would be done for the moment except to support UN
activities and encourage the Congolese leaders to settle their
disputes peacefully. However, there was a marked pro-Kasavubu,
anti-Lumumba attitude in the deliberations, which was to become
public knowledge at the second conference.

The Algerian problem led to intense debate among the
participants at the conference, with several delegations--partic-
ularly Cameroun, Upper Volta, and Dahomey--advocating that the
right to independence of Algeria be asserted. The other delegations, while favoring independence for Algeria, advocated discre-
tion in order not to antagonize France. Senegal, in particular,
argued strongly against supporting the Algerian demand for a UN-
supervised referendum. In the end, the conference agreed to send
Senghor and Houphouet to express its concern to de Gaulle, with
the implication that unless France moved quickly to terminate the

---

[20]*Le Monde*, October 27, 1960.

conflict, stronger positions would be adopted. To underline their support for Algeria, President Hamani Diori of Niger and Mamadou Dia, the Prime Minister of Senegal, were sent to Tunis to report on the conference to President Habib Bourguiba of Tunisia and Ferhat Abbas, President of the provisional government of Algeria. Diori and Dia were also to urge that French interests be given a fair deal in independent Algeria. Finally, it was agreed that the Afro-Asian resolution advocating a UN-supervised referendum in Algeria would be opposed, and that no public condemnation of French atomic tests in the Sahara would be made, in order not to antagonize France.

All in all, the Abidjan conference provided a good opportunity for the participants to develop a feeling for the attitudes and orientations of their prospective partners. They came away reasonably satisfied with the directions taken by the conference and impressed by the willingness to compromise of the other participants. This positive experience was highly favorable to the subsequent decision to create a permanent organization.

It had been hoped that the Brazzaville conference of December 15-19, 1960, would be devoted to matters of interstate cooperation, but this was prevented by the deepening crisis in the Congo, to which the conference devoted half its time.[21] This time, the presidents of all twelve member-states were present, and there were eighteen observers from Congo-Leopoldville, including Kasavubu and Moïse Tshombe, President of the Republic of Katanga (now part of Zaire). Guinea and Mali were asked by Youlou to send observers, but they refused. As was the case in Abidjan, most of the discussions were held in private meetings among the heads of state.

The Brazzaville conference unanimously adopted a resolution supporting the admission of Mauritania to the UN and criticizing the Soviet Union for having vetoed Mauritania's admission. The resolution on Algeria was much stronger than the one adopted at Abidjan, but largely through the efforts of Senghor, Houphouet, and Tsiranana, it did not go as far as leaders like Yameogo and Ahidjo desired. It strongly urged that France end the war by the end of 1961 and honestly apply the principle of self-determination. This was to be preceded by fresh negotiations between France and the Algerian leaders, in which each side would give political guarantees to the other. The idea of a UN referendum was again rejected. Not included in the resolution was the understanding, conveyed privately to France, that the participants at the Brazzaville conference would grant diplomatic recognition to the provisional government of Algeria if the resolution was not implemented.

---

[21] Tevoedjre, p. 11.

A workable solution to the Congo-Leopoldville problem was more difficult to arrive at. All agreed in denouncing what they perceived to be the efforts of the East-West blocs to recolonize the Congo through the use of African and Asian states as intermediaries. While praising the UN efforts in the Congo and thanking UN Secretary-General Dag Hammarskjöld personally, they called for more UN technical aid and urged that all states refrain from interfering in the domestic affairs of the Congo. However, the basic problem of how to reconcile the warring factions in the Congo remained. Youlou had hoped that the conference would designate him as the head of a group of arbitrators or mediators. This idea was strongly opposed by Kasavubu, who argued that the way to peace was through a conference of all domestic parties to the Congo dispute. In the end, the conference merely endorsed Kasavubu's position. After the close of the conference, some participants remained in Brazzaville for further discussion of the Congo-Leopoldville situation, but they contributed little or nothing to the solution of the problem.

When the conference finally took up the question of co-operation among the member states, they had little trouble in agreeing. As noted earlier, the failure of the Mali Federation, and the perceived success of the Conseil de l'Entente, had convinced the participants that looser forms of association were superior to those demanding the surrender of sovereignty to a new body. Prior to the conference, it had been rumored that a common market would be created.[22] These rumors were laid to rest when Youlou, in his opening address, said in reference to the project that "it is not a real 'common market' which would group economies that are more competitive than complementary."[23] The discussions were much more specific, dealing with economic issues such as the stabilization of prices of raw materials and guarantees for private investments. It was in this context that it was decided that "if the realization of these objectives necessitated a regional organization, this organization would have to respect the political individuality of the member states, whose sovereignty was in no way to be called into question."[24] To further investigate the economic problems discussed at the conference, and draft a treaty for a regional organization to deal with them, it was decided that experts from the member states would meet at Dakar in January 1961. The experts were to draw up a charter for the creation of the Organisation Africaine et Malgache de Coopération Economique (OAMCE) and suggest solutions to

---

[22] Le Monde, December 16, 1960.

[23] Afrique Nouvelle, December 21, 1960.

[24] Tevoedjre, p. 11. Emphasis in original.

problems relating to the following: money and credit; support of the agricultural and industrial products of members by means of price stabilization funds; reinforcement and enlargement of regional customs unions; fiscal harmonization and better coordination of commercial exchanges; harmonization of different national economic plans and of their financing; an investment code containing guarantees to private investments; a solidarity fund for economic and social development; and an investment bank. The experts were also to study questions relating to membership in the European Economic Community (EEC) and other international economic and financial organizations from the perspective of safeguarding the infant economies of the members. Finally, all matters relating to the industrialization of members were to be discussed.[25] The scope of reference for the meeting was thus extremely broad, and related to almost all the salient aspects of the economies of the members. The crucial limitation was the provision that the sovereignty of members be respected absolutely in whatever organization was proposed--a provision that subsequently seriously hindered the chances of arriving at joint solutions to problems.

The final resolution adopted by the Brazzaville conference outlined the principles of international behavior of members. These were: (1) obstinate search for peace; non-resort to war and refusal to join hostile coalitions directed against other members; mutual help in case of aggression against a member; acceptance as sacred of territorial boundaries existing at the time of independence; (2) noninterference in the internal affairs of members; prevention of provisional governments from aiming at the overthrow of the government of another African state and prevention of subversive plots against other states; (3) economic and cultural cooperation based on equality; (4) concerted diplomacy with a view to common international policies.[26] The ready agreement on these principles strengthened the feelings of trust among members and further enhanced the willingness to engage in a more permanent form of cooperation.

The meeting of experts was held at Dakar from January 30 to February 4, 1961. Ten of the delegations were headed by ministers, while those of Congo and Cameroun were headed by the Director of Economic Affairs and the Secretary of State for Foreign Affairs respectively. Each delegation had from three to five experts on economic and fiscal matters. The items on the conference agenda were as follows: (1) money and credit as factors of development, and the formation of an inter-African

---

[25] La Documentation Francaise, January 19, 1961.

[26] Afrique Nouvelle, December 21, 1960.

and Malgache bank of development and a solidarity fund; (2) a customs union, fiscal harmonization, and common commercial policies with respect to major items of export; (3) harmonization of development plans, inter-African and Malgache technical cooperation, and coordination of industrial development plans and the financing of plans; (4) Air Afrique, territorial waters, common nationality, and common attitudes toward international organizations for economic cooperation. The question of money and credit was not discussed, however, because the Conseil de l'Entente states were negotiating cooperation agreements with France, and the conference did not want to influence these negotiations. The other matters were discussed in subcommittees and then in plenary sessions.

Two different perspectives prevailed at the conference, which were best expressed by Jacques Rabemananjara, the Madagascar Minister of Economy, and Dia, Prime Minister of Senegal. On his way to Dakar, Rabemananjara said in Paris that if Madagascar had a feeling of solidarity toward other African states, it must be taken into account that its geographic position made it a crossroads between Africa and Asia--and even of Europe. Thus, of necessity Madagascar had to consider the problems to be discussed from a special angle.[27] The implication was that Madagascar (and presumably other states as well) must not be expected to agree to close links with the other states. Senegal's position was essentially opposite to that of Madagascar. In opening the conference, Dia described Senegal's position as follows: "These structures of cooperation which we wish to establish among us will only acquire meaningful form if we try to define, in order to vitalize it, in order to give it force and life, a schema for common development."[28] Senegal, in other words, was proposing a high level of joint decision-making in the economic sector. These opposing perspectives were manifested in much of the debate that occurred in Dakar. We will examine their impact upon two of the major issues taken up by the conference.

First: At Brazzaville, the idea of creating the OAMCE, with a broad scope but no supranational power, had been agreed to. The delegates at Dakar, in the course of drawing up the OAMCE charter, had to decide on the extent to which the states would be required to implement decisions arrived at in the OAMCE context. The Conseil de l'Entente states, led by the Ivory Coast, insisted that for the time being the states should be given a certain degree of liberty of action and choice with respect to the application of OAMCE decisions. This position had the support

---

[27] AFP Special Outre-Mer, January 27, 1961.

[28] Combat, January 31, 1961.

of Madagascar, Gabon, and Mauritania. Senegal, with the support
of Cameroun, called for immediate commitment to the implementation
of such decisions. Chad, Central Africa, and Congo did not take
a strong stand on this issue, but apparently were inclined to the
position taken by Senegal and Cameroun. In the end, the principle
of a low level of commitment to implementation of joint decisions
won out.

A related question that had to be decided was whether
coordination and harmonization of policies would be attempted at
the level of OAMCE or at the level of the two customs unions
within OAMCE. The same split was manifested with respect to
this question, except that Chad, Central Africa, and Congo supported the position of the Conseil de l'Entente states that
coordination and harmonization should be sought principally at
the levels of the Union Douanière Equatoriale (UDE), made up of
Chad, the Republic of Central Africa, Gabon, and the Republic of
Congo, and the Union Douanière des Etats de l'Ouest (UDEAO), made
up of Mauritania, Mali, the Ivory Coast, Senegal, Dahomey, Upper
Volta, and Niger. This led to a decision to strengthen the two
customs unions, particularly the UDEAO, which was to be provided
with a permanent secretariat composed of three members and a
headquarters in Abidjan.[29]

The second major issue in which the split concerning the
level of commitment was manifested related to the role of OAMCE
in the area of foreign aid. Senegal presented a proposal for
the creation of a Fond Africain de Solidarité et de Développement.
The funds for this body were to come from long-term loans with
low interest rates from organizations such as the EEC and the
Organization for Economic Cooperation and Development (OECD), and
from states such as France, West Germany, and the U.S. These
funds were to be used for infrastructure projects that would
yield profits, such as ports and railroads. Profits from these
projects would then be divided among the OAMCE states for use
in their agricultural development plans. The Ivory Coast saw
this as a first step in giving OAMCE preeminence in the foreign
aid field and the power to engage in the redistribution of resources by using profits derived from one country to support other
states. Confident of its own ability to attract foreign aid, the
Ivory Coast strongly opposed Senegal's proposal. Other members
of the Entente, less confident of their abilities to attract
foreign aid, were disposed to support Senegal, but refrained from
doing so in order not to antagonize the Ivory Coast. Gabon and
Cameroun, for reasons similar to those of the Ivory Coast, and
Madagascar, which feared that its geographical isolation from the
others would hinder its chances of getting a fair share of the

---

[29]Le Monde, February 5, 1961.

funds, also opposed the proposal by Senegal. Only Chad and Central Africa spoke out in favor of the proposal, which was therefore indefinitely shelved.

When completed, the Dakar conference had adopted two treaties and nine resolutions, all of which were to be sent to the next conference of heads of state for ratification. The first treaty created the OAMCE, and the second provided for a joint airline in which Air France and the Union Aéromaritime de Transport (UAT) would participate. Madagascar refused participation in the airline company on the grounds that because of its geographical position the project would provide it with no benefits. Chad opposed the idea of creating the airline on the grounds that it had a national airline which would be adversely affected by the new multi-national airline, and withheld final commitment to the project. The nine resolutions adopted were as follows: (1) strengthen the customs unions and regular liaison among the associated organs of each state or group of states; (2) adopt a multilateral convention eliminating double taxation, with experts to meet in 1961 to consider ways of harmonizing rules of taxation and legislative and regulative rules then in force; (3) study methods for the commercialization and stabilization of the prices for coffee and groundnuts; (4) create an inter-African development bank to serve as a coordinating agency for all national development banks; (5) compare objectives of various development plans with respect to production, consumption, exportation, research, and higher technical training, as well as study means for financing development plans and defining positions to be taken with respect to private investment; (6) adopt a convention granting dual citizenship to citizens of member states and reciprocal rights of settlement (établissement); (7) cooperate in the judicial domain; (8) adopt a plan for the coordination of transport and for joint delimitation of territorial waters; (9) henceforth jointly conduct negotiations with the European Economic Community (EEC).

This list of resolutions indicates that the understanding reached at Brazzaville that whatever union was created would have a broad scope was followed at Dakar. In fact, the resolutions reveal a higher level of commitment to joint policy-making than was present at earlier conferences. (This phenomenon will be treated in greater detail in later sections of this chapter.)

The last of the preparatory conferences was held by the heads of state at Yaoundé from March 25-28, 1961. All twelve heads of state were present, and the focus was on interstate cooperation--specifically, the resolutions adopted earlier at Dakar. The treaty creating the OAMCE was adopted, but the signing was postponed until the next conference. Also adopted (and signed) was the treaty creating a joint airline, to be called Air Afrique. Chad, which had opposed the project at Dakar, withdrew its opposition when assured that the interests of its national airline would be protected. The nine resolutions of the Dakar conference were ratified, but in some cases implementation was postponed until the OAMCE structures were established, and in some cases the level of commitment was reduced. Cameroun was asked to study the question of nationality and citizenship and to prepare a multilateral convention of settlement, while Senegal was assigned to examine the question of creating an economic council and prepare an agreement on mutual aid in judicial matters. Two matters not discussed at Dakar which arose at the conference were set aside for further study: the Ivory Coast was to explore the question of joint diplomatic representation and draw up a proposal for an agreement in this area, and Niger was to do the same with respect to the coordination of telecommunications. These reports were to be distributed to members, who were to forward their comments and amendments to the states preparing the reports by June 15, 1961. It was agreed that experts from member states would meet at the Cameroun Embassy in Paris on April 25, 1961, to work out the technical basis of forthcoming negotiations with the EEC.

Two other new matters taken up by the conference related to cooperation in the area of defense and postal policies. A defense agreement was proposed by the Ivory Coast and the Entente states because of their concern with aggression and subversion from the Communist and radical African states. Only lukewarm support was given to this proposal, which was opposed by Senegal, but it was nevertheless decided that experts from member states would meet at Tananarive on June 30, 1961, to elaborate a defense arrangement. The idea of cooperation in postal matters came from the Equatorial states, which had already formed the Office Equatorial des Postes et Télécommunications. A proposal was made to harmonize policies relating to postal and telecommunications equipment and procedures, in order to improve communication links among the members. This proposal was favorably received, and it was decided that experts would meet at Fort-Lamy on June 15, 1961, to draw up a treaty for a postal and telecommunications union.

The final economic issue discussed related to the question of private investments. On this subject, the heads of state disappointed the expectations of the experts at Dakar that there would be an attempt at establishing similar investment codes among members. The conferees reaffirmed their willingness to provide private investments with security guarantees, and proposed the creation of international or national guarantee fund(s) in which members would participate in a manner to be determined by the OAMCE. It was agreed that harmonization would be attempted in the following areas: exemption from external and internal fiscal taxes; stabilization of fiscal policies; a convention of settlement guaranteeing the transfer of capital and profits; advantages granted for reinvestment of profits; and an arbitration procedure.

The efforts at harmonization in these areas were to take account of the differences in resources among the states as well as the differences in the nature of the private investments involved. Further, in order not to deprive a state of its fiscal resources, each member was to retain the right to take measures to partially or totally protect these resources. Experts were to meet in Paris on June 6, 1961, to formulate proposals in these areas and submit them to the conference of heads of state no later than September 15, 1961. Prior to the Paris meeting of experts, the states were to communicate to each other by May 15 a complete list of all advantages granted to private investments, and a list of all enterprises benefitting from these advantages. Within each customs union, the members were to communicate lists of planned investments which might qualify for special treatment.

When the conference turned its attention to international problems, agreement was reached more readily. The usual support for Mauritania's admission to the UN was expressed, and Cameroun's position on unification with North Cameroun was supported.[30] The resumption of direct negotiations between France and Algeria was hailed as an important step toward peace, while the agreements on cooperation in defense, education, and other matters between France and the Entente states were commended. Also applauded was the Tananarive conference on the Congo, while policies designed to promote conflict among Congolese were condemned, as was the South African policy of apartheid. Finally, the conference noted with satisfaction that its audience was increasing and that the significant progress in cooperation which had occurred among members "had just led to the birth of the Union Africaine et Malgache." This statement was the only reference to the creation of another organization, whose charter was not to be drawn up until the Tananarive conference in September 1961.

As Tevoedjre noted, by the Tananarive conference of September 1961, "the UAM was functioning as a regional organization equipped with the administrative structures and techniques which made it one of the most important organs of solidarity on the continent of Africa."[31] To be sure, charters that had previously been approved still had to be signed and new ones adopted. This the Tananarive conference did, as well as take up more specific questions. Thus, by September 1961 the preparatory period had ended and the UAM system had come into being.

---

[30] Britain had organized a referendum in North Cameroun on unification with either Nigeria or Cameroun. The results of this referendum, which favored association with Nigeria, were being challenged by Cameroun.

[31] Tevoedjre, p. 13.

THE UNION AFRICAINE ET MALGACHE SYSTEM

During the period between October 1960, when the first conference was held in Abidjan, and September 1961, when the preparatory period ended, there were several interesting developments. Interest in cooperation remained widespread, but there were divergent views on the level of commitment required to promote cooperation, with the Ivory Coast the spokesmen for a low level of commitment and Senegal the advocate for a high level of commitment. Experts seemed more willing to engage in joint policy-making and implementation on a high level than did the heads of state. Discussions of international problems, with the exception of the Algerian question, and general economic matters provoked little controversy, but the opposite was the case when specific measures for economic cooperation were raised, owing to concerns about possible economic losses. In general, economic cooperation was seen as a way of promoting the economic development of members, but the how and why were never systematically examined. Ultimate decision-making remained in the hands of the heads of state, with ministers and experts relegated to the role of making proposals. The scope of the Union remained wide, and numerous meetings were held that entailed significant costs in time and personnel. As we shall see, this was to prove to be a burden for states with limited supplies of qualified civil servants.

The nature of the Union Africaine et Malgache as provided for in the various treaties is our next concern in this chapter.

The Treaties of the UAM

In an interview with journalists over Abidjan radio soon after the Yaoundé conference, Raphael Saller, the Ivory Coast Minister of Finance, said:

> The OAMCE is in no way a supranational organ, but an organ which only aims at reinforcing the solidarity among the member states. The functioning of the OAMCE does not in any way infringe on the sovereignty of member states. Its Council is its sole organ of decision. . . . Only decisions unanimously made commit the nations represented. As for the Secretary-General, his role is to assist the Council, of which he is only an executive agent in the administrative domain; he possesses no power of his own.[32]

This statement was not only an accurate description of the OAMCE, but it was also equally valid for the other institutions that made up the UAM system.

---

[32] *AFP Special Outre-Mer*, April 12, 1961.

POLITICAL INTEGRATION IN FRENCH-SPEAKING AFRICA

In the first article of the charter of the UAM, signed at Tananarive on September 12, 1961, the UAM was described as a union of independent and sovereign states open to all independent African states; unanimity was required for admission of new members.[33] In Article 2 the organization was described as founded on the solidarity uniting its members, and its goal was specified in the following terms: "To organize the cooperation of its members in all domains of foreign policy, in order to reinforce their solidarity, to assure their collective security, to assist in their economic development, to maintain peace in Africa, in Madagascar, and in the world."

According to Article 4, the general policy of the UAM was to be determined by a conference of heads of state holding two ordinary sessions annually; extraordinary sessions could be held at the request of any state with the support of a majority of the UAM members. Provision was also made for meetings of the appropriate ministers, experts, or permanent delegates to the UN between sessions of the conference of heads of state. Article 4 also stipulated that "motions shall be adopted by a simple majority. Discipline shall be obligatory in all questions relating to decolonization." A General Administrative Secretariat, with headquarters at Cotonou, was provided for in Article 3. The Administrative Secretary-General was to be appointed for two years by the conference of heads of state on the nomination of the President of Dahomey. Responsibility for adopting the budget of the Secretariat rested with the heads of state, and the contribution to this budget of each member was to be proportional to its operating budget. A UAM group at the UN was also provided for; Article 5 stipulated that "this group shall hold compulsory meetings to concert action before all important decisions." The final article of the charter provided for its publication in the Journal Officiel of each member.

Signed on the same day as the UAM charter was the treaty creating OAMCE. The preamble to this treaty is of particular interest for the reasons it gives for the creation of the OAMCE and for its description of the type of organization that was being created. It reads as follows:

The governments of the twelve member states:

Considering the necessity of affirming their political independence through the economic and social advancement of their populations;

---

[33]The charters of the UAM, OAMCE, Union Africaine et Malgache de Défense (UAMD), and the Union Africaine et Malgache des Postes et Télécommunications (UAMPT) are to be found in La Documentation Francaise, Documentation UAM (Paris: Imprimerie d'Haussy et Cie., 1963), pp. 21-113.

Observing that at the present time there is no need to proceed in the creation of an organ with a supranational character, entailing the transfer of sovereignty, since the realization of the said objectives could be obtained by a concerted action respecting the political personality of the states, undertaken through their initiative and under their responsibility;

Considering that the realization of these objectives demands a concerted action respecting their political personality, conducted with their initiative and under their responsibility;

Wishing to harmonize their economic policies and thus make a contribution to the enhancement of Afro-Madagascar solidarity by the reinforcement of the economic ties which unite them while respecting the international engagements to which they have subscribed . . . .

The first section of the treaty, comprised of Articles 1-5, outlined the general nature of the OAMCE. Its goal was to be "to reinforce the profound solidarity and the desire for close cooperation of the African and Madagascar states in order to permit them to accelerate the elevation of the standard of living of their populations." Membership was open to all African states subscribing to this principle. In pursuit of the above goal, the organization was to seek to bring progressively closer the economic policies of its members and coordinate their development plans. This task was to be undertaken in all aspects of economic policy, particularly in the following areas: production (coordination of agricultural production, transformation of techniques); industrialization and its financing (credit, fiscal policies, investment codes, Fond Africain et Malgache de Développement et de Solidarité); internal and external trade (prices, markets, customs duties and commercial policies, inter-African commercial circuits); money (Afro-Malgache cooperation and common monetary policy vis-à-vis the exterior); relations with regional or international economic organizations. In undertaking the above tasks the OAMCE was to utilize all means at its disposal, particularly the following: the elaboration of conventions; presenting recommendations for harmonizing internal economic policies to members; undertaking common projects, from common funds, and for the common benefit, when this proves to be necessary at the multinational level; coordination of scientific and geological research up to the point of creating multinational institutes and cooperating with foreign and international institutes; standardization, centralization, and distribution of information documents; negotiating, in the name of each member, with third countries or organizations. Finally, the institutions of the OAMCE were to be the Council, the General Secretariat, and the technical committees.

The second section of the treaty, comprising Articles 6-14, was devoted to the Council. Consisting of one delegate

from each member, it was to be the supreme decision-making organ.
The Council was granted the power to speak out on all questions
affecting the organization and call the attention of the technical
committees to matters it considered opportune for realizing common
objectives. Further, the Council was responsible for appointing
the Secretary-General, adopting the budget and determining each
member's contribution to it, and establishing the working rules
of the different organs of the OAMCE. Decisions and recommendations of the Council required unanimity, with each state having
one vote. Members pledged attendance at Council meetings, failing
which they would ask another member to represent them. Article
11 provided that "if a member state is not present or represented
at a meeting of the Council, it will be presumed to have accepted
the decisions taken in its absence if, within a period fixed by
the Council, it has not declared itself opposed to the decisions;
in this case [if it declares its opposition] the decisions will
not be implemented. However, members who participated in these
decisions can decide that they will be applicable for them."
Finally, this section provided that the Council would hold an
ordinary session every six months with a President who would
rotate among members from one ordinary session to another; meetings of the Council were also to rotate among members.

The third section of the treaty dealt with the Secretariat,
whose headquarters were to be in Yaoundé. The role of the Secretary-General, appointed for two years, was to assist the Council,
under whose supervision he was also to oversee the administrative
workings of the Secretariat. A responsibility of the Secretary-
General specified in the treaty was the presentation of an annual
report and a report at the opening of each session of the Council.
The Council was to specify the powers of the Secretary-General;
the section stated that "the Secretary-General and the personnel
of the Secretariat placed under his authority will receive and
solicit directives only from the presiding President of the
Council."

The fourth section of the treaty dealt with the technical
committees, four of which were listed: Committee for Scientific
and Technical Research, Committee for the Study of Financial and
Monetary Problems, Committee of Foreign Trade, and Committee of
Economic and Social Development. Other committees were to be
created at the initiative of the organization or of several
states to study general, regional, or specific problems. Further,
it was provided that whenever necessary, any African state with
the need to do so could meet under the auspices of the organization and deal with common, specific matters. Decisions in this
context, though, were not to run contrary to those of the organization. These states could ask for the formation of regional
secretariats or technical committees devoted to the study of
their specific problems, and the organization could assign them
the task of undertaking regional programs.

THE UNION AFRICAINE ET MALGACHE SYSTEM

The final section of the treaty contained general provisions. The Council was required, at its last yearly session, to study means for harmonizing the institutions of the organization with the evolution of its objectives as specified in the treaty. Decisions on the admission of new members were made the responsibility of the Council. Members made the following pledge: "The member states will take all appropriate measures to assure the execution of the provisions of the present treaty or those which result from actions taken by the institutions of the organization." The last two articles of the treaty dealt with procedures for ratification and the depositing of instruments of ratification with the government of Cameroun. The treaty was to be effective from the receipt of instruments of ratification by the government of Cameroun.

Attached to the OAMCE treaty were four protocols creating the four technical committees provided for in the treaty, a protocol creating and organizing the Secretariat, and a convention on the privileges and immunities of the OAMCE; all of these documents were signed at Tananarive on September 12, 1961. The task of adopting the founding documents of the OAMCE was completed at the first ordinary session of the OAMCE Council at Yaoundé in June 1962 with the acceptance of the governing rules for the OAMCE Council and the technical committees.

The protocols creating the technical committees gave each one powers to discuss a very wide range of topics within its area. However, they were empowered only to present opinions and recommendations, for which a two-thirds majority (each state having one vote) was necessary, to the Council. The OAMCE Secretary-General was made responsible for the Secretariats of the Committee of Economic and Social Development and the Committee for the Study of Financial and Monetary Problems; the Secretariats of the remaining two committees--Foreign Trade and Scientific and Technical Research--were to be managed by an employee of the OAMCE Secretariat. Each technical committee was centered at the headquarters of the OAMCE Secretariat, and each was to hold two ordinary sessions annually. Each state was responsible for the cost of its representatives attending meetings of the technical committees. A Committee for the Coordination of Transport, with provisions identical to those of the other technical committees, was created in September 1962.

There was little that was new in the protocol creating and organizing the OAMCE Secretariat, except for an interesting provision in Article 5 that, as much as possible, nominations for Assistants to the Secretary-General would take into account the principle of equitable geographical distribution. The convention on the privileges and immunities of the OAMCE endowed the organization with a juridical personality and specified the diplomatic privileges it and its personnel were entitled to. The governing rules of the OAMCE Council dealt with the internal workings of this body, among which was a proviso that representatives must have the rank or exercise the functions of a minister in the governments. No representative may represent more than one other state.

Similar in nature to the UAM and the OAMCE documents was the UAM Defense Pact (UAMD). In reference to this pact, Houphouet said soon after the Yaoundé conference of March 1961 that "the common defense that we are going to organize in the midst of the UAM is the most important decision of the conference of Yaoundé."[34] A glance at the UAMD pact shows why Houphouet made this statement.

The UAMD committed its members to the regulation of all their international disputes by peaceful means, and to the promotion of peaceful and friendly international relations. To assure the achievement of these goals, the parties were to maintain and increase their individual and collective capacities to resist all forms of aggression. Whenever in the opinion of one of the members the territorial integrity, political independence, or security of one of the parties was threatened, the members were to engage in mutual consultations on the measures to be taken. But no action was to be taken on the territory of a member and no diplomatic move was to be undertaken on its behalf except at its request or with its consent; this provision was to be suspended, however, if the magnitude, violence, or rapidity of the aggression prevented the free functioning of the institutions of the state concerned. Members agreed that a case of acknowledged aggression against one would be considered an aggression against all, necessitating the immediate implementation of measures previously agreed to; subsequently, and after consultations, other required measures--including the use of force--would be undertaken. The term aggression was not limited to nuclear or conventional armed attack, but included subversive actions directed, inspired, or supported from the outside.

The task of establishing the general policies of the UAMD was the responsibility of a conference of heads of state. The pact provided for a Supreme Council of the pact, in which each state would be represented by one plenipotentiary. It was to be the responsibility of the Supreme Council to study all measures relating to the application of the pact and, within the limits specified by the conference of heads of state, decide on the measures that needed to be taken. Decisions of the Supreme Council required a majority of two-thirds of the members, and a Secretariat was to be created to assist the Council. Other provisions of the UAMD pact made it open to all African states, and required a review of the pact every five years for possible

---

[34]Le Figaro, March 31, 1961.

revisions. Ten years after it went into effect, any member was to be free to withdraw from the pact after giving a year's notification of its intention to do so.

The purpose of the UAM Post and Telecommunications Organization (UAMPT) was to promote coordination and cooperation among members in matters of post and telecommunications in order to improve the services in these areas, as well as to elaborate and present joint proposals to international conferences on post and telecommunications. These tasks were to be undertaken by three institutions: (1) a Committee of Ministers responsible for post and telecommunications, the supreme organ of the union, (2) a General-Secretariat, and (3) administrative and technical studies commissions. The Committee of Ministers was to hold one ordinary session each year; it was to be headed by a President who would rotate among the various countries every year and to whom some of the powers of the Committee of Ministers could be delegated. Decisions of the Committee of Ministers were to be made by a two-thirds majority. The Secretariat, with its headquarters in Brazzaville, was a technical and administrative organ under the direct authority of the President of the Committee of Ministers. The Secretary-General and the experts of the Secretariat were to be appointed by the Committee of Ministers. Among other things, the Secretary-General was made responsible for coordinating all matters relating to post and telecommunications between sessions of the Committee of Ministers, distributing information relating to the functioning and improvement of postal and telecommunications services, preparing and submitting relevant proposals to the Committee of Ministers, and undertaking studies requested by members. The administrative and technical studies commissions were to meet when requested by the Committee of Ministers and examine matters specified by the Committee or its President. Each state was responsible for the cost of sending its representatives to UAMPT meetings, while the cost of the Secretariat was to be met from equal contributions from each member.

Students of the process of regional political integration have described the several features of a regional union that are essential if it is to make rapid progress in integration.[35] These are (1) supranational decision-making organs, (2) functionally

---

[35] See in particular Ernst B. Haas, "International Integration: The European and the Universal Process," and Ernst B. Haas and Philippe C. Schmitter, "Economics and Differential Patterns of Political Integration: Projections about Unity in Latin America." Both articles are to be found in International Political Communities (New York: Doubleday and Co., 1966).

specific economic tasks with high spill-over potential into vital areas of welfare policy, (3) built-in or automatic integration based on a firm schedule for the rate and amount of dismantling of obstacles to factor movements, and (4) the presence of identical or converging economic aims with a strong commitment to political unification. The UAM system fell far short of each of these requirements.

The framers of the various founding documents of the UAM were explicit in rejecting all aspects of supranationality. Thus they consistently made references to an Administrative Secretary-General and General Secretariat to indicate that the individuals and institutions concerned had no policy-making powers. Attention was often called to the fact that the union entailed no surrender of sovereignty and that the principle of the equality of the states was to be respected. On most issues--and certainly on all important issues--the principle of unanimity was maintained. Even with respect to decisions unanimously arrived at, the degree of obligation of members to implement them was left vague, with the exception of decisions relating to matters of decolonization. Ultimate responsibility for decision-making was kept in the hands of politicians, with experts confined to making proposals, and with no provision for participation by voluntary associations. Finally, although this was not consciously planned, the creation of several secretariats meant that rivalries among them were more likely than the emergence of one of them as a nucleus of a political union.

With some exceptions in the case of the UAMPT, the founding documents provided for cooperation in only very broad and diffuse areas, such as the coordination of economic development plans and the pursuit of concerted foreign policies. On the other hand, the tasks assigned to the UAMPT seem to fall into the category of issues which Ernst Haas says "may be so trivial as to remain outside the stream of human expectations and actions vital for integration."[36]

There was little in the founding documents that committed the members of the UAM to do specific things at specific times. Instead, the documents referred merely to efforts at cooperation, coordination, and harmonization, thus making it necessary to negotiate each specific policy measure. The OAMCE treaty made it easy for states opposed to policy measures enjoying wide approval to be recalcitrant by making it possible for policies to

---

[36]Haas, "International Integration . . .," p. 102. Examples of issues cited by Haas are the standardization of railway rolling stock and the installation of uniform road signs. The similarities between these and the UAMPT tasks are obvious.

be adopted which engaged only some members. The need to follow
the path of negotiated integration meant that (1) there was no
provision for accelerating the process of integration, and
(2) there was no locking-in system to ensure progress and prevent
stagnation or regression.[37]

Finally, the basic documents of the union made it clear
that ultimate political union was explicitly ruled out. On the
contrary, the emphasis was on the preservation and the strengthening of the sovereignty and independence of member states. The
UAM system, in other words, was designed to facilitate the state-
building activities of its members--not to supplant them. Economic aims shared the spotlight with political and personal aims,
and in each case the aims conflicted as often as they converged.
Where aims could be said to be identical, as with respect to a
better deal from the international economic system, they were so
general as to be meaningless. Thus the UAM system was, at best,
characterized by converging economic aims with a weak commitment
to political unification.

---

[37]References to these two strategies of integration, which are
contained in the Treaty of Rome creating the EEC, are to be found
in Amitai Etzioni, "European Unification: A Strategy of Change"
in International Political Communities, pp. 186-187.

Chapter 3

CHANGES IN INTEGRATIVE CONDITIONS:
1960-1964

It will be recalled that the main factors responsible for the creation of the UAM system were the similarities in the nature of the units involved. They all had very close ties with France, on whom they were very dependent and whose preeminence in the member states was unquestioned.

Each state had a strong presidential system of government with a political system that was authoritarian in nature, or moving in that direction. Pluralistic tendencies were poorly developed, with the political leaders seeking to lessen the autonomy of the main domestic groups (trade unions and student movements, for the most part) and convert them into arms of the government. The various countries were headed by political elites that were highly congenial, with ideologies that were reformist and of the liberal-conservative variety.

All twelve states had limited economic capacities with weak industrial sectors, and each member perceived itself to be largely dependent on the external environment for its economic development. However, capabilities were unevenly distributed within the group of countries, and perceptions differed concerning the extent to which national as opposed to regional efforts in dealing with the external environment would be more successful in promoting the economic development of the individual states. The external environment was generally perceived as compelling. There were, however, differences in the intensity of this feeling and in the perception of the nature of the environment's influence.

Our immediate concern is with the extent to which these factors changed during the life of the UAM system, which ended at the Dakar conference of March 1964 with the decision to suppress the UAM as a political organization and replace it by the Union Africaine et Malgache de Coopération Economique (UAMCE)--an organization devoted entirely to economic and technical cooperation. Questions relating to the character of transactions among members, including the fate of supranational voluntary associations, will be handled when the degree of economic and social integration achieved by the UAM system is discussed.

New Members

It is not surprising that the original integrative conditions remained remarkably stable during the two-and-one-half years of the existence of the UAM system. During this period, none of the original twelve members withdrew from the union, and as we shall see, significant changes occurred only in the Republic of Congo. Two new members were added to the union: Rwanda at the Ouagadougou conference of March 1963 and Togo at the Cotonou conference of July 1963. This increase in membership came during the last year of the union, when its continued existence was greatly in doubt. Thus there was little time for whatever disintegrative factors might have been inherent in the expansion of the union to come into play; however, the two new members were not dissimilar from the founding members.

Neither in its economy nor in the nature of its domestic polity did Togo differ significantly from the founding members of the UAM system. The only major difference between Togo and the UAM members related to its ties with France. Togo was a French Trust Territory prior to independence in April 1960, and close ties between the two countries continued after independence. However, even though it was a member of the Franc Zone and an associated member of the EEC, Togo maintained an "open door" commercial policy. It was significant that Olympio had a Franco-English education, enjoyed closer ties with political leaders in Ghana than with political leaders in the French-speaking areas, "looked askance at anything in Africa representing or recalling French colonization," and "had never set foot in the Palais Bourbon and preferred to speak English at Pan-African conferences."[1] Concern that the emerging UAM group would be too closely linked with France, it will be recalled, was largely responsible for Togo's original refusal to join it.

This obstacle to Togo's membership in the UAM was removed when noncommissioned officers in the Togolese army staged a coup and assassinated Olympio in January 1963. Olympio was succeeded by Nicolas Grunitzky, then in self-imposed political exile in Cotonou. Grunitzky had been the leader of the major party in Togo up to 1958--the Parti Togolais du Progrès (PTP)--and a member of Senghor's Indépendants d'Outre-Mer (IOM). The PTP was in electoral competition with Olympio's Comité de l'Unité Togolaise (CUT), and was receiving support from France. The leaders in the coup were "former NCOs in the French Army, who had traveled and thought a little and were becoming ashamed of the small part played by their country on the international stage, of its isolation and poverty, and were furious that Olympio had refused

---

[1]Tevoedjre, p. 41.

to join the Union Africaine et Malgache."[2] Thus the anti-French and anti-UAM elements were removed from Togolese policies, and the stage was set for joining the UAM system.

If the new government of Togo was eager to join the UAM, the circumstances behind its desire to enter--particularly the assassination of Olympio--and concern by the Ivory Coast that there was a link between the Togo coup and the discovery of a plot in Abidjan meant that some UAM members were not eager to have Togo in their midst. In fact, the new government of Togo had great difficulties in securing even de facto recognition from many UAM and non-UAM African states.[3] Senegal was one of the first states to recognize the new government of Togo. Joining Senegal in urging the recognition of Togo were Cameroun and Dahomey, while the Ivory Coast and Upper Volta led the opposition. This opposition remained firm until some weeks after elections in Togo in which Grunitzky was elected President. Then all African states recognized the Grunitzky government, and Togo was admitted as the fourteenth member of the UAM.

The admission of Rwanda to the UAM posed little difficulty. Rwanda had been jointly administered with Burundi as a Belgian Trust Territory, but the two territories achieved independence separately on July 1, 1962. This occurred "amid suspicions between the new states . . . and dire predictions of crises to come to these poor, overcrowded new states."[4] Ahidjo, President of the UAM from March-September 1962, was concerned that the kind of internal collapse which occurred in the Democratic Republic of the Congo after the Belgians withdrew might also occur in Rwanda. There was another consideration in the mind of Ahidjo, who was unhappy with the close identification between France and the UAM--a feeling he shared with the then Secretary-General of the UAM, Tevoedjre: "If Rwanda, which had never been a French colony, would adhere to the UAM, to my mind it [would be] a great step toward an Africanization of the organization, a means of establishing a certain psychological distance vis-à-vis Paris. . . ."[5] Ironically, then, what made the prospect of bringing Rwanda into the union appealing to Ahidjo and Tevoedjre

---

[2]De Lusignan, p. 175.

[3]The debates triggered by the Togo coup are treated in Tevoedjre, pp. 44-50.

[4]Arnold Rivkin, The African Presence in World Affairs: National Development and Its Role in Foreign Policy (New York: The Free Press of Glencoe, 1963), p. 10.

[5]Tevoedjre, p. 26.

was that in one significant respect it was different from the other members of the union. However, we must not lose sight of the fact that Rwanda retained close links with Belgium and was an associate member of the EEC; thus its external orientation, which was conservative, and its ties were not different from the members of the UAM. It was in this context that Ahidjo sent Tevoedjre to examine the prospects for cooperation between the UAM and Rwanda.

Rwanda was receptive to the idea of membership in the UAM, in part because of its poverty and the hope that there would be economic rewards in joining. Another factor was that its "fairly conservative foreign policy and internal social revolution had led it to feel somewhat isolated among its immediate neighbors."[6] Thus discussions between Tevoedjre and President Kayibanda of Rwanda went very well, and resulted in the latter's attending the UAM Libreville conference of September 1962 as an observer. At this conference, the UAM states made the following decisions concerning aid to Rwanda: Members would open their universities to students from Rwanda, who were to be provided with scholarships and other facilities; experts of Air Afrique and the UAMPT would be sent to Rwanda in order to improve the system of communication and telecommunications with Rwanda; members would supply Rwanda with middle-level civil servants.[7] With these inducements Rwanda was ready to take the plunge and join the UAM prior to the Addis Ababa conference of May 1963, as Kayibanda had promised Tevoedjre. Rwanda was warmly welcomed by the other states, who saw this move as strengthening their organization and increasing its prestige.

Thus the two new members were similar to the original members of the UAM system in their conservative foreign and domestic policies and in their low levels of economic development. Their membership, though, did not increase the resources available to the group; in fact, the contrary was the case, as the decisions with respect to aid to Rwanda indicate. At the same time, given their low capabilities and the lack of prestige of their leaders, who were hardly known, Rwanda and Togo would not challenge the prevailing distribution of power within the UAM. All things considered, the admission of these new members was not likely to introduce elements of instability into the UAM system.

---

[6] Immanuel Wallerstein, Africa: The Politics of Unity (New York: Random House, 1967), p. 61.

[7] Decision No. Lib/003 bis/UAM. See Union Africaine et Malgache, Compte-rendu des travaux de la Conférence de Libreville, 10-13 Septembre 1962 (Cotonou: Secrétariat Général de l'UAM, n.d.), p. 143.

POLITICAL INTEGRATION IN FRENCH-SPEAKING AFRICA

External Ties

Commenting on the ties between France and the UAM states, Tevoedjre made the following observation: "The greatest shortcoming of the UAM in diplomacy was the impression it sometimes gave of an excessive dependence on France. The ties between each of the UAM states and France were in effect so close as to give the impression that the organization itself drew its every inspiration from the former metropole."[8] Table 9 gives some idea of the extent of this dependence.

From Table 9 it is clear that for the members of the UAM, France remained the dominant trading partner, the major source of foreign aid, and the main provider of higher education. Unfortunately, figures are not available on the total number of foreign technical assistance personnel serving in each of the twelve countries. We are thus unable to say what proportion of these personnel came from France, but it is clear that this proportion would be very high. Equally interesting, but also difficult to get data on, is the total number of Frenchmen employed in various capacities in the twelve countries. The available data for the Ivory Coast and Mauritania are presented in Table 10. If it is assumed that most of the foreigners occupying top-level positions in the Ivory Coast and Mauritania are Frenchmen (an assumption warranted by the available evidence), then it is clear that domestic management of the economies of the two countries was still very much in the hands of the French. (This was also the situation in the other ten countries for which data are not available.)

As we saw in Chapter 2, the links between France and the members of the UAM covered many more areas than those we have discussed thus far. Two other areas that should be touched on are the monetary links with France and agricultural price support for the exports of the twelve states. During the life of the UAM system, the twelve states remained members of the Franc Zone, and their currency remained freely convertible with the French franc. Agricultural exports from the twelve to France continued to enjoy prices well above their world market prices; Table 11 gives an idea of the sums involved. When we note that the list of items in Table 11 includes about 80 percent of the exports of some of the states concerned (Chad and Dahomey), it becomes obvious that very important interests were involved in the French subsidies.

Thus a great dependence on France, to the virtual exclusion of important ties with other third parties, was characteristic

---

[8]Tevoedjre, p. 19.

Table 9

SOME INDICATORS OF THE DEPENDENCE OF THE UAM STATES ON FRANCE

Country	Trade with France as Percent of Total Trade in 1962		Percentage of Total Foreign Aid from France and EDF[a]		French Technical Assistance Personnel as of:		Percentage of Students Overseas Who Are in France (c. 1964)
	Exports	Imports	France	EDF	7/1/60	1/1/64	
Cameroun	60%[b]	55%	57%	38%	830	707	78%
Central Africa	57	61	64	18	403	427	73
Chad	50	51	54	36	424	457	80
Congo	20	67	71	29	492	518	81
Dahomey	70	59	54	24	482	221	40
Gabon	59	63	60	30	324	367	94
Ivory Coast	46	43	62	32	1,313	1,364	84
Madagascar	54	75	53	39	2,277	1,738	91
Mauritania	48	72	72	2	210	230	51
Niger	64	54	50	26	379	348	79

Table 9 (continued)

Country	Trade with France as Percent of Total Trade in 1962		Percentage of Total Foreign Aid from France and EDF[a]		French Technical Assistance Personnel as of:		Percentage of Students Overseas Who Are in France (c. 1964)
	Exports	Imports	France	EDF	7/1/60	1/1/64	
Senegal	86%	65%	60%	27%	1,062[c]	1,357	76%
Upper Volta	18	52	61	30	410	341	89

[a]These figures are not very accurate because of the difficulties in securing data on aid from sources other than France and the European Development Fund (EDF). Thus the percentages in the table are slightly high. The dates are 1964 for the Ivory Coast, Mauritania, Central Africa, Congo-Brazzaville, Gabon, and Chad; 1965 for Senegal and Upper Volta; 1966 for Cameroun and Madagascar; 1966-67 for Niger; and 1967 for Dahomey.

[b]Trade figures for Cameroun are for East Cameroun only; figures for West Cameroun are not available.

[c]The July 1960 figure for Senegal leaves out the technical assistance personnel assigned to the Mali Federation.

Sources: International Monetary Fund, Surveys of African Economies, Volumes 1 and 3 (Washington, D.C., 1968 and 1970); République Malgache: Ministère des Finances et du Commerce, Inventaire Socio-Economique de Madagascar, 1960-1965; France: Ministère de la Coopération, Cinq ans de fonds d'aide et de coopération; France: Comité Monétaire de la Zone Franc, La Zone Franc en 1964; République du Dahomey: Ministère de l'Economie et du Plan, Annuaire Statistique du Dahomey (3e volume, 1969); and figures supplied by embassies of the twelve countries in Washington, D.C., and the Organisation Commune Africaine et Malgache (OCAM) Secretariat in Yaoundé.

CHANGES IN INTEGRATIVE CONDITIONS: 1960-1964

Table 10

DISTRIBUTION OF WAGE EARNERS IN THE IVORY COAST AND
MAURITANIA BY QUALIFICATION AND ORIGIN: 1964

(in percentages)

Ivory Coast

Employment Category	Ivorian Nationals	Foreigners of African Origin	Foreigners of Non-African Origin
Managerial staff	10.1%	4.5%	85.4%
Technicians	15.7	2.5	81.7
Foremen	28.3	11.1	60.5
Employees	69.6	21.9	8.4
Skilled workers	69.2	30.0	0.8
Apprentices and unskilled workers	33.7	66.3	--
Total	47.5	45.7	6.8

Mauritania

Employment Category	Mauritanian Nationals	Non-Mauritanians
Management	6%	94%
Supervisors	6	94
Skilled employees	45	55
Skilled workers	50	50
Apprentices	78	22
Unskilled workers	96	4
Total	67	33

Sources: International Monetary Fund, Surveys of African
Economies, Volume 3 (Washington, D.C., 1970), pp.
261 and 348.

Table 11

FINANCIAL ADVANTAGE (OR SURPRISE) FOR AFRICAN AND MALAGASY
STATES (GROSS):   1961

(in million francs)

Coffee, robusta	202.69
Coffee, arabica	5.09
Groundnuts	20.10
Groundnut oil	41.18
Palm oil	0.86
Bananas	26.37
Sugar	25.20
Rice	7.80
Cotton	10.10
Others	3.60
All products	342.99

Source: Teresa Hayter, French Aid (London: Overseas Development
Institute, Ltd., 1966), p. 75.

of the twelve states during the life of the UAM system. This
was no doubt in part a result of the stability of the domestic
polities of the members during this period--a subject to which
we now turn.

The Domestic Polities

        The twelve heads of state present or represented at the
Tananarive conference of September 1961 were Ahidjo (Cameroun),
Youlou (Congo), Maga (Dahomey), Mba (Gabon), Yameogo (Upper Volta),
Tsiranana (Madagascar), Ould Daddah (Mauritania), Diori (Niger),
Senghor (Senegal), Tombalbaye (Chad), Houphouet-Boigny (Ivory
Coast), and Dacko (Central African Republic). At the final UAM
conference at Dakar in March 1964, all these men except Maga and
Youlou were still the leaders of their countries. Maga was over-
thrown by an army coup in October 1963 that led to Justin Ahomadeg-
be becoming the Vice-President and head of government while Sourou
Apithy, a long time rival-ally of Maga, became President. This
situation lasted until November 1965, when a second coup led to
Christophe Soglo becoming President. Youlou was overthrown by a

revolution led by the trade unions in August 1963 and replaced
by Alphonse Massemba-Débat, who had been President of the National
Assembly in 1959-61 and Minister of State until his dismissal a
few months before the revolution.[9]

   From these dates it is clear that the leadership changes
in Dahomey and Congo occurred during the last year of the UAM,
after the possible dissolution of the union had been discussed at
length and seriously considered at the Cotonou conference of
July 1963. Thus these changes were not likely to affect the
day-to-day workings of the UAM system. More important is the
fact that the leadership changes in Dahomey did not affect the
nature of the polity concerned; the opposite was the case with
respect to the leadership change in Congo.

   Apithy desired to move Dahomey leftwards, particularly
in the foreign policy area. He felt that France should remain
the privileged ally of Dahomey, but he also wanted to establish
ties with the East and recognize Communist China. This was opposed by Ahomadegbe, who wanted to follow the foreign policy
orientation of the Ivory Coast and the Entente states. (The
domestic economy was in the hands of Ahomadegbe, who reduced
civil service salaries by 20 percent and imposed other austerity
measures to reduce deficits and end a recession.) In general,
the political life of Dahomey between 1963 and 1965 was very
unstable, with Apithy and Ahomadegbe engaged in a continuous
struggle with each other. This ended in November 1965 when the
army under Soglo intervened and the two leaders were forced to
resign.

   The Congo revolution, on the other hand, led to a dramatic
shift to the left. Initially, some moderates were represented
in the government, but they were soon forced to resign and were
replaced by socialists. A single party--the Mouvement National
de la Révolution--was created, as were other "leftist" organizations, such as the Jeunesses Ouvrières, which was a civilian
militia under the control of the political bureau of the party.
Ties were established with the Eastern bloc which resulted in
foreign aid from these countries. Thus in 1965 the U.S.S.R.
made available a 12-year low interest loan of 8 million rubles
to finance various projects, while in January 1965 Communist
China gave a 16-year interest free loan of 5 billion CFA francs.[10]

---

[9] On the Dahomey coup and the Congo revolution, see Emmanuel
Terray, "Les Révolutions congolaise et dahoméenne," _Revue
Francaise de Science Politique_ (Octobre 1964).

[10] International Monetary Fund, _Surveys of African Economies_,
Vol. 1, p. 246.

Congo thus ceased being one of the moderate African states and became one of the radical ones.

The political systems of the remaining ten states remained essentially what they were in 1960-61. Power remained centralized in the hands of the President, with varying degrees of opposition from other political leaders. Voluntary associations remained weak and had no continuous, legitimate participation in governmental decision-making. Workers and students were concentrated in the capital cities and were more politically aware and involved; in the absence of official channels of political communication, they resorted to anomic forms of protest. However, the observation of two scholars that "the unions in Tropical Africa were of even less significance after independence than they had been before, at least in domestic politics," and that "almost everywhere in the continent, labor organizations were taken over by the governing parties, once independence was achieved"[11] was true not only of trade unions in the UAM states, but also of student organizations. The leaders continued to display very limited concern with ideology, pursued a gradual and adaptive pattern of domestic change, and retained close ties with the Western countries.

In summary, the political systems of the UAM members remained stable during the life of the system. Presidents were changed in two countries, but in only one of them did this result in a change in the nature of the polity. What then about the economies of the member states? The next section is devoted to this subject.

The Economies

In Chapter 2 we saw that the economies of the member states were characterized by underdevelopment and substantial dependence on France; the ties between France and the UAM members during the UAM period were as great as during the colonial period. Further, there were significant disparities in the economic capabilities of the various member states. In Tables 12-16 we will indicate the capabilities of the UAM members and the extent to which the economic disparities increased or decreased.

Perhaps the first thing that is evident from the data in Tables 12-16 is that members of the UAM system remained

---

[11]Elliot J. Berg and Jeffrey Butler, "Trade Unions" in James S. Coleman and Carl G. Rosberg, Jr., eds., Political Parties and National Integration in Tropical Africa (Berkeley: University of California Press, 1964), p. 366.

Table 12

SIZE, GROWTH, AND DISTRIBUTION OF THE GDP AND THE GDP PER CAPITA: C. 1959 AND C. 1964

(Current prices)

Country	Distribution of GDP		Average Annual Increase in GDP		GDP Per Capita		Average Annual Increase in Per Capita GDP	
	C. 1959[a] Value in Billion CFA	C. 1964[b] Value in Billion CFA	Value in Billion CFA	Per-cent	C. 1959[a] Value in CFA Francs	C. 1964[b] Value in CFA Francs	Value in CFA Francs	Per-cent
Cameroun	99.3	156.5	14.3	14.4%	29,650	30,388	184	0.6%
Central Africa	34.1	41.4	2.4	7.1	28,196	29,571	458	1.6
Chad	39.5	52.6	2.6	6.6	15,200	15,939	148	1.0
Congo	23.8	34.2	2.1	8.7	30,500	42,750	2,450	8.0
Dahomey	33.2	41.8	2.2	6.5	16,600	18,174	394	2.4
Gabon	31.4	47.7	4.1	13.0	69,800	101,489	7,922	11.4
Ivory Coast	142.6	239.7	24.3	17.0	41,214	63,920	5,676	13.8
Madagascar	140.8	147.0	3.1	2.2	26,220	26,534	157	0.6
Mauritania	14.5	34.6	4.0	27.7	17,000	33,573	3,315	19.5
Niger	47.8	66.0	6.1	12.7	15,950	20,308	1,453	9.1
Senegal	133.0	187.7	10.9	8.2	45,900	55,209	1,862	4.0
Upper Volta	42.6	56.4	2.3	5.4	10,150	11,874	287	3.0
Totals	782.6	1,105.6			346,380	449,729		

[a]Years are 1958 for Congo and Chad; 1959 for Mauritania, Senegal, Dahomey, Upper Volta, and East Cameroun; 1960 for the Ivory Coast, Niger, Gabon, and Madagascar; and 1961 for Central Africa.

[b]Years are 1962 for Madagascar; 1963 for Dahomey, Niger, Congo, and Chad; 1963-64 for the Federation of Cameroun; 1965 for Upper Volta; and 1964 for Senegal, the Ivory Coast, Mauritania, Central Africa, and Gabon.

Sources: See page 83 below.

Table 13

COMPOSITION AND SECTORAL GROWTH OF THE GDP: C. 1959 AND C. 1964

(Current prices)

Country	Share of Secondary Sector in GDP				Average Annual Increase in Size of Secondary Sector		Production of Energy and Manufactured Goods				Average Annual Increase in Production of Energy and Manufactured Goods	
	C. 1959[a]		C. 1964[b]				C. 1959[a]		C. 1964[b]			
	Value in Billion CFA	Per-cent	Value in Billion CFA	Per-cent	Value in Billion CFA	Per-cent	Value in Billion CFA	Percent of GDP	Value in Billion CFA	Percent of GDP	Value in Billion CFA	Per-cent
Cameroun	8.6	8.7%	19.6	12.5%	2.8	32.0%	5.8	5.8%	14.1	9.0%	2.1	35.8%
Central Africa	5.3	15.5	6.9	16.7	0.5	10.1	3.0	8.8	3.4	8.2	0.1	4.4
Chad	3.5	8.9	7.5	14.2	0.8	22.9	2.6	6.5	2.9	5.5	0.1	2.7
Congo	3.9	16.4	5.8	17.0	0.4	9.7	2.6	10.9	n.d.	n.d.	n.d.	n.d.
Dahomey	2.8	8.4	4.1	9.8	0.3	11.6	0.9	2.7	1.3	3.1	0.1	11.1
Gabon	9.7	30.9	13.6	28.5	1.0	10.1	1.4	4.6	3.0	6.3	0.4	27.1
Ivory Coast	19.9	14.0	36.0	15.1	4.0	20.2	13.1	9.2	25.0	10.4	3.0	22.7
Madagascar	17.6	12.5	18.7	12.7	0.6	3.1	11.1	7.9	11.8	8.0	0.3	3.0
Mauritania	0.7	4.8	8.7	25.1	1.6	228.6	0.1	0.6	0.4	1.1	0.1	75.0
Niger	5.8	12.1	7.6	11.5	0.6	10.3	2.2	4.7	3.0	4.6	0.3	11.9
Senegal	24.2	18.2	33.5	17.9	1.9	7.7	14.2	10.7	19.5	10.4	1.7	.7.5
Upper Volta	3.7	8.7	5.5	9.8	0.3	8.1	1.2	2.8	3.0	5.3	0.3	25.0
Totals							58.2		87.0			

[a] See notes for Table 12.

[b] See notes for Table 12.

Table 13 (continued)

Country	Per Capita Production of Energy and Manufactured Goods		Average Annual Increase in Per Capita Production of Energy and Manufactured Goods	
	C. 1959[a] Value in CFA Francs	C. 1964[b] Value in CFA Francs	Value in CFA Francs	Percent
Cameroun	1,662	2,738	269	16.2%
Central Africa	2,500	2,429	-24	-1.0
Chad	970	879	-18	-1.9
Congo	3,291	n.d.	n.d.	n.d.
Dahomey	435	565	33	7.6
Gabon	3,236	6,383	787	24.3
Ivory Coast	3,786	6,667	720	19.0
Madagascar	2,067	2,123	28	1.3
Mauritania	106	369	53	50.0
Niger	759	935	59	7.8
Senegal	4,649	5,741	218	4.7
Upper Volta	275	632	59	21.5
Totals	23,736	29,461		

Sources: See pp. 83 below.

Table 14

SIZE AND GROWTH OF TOTAL EXPORTS AND PER CAPITA EXPORTS: C. 1960-1964

(Current prices)

Country	Total Exports		Average Annual Increase in Exports		Per Capita Exports		Average Annual Increase in Per Capita Exports	
	Value in Billion CFA C. 1960	Value in Billion CFA C. 1964	Value in Billion CFA	Percent	Value in CFA Francs C. 1960	Value in CFA Francs C. 1964	Value in CFA Francs	Percent
Cameroun	23.950ᵃ	34.523ᵇ	2.643	11.0%	6,862ᵃ	6,703ᵇ	-40	-0.6%
Central Africa	3.425	7.141	0.929	27.1	2,854	5,101	562	19.7
Chad	3.270	6.544	0.819	25.0	1,239	1,983	186	15.0
Congo	4.430	11.703	1.818	41.0	5,608	14,628	2,255	40.2
Dahomey	4.510	3.255	-0.314	-0.7	2,179	1,415	-191	-8.8
Gabon	11.825	23.169	2.836	24.0	26,573	49,295	5,681	21.4
Ivory Coast	37.330	74.501	9.293	24.9	10,789	19,867	2,270	21.0
Madagascar	18.485	22.654	1.042	5.6	3,442	4,089	162	4.7
Mauritania	0.435ᶜ	11.310	3.625	833.0	576ᶜ	10,981	3,468	602.1
Niger	3.110	4.665	0.389	12.5	1,054	1,435	95	9.0
Senegal	30.655ᶜ	30.243	-0.137	-0.4	10,051ᶜ	8,895	-385	-3.8
Upper Volta	1.065	3.314	0.562	52.8	244	697	113	46.4
Totals	142.490	233.022			71,471	125,089		

ᵃEast Cameroun only.

ᵇFederation of Cameroun.

ᶜ1961.

Sources: See p. 83 below.

Table 15

SIZE AND GROWTH OF TOTAL AND PER CAPITA GOVERNMENTAL REVENUES: ORDINARY BUDGET, C. 1960-C. 1964

(Current prices)

| Country | Government Receipts | | Average Annual Increase in Government Receipts: C. 1960-C. 1964 | | Per Capita Government Revenues | | Average Annual Increase in Per Capita Government Revenues | |
	C. 1960 Value in Billion CFA	C. 1964 Value in Billion CFA	Value in Billion CFA	Percent	C. 1960 Value in CFA Francs	C. 1964 Value in CFA Francs	Value in CFA Francs	Percent
Cameroun	15.99[a]	24.44[b]	2.82	17.6	4,581[a]	4,746[b]	55	1.2
Central Africa	2.80	7.62	1.21	43.2	2,333	5,443	778	33.3
Chad	3.86	7.04	0.80	20.7	1,462	2,133	168	11.5
Congo	3.90	9.78	1.47	37.7	4,937	12,225	1,822	36.9
Dahomey	5.40	7.17	0.44	8.1	2,609	3,117	127	4.9
Gabon	4.01	8.31	1.08	26.9	9,011	17,680	2,167	24.1
Ivory Coast	26.37	34.90	2.13	8.1	7,621	9,307	422	5.5
Madagascar	16.49	32.07	3.90	23.7	3,071	5,789	680	22.1
Mauritania	2.99	4.33	0.34	11.4	3,960	4,204	61	1.5
Niger	5.33	6.94	0.40	7.5	1,807	2,135	82	4.6
Senegal	32.15	34.30[c]	0.48	1.5	10,541	10,088[c]	-101	-1.0
Upper Volta	5.22	8.69	0.87	16.7	1,195	1,829	159	13.3
Totals	124.51	185.59			53,128	78,696		

[a]East Cameroun in 1961-62 fiscal year.

[b]Federation of Cameroun in 1964-65 fiscal year.

[c]1964-65 fiscal year.

Sources: See p. 83 below.

Table 16

GDP PER CAPITA IN U.S. DOLLARS AT 1960 PRICES: 1960-1966

| Country | GDP Per Capita | | Average Annual Increase or Decrease | |
	1960 Value in U.S. Dollars	1966 Value in U.S. Dollars	Value in U.S. Dollars	Percent
Cameroun	106	116	1.7	1.6
Central Africa	95	90	-0.8	-0.8
Chad	59	56	-0.5	-0.8
Congo	136	123	-2.2	-1.6
Dahomey	72	68	-0.7	-1.0
Gabon	288	357	11.5	4.0
Ivory Coast	179	225	7.7	4.3
Madagascar	101	95	-1.0	-1.0
Mauritania	81	124	7.2	8.9
Niger	71	71	0.0	0.0
Senegal	190	187	-0.5	-0.3
Upper Volta	43	39	-0.7	-1.6
Totals	1,421	1,551		

Sources: See p. 83 below.

Sources for Tables 12-16

France: Comité Monétaire de la Zone Franc, La Zone Franc, 1959, 1960, 1962, and 1964.

France: Ministère de la Coopération, Planification en Afrique, Vols. 4 and 5.

France: Ministère de la Coopération, Perspectives de population dans les pays africains et malgache d'expression francaise.

France: Ministère de la Coopération, République Centrafricaine: Economie et Plan de Développement (July 1969).

France: Ministère de la Coopération, République Islamique de Mauritanie: Economie et Plan de Développement (December 1963).

République Malgache, Inventaire Socio-Economique de Madagascar, 1960-1965.

République du Sénégal, Comptes Economiques: Années 1959-1960-1961-1962 (December 1963).

Organisation Commune Africaine et Malgache, Bulletin Statistique de l'OCAM (No. 7, September 1967, and No. 8, March 1968).

United Nations Economic Commission for Africa, Economic Cooperation and Integration in Africa: Three Case Studies (ST/ECA/109) (New York, 1969).

United Nations Economic Commission for Africa, African Economic Indicators, 1968 (n.d.), Graph II.

International Monetary Fund, Surveys of African Economies, Vol. 1 (Washington, D.C., 1968).

International Monetary Fund, Surveys of African Economies, Vol. 3 (Washington, D.C., 1970).

Bulletin de l'Afrique Noire, Memento Statistique de l'Economie Africaine (No. 413, 1966; No. 509, 1968; No. 557, 1969).

economically underdeveloped. Per capita productivity, exports, and governmental revenues remained very low, as did the size of the secondary sector and the production of energy and manufactured goods. Even the comparatively wealthier countries, such as Senegal, the Ivory Coast, and Gabon would rank (on a per capita basis) among the poorest and least developed countries on a global scale.

A second feature evident in Tables 12-16 is that the economic resources in the region were very unevenly distributed. Around 1959, for example, the ratio between the highest and the lowest GDP was about 10:1, while that for the GDP per capita was about 7:1. The respective figures around 1964 were 8:1 and 9:1. Comparable ratios existed during the two time periods for all the measures of levels of economic development.

In terms of the total values involved, Senegal, the Ivory Coast, Madagascar, and Cameroun were far ahead of the remaining states with respect to the GDP, secondary sector, production of energy and manufactured goods, exports, and governmental revenues at both time periods. Gabon reached their level with respect to the size of its secondary sector and the value of its exports in 1964. If we examine the share of the secondary sector and the production of energy and manufactured goods in relation to the GDP, we find the picture more confusing. Largely due to its mineral resources, Gabon had the largest secondary sector, with Mauritania ranked second in 1964 (it was last in 1959) because of large-scale iron ore mining begun in the early 1960's; but when we limit our attention to the production of energy and manufactured goods, these two countries are no longer in the top positions. Diamond mining was responsible for the high position of Central Africa with respect to the size of the secondary sector in relation to the GDP, and the development of textile manufacturing resulted in its being among the top countries with respect to the share of energy and manufactured goods in the GDP. Congo was very high in both these measures because of the importance of its manufacturing activities, which around the mid-1960's were said to rank fourth among the UAM states--after Senegal, the Ivory Coast, and Cameroun.[12] Senegal, the Ivory Coast, Cameroun, and Madagascar were high in these two measures (though Cameroun was somewhat low around 1959).

If we examine per capita values rather than total values, Gabon was highest in all measures except those for the production

_____

[12]Bulletin de l'Afrique Noire, Memento de l'Industrie Africaine, 1966 (Numéro Spécial, No. 413), p. 103. Because of the manner in which the Congolese government collected its economic statistics, it was impossible to determine the value of energy and manufactured goods produced around 1964.

of energy and manufactured goods and governmental revenues around 1960. Second and third highest positions were for the most part occupied by Senegal and the Ivory Coast, with the Ivory Coast rather than Senegal in the second position during the period around 1964 in most instances; Congo occupied the fourth position in all but one case (per capita exports around 1960). The middle positions were invariably occupied by Cameroun, Madagascar, and Central Africa; Mauritania joined this middle group around 1964 with respect to all measures except that of per capita production of energy and manufactured goods. Dahomey, Upper Volta, Niger, and Chad almost always ranked as the least developed of the UAM states.

Analysis of the average annual growth rates tells much the same story, but with some significant differences. Due to the investments and other activities connected with the start of mining activities, Mauritania enjoyed fantastically high growth rates in all measures except total and per capita governmental revenues. For example, exports increased by an annual average of 833 percent, the secondary sector by 228.6 percent, and the GDP by 27.7 percent. However, Mauritania was so low on the scale of economic development around 1959 that even with these growth rates it ranked among the top five states in 1964 in only two measures (GDP per capita and per capita exports). Apart from Mauritania, only the Ivory Coast and Gabon experienced significant growth rates in most of the measures. Cameroun ranked after the Ivory Coast and Gabon in terms of growth rates, and would have ranked higher; however, the merger between East and West Cameroun in 1961 resulted in low growth rates for the Federation of Cameroun in 1964 because West Cameroun was not as prosperous as East Cameroun. The lowest growth rates were usually those of Madagascar, and the growth rates for Senegal, except for GDP per capita, were in the lower half of the group. Congo's growth rates, with one exception (the secondary sector), were consistently among the highest six. Upper Volta, Central Africa, Chad, and Niger had reasonably high growth rates in several of the measures, while Dahomey experienced no significant growth rates in any of the measures.

These growth figures indicate that the wealthier countries, with the exception of Senegal and Madagascar, were growing much faster than the poorer ones--increasing the disparity in resources between the two groups. The economic decline of Senegal is particularly noteworthy, and we will have cause to call attention to it when discussing policies advocated within the UAM system.

Table 16 inspires a note of caution in our interpretation of growth rates among the UAM states. Tables 12 to 15 are based on "current prices"; thus it is difficult to say whether increases in values were the reflection of real growth or merely the reflection of increases in prices. Unfortunately, data on increases in prices during the 1960-1964 period that will permit the computation of real growth rates are generally not available. On the other hand, Table 16 covers the period 1960-1966, extending beyond the years we are concerned with here. However, if we assume that Table 16 describes the 1960-1964 period as well as it describes the period 1960-1966 (an assumption supported by the scattered information available on the rate of inflation in the region), then only Mauritania, the Ivory Coast, Gabon, and Cameroun experienced any growth in per capita GDP during the UAM period. The economy in Niger was stagnant, while those of the other states declined.

Differential growth rates lead us to the third feature that characterized the economies of the UAM states during the 1960-1964 period--increasing disparities in the distribution of resources. The states which most often increased their share of regional resources were Mauritania, the Ivory Coast, and Gabon, followed by the Congo. Senegal, Niger, Dahomey, Chad, and Madagascar remained stagnant or declined with respect to their share of regional resources in all but one or two of the measures used. The remaining three states registered gains in four or five of the measures, but these were not significant.

We can now summarize what happened to the integrative conditions with respect to the size of capabilities and the manner of their distribution. Capabilities during the UAM period remained weak and, on the basis of Table 16, might even have declined in almost all the members of the union. The disparities in the distribution of resources which existed at the beginning of the period were increased rather than decreased. The redistribution of resources was in part at the expense of two of the better-endowed states--Senegal and Madagascar--and in part at the expense of the poorest members of the region--Chad, Dahomey, and Niger.

Significantly, the states that benefitted most from this process of uneven growth were the three most opposed to a high level of regional political integration--Mauritania, the Ivory Coast, and Dahomey. Moreover, these three states were the ones that felt most confident of their abilities to promote their economic development by national, as opposed to regional, measures. Finally, and most important, neither among the gainers nor among the losers did the feeling prevail that the existence or functioning of the UAM system affected the growth rates of its members. (Within the UDE, there was some feeling that the higher growth rates of Congo were due to the UDE, but this related to the functioning of the UDE and not of the UAM.) As we shall see, there was little economic coordination in the UAM, and growth rates were perceived as the result of national efforts. Our conclusion, therefore, is that with respect to the size and

distribution of resources, background conditions were even more
unfavorable to regional political integration during 1960-1964
than they were prior to 1960.

To the phenomena of marginal increases in resources (if
not a decline in resources) must be added the problem of increasing burdens. First, there was the new burden arising from state-
hood and independence. This involved the costs of maintaining a
foreign service, membership in various international organizations,
and attendance at various international conferences. It is impossible to determine the sums expended on these activities, but
given the small resources available and the numerous inter-African
conferences held between 1960 and 1964,[13] it is safe to assume
that they were not insignificant for any of the countries. Moreover, as we shall see, some of the issues discussed among the UAM
states related to the use of joint diplomatic representations to
reduce costs and measures to be taken to persuade international
organizations to reduce the financial burdens of membership for
poor states.

A second aspect of the problem of increasing burdens
relates to the cost of membership in the UAM system. This involved (1) contributions to the various budgets, (2) providing
personnel to staff the various secretariats, (3) sending delegates
to conferences, and (4) playing host to one or more of the various
conferences. The costs of the first two items did not amount to
much: the budget of the UAM system was quite small, amounting
to only 153 million CFA in 1962 and 284 million CFA in 1963, and
the demand for personnel from any state for the secretariats never
exceeded four or five. The situation was quite different with
respect to the remaining two items. According to Tevoedjre, "the
Bangui Conference (March 1962) cost over 50 million francs CFA;
Libreville (September 1962) over 80 million; and Ouagadougou
(March 1963) over 100 million. Delegates, never fewer than 200,
were lodged and fed by the particular state which was sponsoring
the Conference."[14] Thus for the countries in which heads of state
conferences were held from 1960-1964 (and this included all but
Mauritania, Niger, and Chad), the costs must have been very substantial. The costs of participating in these conferences were
also high, as Yameogo observed in February 1962:

> The government of Upper Volta is becoming more and more pre-
> occupied with the very high number of ministerial and special
> conferences in which our government has to be represented.
> To the ministerial conferences, whether belonging directly to
> the activity of the UAM or whether belonging to the activity

---

[13]See Zartman, pp. 18-19, for a list of the inter-African conferences held during this period.

[14]Tevoedjre, pp. 17-18.

of the specialized secretariats, are added the meeting of the
technical committees and committees created ad hoc as needs
arise. These increases are costly and make it more difficult
for the heads of ministerial departments to accomplish the
duties for which they are held responsible in their respective
governments.[15]

This concern was widely shared. In short, membership in the UAM
system entailed increasing economic burdens but no increasing
economic rewards.

The third and final facet of increasing burdens derives
from domestic pressures for improvement in standards of living.
Economic dissatisfactions were largely responsible for governmental changes in Dahomey and Congo; they were also strong in
Upper Volta, Central Africa, and Senegal, and resulted in the
overthrow of the governments of the first two in January 1966.
Such pressures were not as great in the other states, but they
existed and were of growing concern to the leaders. Because of
low and sometimes declining resources, the states were not in a
position to satisfy the economic demands.

Our discussion of the integrative economic conditions has
touched on two crucial process conditions cited in the literature
on regional political integration. According to Deutsch, successful regional political integration requires significant growth
in capabilities among all participating units, a situation often
associated with superior growth in one of the units, which then
acts as the core area around which integration occurs.[16] Neither
of these two requirements was met in the UAM system. In general,
unit capabilities did not experience significant growth and might
even have declined. In those countries in which growth clearly
occurred, the magnitude of growth was not very substantial. On
the basis of the data in Table 16, only Mauritania met and sur-
passed the 5 percent growth rate in per capita GDP established as
the target in the UN resolution declaring the 1960's the decade
of development. Whether other process conditions that emerged
were just as detrimental to regional political integration will
concern us in subsequent sections of this chapter.

The Compellingness of the External Environment

Insecurities resulting from newness in the international
scene, fear of externally induced subversion, the existence of

---

[15] Ibid., p. 16.

[16] Karl W. Deutsch et al., Political Community and the North
Atlantic Area (Princeton: Princeton University Press, 1957),
pp. 37-43.

rival blocs in Africa based on competition for prestige, disputes
over the pattern of domestic development in Africa and the nature
of the ties that should be maintained with non-African states,
and controversies over the nature of the African subsystem were
among the major factors responsible for the creation of the UAM.
The saliency of these factors varied from state to state, but all
perceived the external environment as threatening. By 1963, however, significant changes in these factors had occurred, and the
extent to which the UAM members perceived the external environment
as threatening had declined considerably. A brief examination
of these changes is necessary.

The first of these factors--insecurities resulting from
newness in the international scene--did not persist for long. As
time elapsed, and as involvement in the international system
deepened, the feeling that the external environment could be
coped with gradually increased. To be sure, it was recognized
that certain capabilities necessary for effective participation
in the international system were lacking, but there was no longer
the feeling of being lost. This was a result of experience which
showed that these matters were not as difficult as they were
assumed to be, the courtship of the new African states by the
major powers in the early 1960's, and the existence of several
forums in which information and other forms of assistance in
foreign policy matters could be sought. (The UAM system was one
such forum.)

Related to this was a decline in the fear of externally
inspired subversion. To be sure, Ghana continued to be regarded
as a center of subversion in Africa, and allegations that third
parties were fomenting subversive activities were made by several
UAM states. But these threats were no longer perceived as being
as intense as they had been in 1960, particularly by Senegal and
Cameroun. A major exception was in January 1963 when Olympio of
Togo was assassinated. This event made a great impression not
only on the UAM states, but on all African leaders, because it
was the first assassination of a head of state in Africa. However, the events in Togo were later perceived as having resulted
from internal factors rather than from external subversion (see
p. 67 above). Further, during the UAM period, fewer and fewer
links were perceived between internal subversion and the Communist
bloc, and the possibilities of direct threats from the Communist
countries, which had weighed heavily in the mind of Houphouet,
were now regarded as remote.

Finally, the period between 1961 and 1963 was dominated
by efforts at eliminating rival blocs in Africa and the creation
of an organization that would include all independent African
states except South Africa, whose central task would be the promotion of African unity. The first step in this process was the
Monrovia conference of May 1961, which was designed to bring

together the Casablanca and Brazzaville groups as well as non-aligned African states. The twelve UAM members were present at the conference, as were Ethiopia, Liberia, Libya, Nigeria, Sierra Leone, Somalia, Togo, and Tunisia (as an observer). The conference failed in its aim of bringing together the radical and moderate African states, but it bridged the French-English-speaking gap. Also, it widened the ranks of the moderates, and the UAM states were greatly reassured by the fact that the participants at the conference shared their views on issues that had previously divided the African states. These issues were the pattern of domestic development, the manner of organizing the African subsystem, and the links between African and non-African states.

A second effort was made to bring all African states together at the Lagos conference of January 1962, but the Casablanca powers again refused to attend, as did Libya, Tunisia, and the Sudan. A draft charter creating an Organization of African States, inspired by the charter of the Organization of American States, was presented by Liberia. While approving the proposal in principle, the Lagos conference deferred its final adoption so that states not present at the conference might have the option of becoming associated with the new group. Thus the moderate states present at Monrovia and Lagos were doing everything possible to keep the door open to the other independent African states.

As previously noted, two major issues were primarily responsible for the division of African states into rival blocs: the Algerian conflict and the Congo crisis. Disputes over these issues, combined with disputes over the way to achieve African unity and competition for prestige, were responsible for the continued existence of the rival blocs through much of 1962 and the failures of the Monrovia and Lagos conferences. In late 1962 and early 1963, significant changes occurred that made it possible for the two blocs finally to meet and create a larger grouping.

First, negotiations between France and Algeria led to Algeria's becoming independent in July 1962, thereby eliminating one of the main issues of inter-African controversy. Second, the Congo crisis was ended in January 1963 with the defeat of Tshombe's forces and the reintegration of Katanga into the Democratic Republic of the Congo. Finally, a minor issue--the conflict between Morocco and Mauritania--lost its importance with the admission of Mauritania into the UN and the evolution of friendly ties between Mauritania and countries like Ghana and Mali. Thus, by early 1963 most of the major issues that divided the Monrovia and Casablanca groups had lost their saliency.

Another factor that contributed to the success of the efforts at regrouping among African states was the disintegration

of the Casablanca bloc. As early as December 1960 Ghana had
recognized Mauritania, and Mali signed a frontier treaty with
Mauritania in February 1963. Thus the principal reason for
Morocco's membership in the Casablanca group--the hope of annex-
ing Mauritania--had been lost. On the Congo issue, the Casablanca
states had also pursued different policies. With the settlement
of the Congo crisis, the basis for a common policy on this issue
no longer existed; this was also the case with respect to the
Algerian problem after July 1962. In short, there were no longer
any major issues to hold the Casablanca group together.

Also contributing to the disintegration of the Casablanca
group was the inconsistency between the profession of its members
to the ideal of African unity and their formation of an organization consisting of only five members. Guinea and Mali felt this
contradiction most acutely, and only pressures from Ghana kept
them from attending the Monrovia and Lagos conferences. The
position of Guinea and Mali was strengthened when President Ben
Bella of Algeria, who had tremendous prestige in Africa, endorsed
the creation of a united front composed of all African states in
order to fight against colonialism in Africa.

It was in this context that Haile Selassie of Ethiopia
and Abubakar Balewa of Nigeria undertook the diplomatic initiatives that resulted in the creation of the Organization of African
Unity (OAU) at the Addis Ababa conference of May 1963. The OAU
brought together the Monrovia and Casablanca groups, which were
henceforth abolished, but the fate of groups like the UAM was
left in doubt as a result of an understanding at the conference
that whereas blocs were forbidden, regional groupings were per-
missible. Whether the UAM was a bloc or a group and what its
fate should be was to become a major concern of the UAM states
after May 1963. The important thing to be noted here is that
the success of the Addis Ababa conference resulted in a euphoric
feeling that inter-African rivalry was a thing of the past; further, because the OAU Charter was based on the attitudes of the
moderate states with respect to African unity, the UAM states
lost their earlier feeling of being isolated within the African
subsystem and of having to cope with pressures from the radical
states. Thus, by early 1963 the factors that were responsible
for the perception of the external environment as threatening
were absent. As we shall see, this was a major factor in the
dissolution of the UAM.

We are now in a position to summarize the changes in
integrative conditions during the period of the UAM system.
Capabilities continued to be weak and may have declined for a
majority of the states. The few states that experienced increases in capabilities did not grow fast enough for any of

them to constitute a core area even if it so desired. At the same time, burdens increased because of internal developments and participation in the UAM and the global system. Even more than in 1960, capabilities continued to be unevenly distributed, with the gap increasing; but this was in no way linked to the functioning of the UAM system in the perception of the actors. The domestic polities and elite values of the member states remained quite similar but somewhat more heterogeneous than was the case around 1960. The degree of pluralism in member states remained low and might even have declined somewhat. External ties and dependencies remained roughly the same as they were in 1960, but there were slight changes in the patterns of these ties and dependencies. Finally, the degree to which the external environment was perceived as compelling declined significantly.

In light of these changes in integrative conditions, our prediction is that efforts at regional political integration will fail unless the process variables are particularly strong. We have already noted that with respect to two such variables--increasing capabilities among all the units and the emergence of a core area--conditions favorable to regional political integration did not emerge in the UAM. Our next task is to examine the workings of the UAM system to determine the nature of the other process variables that emerged and the level of political integration achieved.

Chapter 4

THE UAM IN OPERATION

According to Ernst Haas, "The study of regional integration is concerned with explaining how and why states cease to be
wholly sovereign, how and why they voluntarily mingle, merge,
and mix with their neighbors so as to lose the factual attributes
of sovereignty while acquiring new techniques for resolving conflict between themselves."[1] A central feature of this process
is the emergence of what Leon Lindberg refers to as a collective
decision-making system. It is this process that is of central
importance in the study of regional political integration.

The most elaborate effort at developing classification
schemes for tracing the evolution of a collective decision-making
system is that undertaken by Lindberg.[2] The first and, for us,
the most interesting of Lindberg's schemes deals with the level
of collective decision-making activity--or the extent to which
decisions are actually made as a group. Level is described in
terms of the scope of policy areas treated, the range of decision-
making stage attained, and the degree of decisiveness in each
issue area or decision-making stage.

Lindberg's functional scope of collective decision-making
is reproduced below:

External Relations Functions

1. Military security
2. Diplomatic influence and participation in world affairs
3. Economic and military aid to other polities
4. Commercial relations with other polities

---

[1]Ernst B. Haas, "The Study of Regional Integration: Reflections on the Joy and Anguish of Pretheorizing" in Leon N. Lindberg
and Stuart A. Scheingold, eds., Regional Integration: Theory and
Research (Cambridge: Harvard University Press, 1971), p. 6.

[2]See Leon N. Lindberg, "Political Integration as a Multidimensional Phenomenon Requiring Multivariate Measurement" in Lindberg
and Scheingold, eds., Regional Integration: Theory and Research,
pp. 45-127.

Political-Constitutional Functions

5. Public health and safety and maintenance of order
6. Political participation (i.e., symbolic participation, voting, office-holding)
7. Access to legal-normative system (equity, civil rights, property rights)

Social-Cultural Functions

8. Cultural and recreational affairs
9. Education and research
10. Social welfare policies

Economic Functions

11. Counter-cyclical policy (government expenditure, price and wage controls, budgetary policy)
12. Regulation of economic competition and other government controls on prices and investments
13. Agricultural protection
14. Economic development and planning (including regional policies, aid to depressed industries, public finance, guarantees of investment, etc.)
15. Exploitation and protection of natural resources
16. Regulation and support of transportation
17. Regulation and support of mass media of communications (including post office, television, radio, etc.)
18. Labor-management relations
19. Fiscal policy
20. Balance-of-payments stability (exchange rates, lending and borrowing abroad, capital movements)
21. Domestic monetary policy (banking and finance, money supply)
22. Assurance of free movement of goods, services, and other factors of production (not including capital) within the customs union.[3]

For our purposes, we find it useful to disaggregate some of the issue areas under Lindberg's "external relations functions," and have therefore increased the number in this category to eleven. We have also added one new issue area under "political-constitutional functions." No change appears necessary with respect to social-cultural functions and economic functions. (Our revised list of issue areas is to be found in Table 17.)

An effort at measuring the scope of decision-making in a particular union immediately raises the question of the relative salience of different issue areas. Several suggestions have been

---

[3]Ibid., p. 60.

made as to how this problem can be handled,[4] but in our view none
of them is satisfactory; it is a problem whose solution must await
further progress in the measuring techniques available to political scientists. For the purposes of the present study, the
inability to assess the salience of each issue area is not a
major difficulty. We will be concerned with the same region
over a ten-year period, and can assume that there were no significant changes in the relative salience of different issue areas.
Such an assumption is strengthened by the fact that, with the
exception of the Republic of Congo, the political systems of the
member states hardly changed during the period.

Six stages are listed in Lindberg's range of decision-
making scale; they are as follows:[5]

Score	Stage of Decision
1	Collective problem recognition
2	Specific action alternatives defined collectively
3	Collective decisions on policy guidelines
4	Detailed collective goal-setting; implementation by national rules
5	Decisions on policies and rules directly binding on individuals
6	Collective implementation and enforcement

Lindberg's decisiveness scale--or locus of decision-making
scale--is as follows:[6]

Score	Locus
0	All activity at the national level
1	Preponderance at national level; some collective
2	Substantial activity at collective level, but national dominant

---

[4]See ibid., pp. 61-64, and Joseph S. Nye, "Comparative Regional
Integration: Concept and Measurement," International Organization, Vol. XX, No. 4 (Autumn 1968), p. 869.

[5]Lindberg, "Political Integration . . .," p. 67.

[6]Ibid., pp. 71-72. We have used the most discriminating of
Lindberg's measures in this area. (Compare this scale with the
scale on p. 69 in the same article.)

3	Roughly equal activity at both levels
4	Collective level dominant, but substantial national activity
5	Preponderance of activity at collective level; small national role
6	All activity at the collective level

Both of these scales will be used in this study--with only one alteration. We will include a decision-making stage entailing joint discussion which fails to result in a collective definition of the problem; the score assigned to this stage is 0.

The Scope of Decision-Making

A short description of the decision-making procedure is necessary before presentation of our table on the scope of decision-making in the UAM. Issues arose in the UAM context by their being raised either by one of the member states or by one of the secretariats. The next step in the decision-making procedure was the discussion of the issues by one of the several councils of ministers. There was a high degree of functional specialization within the UAM system. Thus the UAMPT Council of Ministers was essentially concerned with matters relating to post and telecommunications, the UAMD Council of Ministers with defense matters, and the OAMCE Council of Ministers with economic matters. On the other hand, the UAM Council of Ministers, though primarily concerned with political matters, dealt with a wider range of issues, and thus ended up dealing with matters that had been or were being discussed by one of the other specialized agencies. The main overlap between the UAM Council of Ministers and the other councils of ministers was in the area of external relations functions. Thus both the UAM and the UAMPT Councils of Ministers dealt with matters relating to influence and coordination of policies in global or continental organizations concerned with postal and telecommunications matters. The overlap between the UAM and the OAMCE Councils of Ministers were similar in nature, while the overlap between the UAM and the UAMD Councils of Ministers arose from both bodies dealing with the problem of subversion in Africa. The most serious overlap was between the UAM and the OAMCE, and as we shall see, it resulted in a great deal of rivalry between the two secretariats.

Regardless of which council of ministers treated a particular topic, the next step in the decision-making procedure was the formulation of recommendations for ratification by a heads of state conference. In cases in which the council of ministers failed to reach unanimous agreement, the matter would be sent to the heads of state for arbitration. Occasionally, the

council of ministers would refrain from discussing an issue on
the grounds that only the heads of state were competent to deal
with the problem. Also, in a few instances, matters were taken
up directly by the heads of state without having been previously
referred to one of the councils of ministers. There were only
six minor issues on which decisions were made by the councils
of ministers without being referred to a heads of state conference
for ratification. Thus, by focusing on the level of the heads
of state conference, we can get an almost complete picture of the
scope of decision-making in the UAM system.

Table 17 presents data on the number of items treated in
each of thirty issue areas at each of the six UAM heads of state
conferences. The criteria used for including an item are minimal,
entailing no more than its inclusion on the agenda or its being
raised at one of the sessions of the UAM or its subsidiary organizations. This should be kept in mind in evaluating our measure
of the scope of decision-making in the UAM and our treatment of
the relationship between scope and the other two aspects of the
level of collective decision-making.

One feature apparent from Table 17 is the broad scope of
issue areas treated by the UAM. Only four of the 30 issue areas
did not receive any attention whatsoever. If we disregard those
issues which accounted for less than one percent of the total
number of items discussed, there are still nineteen issue areas
which received some treatment in the UAM context. In contrast,
Lindberg and Scheingold found that the scope of the EEC was restricted to seven issue areas in 1957 and nine issue areas in
1968.[7] It should be noted, however, that their criteria of inclusion are more stringent than ours, entailing more than pre-
decisional activities.[8] Since we plan to present a separate
measure for the decision-making stage attained in each issue
area, we think it best to utilize broader criteria for measuring
scope. This will enable us to indicate, among other things, the
relationship between scope and stage of decision-making. Conse-
quently, until we present our data on the stage of decision-
making, a comparison between the scope of the UAM and that of
the EEC is not possible. On the basis of our criteria, though,
the UAM was clearly characterized by a very broad scope.

A second feature evident from Table 17 is the tendency
for the number of items treated under most issue areas to remain
stable from one conference to the next. This is true for all the
economic functions except those dealing with the regulation and

---

[7]Lindberg, p. 74.

[8]Ibid., p. 73.

Table 17

NUMBERS OF ISSUES DISCUSSED AT THE UAM HEADS OF STATE CONFERENCES

Issue Areas	Tananarive (September 1961)	Bangui (March 1962)	Libreville (September 1962)	Ouagadougou (March 1963)	Cotonou (July 1963)	Dakar (March 1964)	Totals Number	Totals Per cent
External Relations Functions								
1. Military security	1	0	1	3	1	0	6	1.5%
2. Conflict resolution and management among members	1	1	0	3	0	2	7	1.8
3. Cold war, arms control and disarmament	2	0	8	0	0	0	10	2.6
4. Decolonization and human rights	9	1	8	3	3	0	24	6.1
5. Diplomatic influence and participation in intra-African affairs	1	4	4	6	4	4	23	5.9
6. Diplomatic influence and participation in global affairs	2	7	32	20	1	10	72	18.4
7. Economic and technical aid to or from other polities	10	7	6	3	2	0	28	7.2
8. Global economic, commercial, scientific and technical arrangements	4	4	3	8	1	6	26	6.7
9. Continental economic, commercial, scientific and technical arrangements	1	3	1	3	2	4	14	3.6
10. Economic, commercial, scientific and technical relations with major trading partners (France, the EEC)	6	10	4	3	0	0	23	5.9

Table 17 (continued)

Issue Areas	Tananarive (September 1961)	Bangui (March 1962)	Libreville (September 1962)	Ouagadougou (March 1963)	Cotonou (July 1963)	Dakar (March 1964)	Totals Number	Totals Per-cent
External Relations Functions (continued)								
11. Economic, commercial, scientific and technical relations with minor trading partners	0	2	2	0	1	0	5	1.3%
Subtotal	37	39	69	52	15	26	238	61.0
Percent	76%	58	76	57	33	55		61.0
Political-Constitutional Functions								
12. Public health and safety and maintenance of order	0	0	0	3	0	1	4	1.1
13. Political participation	0	0	0	0	0	0	0	0.0
14. Access to legal-normative system	3	2	1	0	2	0	8	2.1
15. Organization and administration of the civil service	2	0	0	3	2	0	7	1.8
Subtotal	5	2	1	6	4	1	19	5.0
Percent	10%	3	1	7	9	2		5.0
Social-Cultural Functions								
16. Cultural and recreational affairs	0	0	1	1	0	0	2	0.5
17. Education and research	3	3	4	5	7	14	36	9.2
18. Social welfare policies	0	0	1	0	0	0	1	0.3
Subtotal	3	3	6	6	7	14	39	10.0
Percent	6%	5	7	7	15	30		10.0

Table 17 (continued)

Issue Areas	Tananarive (September 1961)	Bangui (March 1962)	Libreville (September 1962)	Ouagadougou (March 1963)	Cotonou (July 1963)	Dakar (March 1964)	Totals Number	Totals Per-cent
Economic Functions								
19. Counter-cyclical policy	0	0	0	0	0	0	0	0.0%
20. Regulation of economic competition and other government controls on prices and investments	1	1	0	0	0	1	3	0.7
21. Agricultural protection	0	0	0	0	0	0	0	0.0
22. Economic development and planning	1	3	2	1	1	3	11	2.7
23. Exploitation and protection of natural resources	0	0	1	0	0	0	1	0.3
24. Regulation and support of transportation	1	6	9	3	0	1	20	5.0
25. Regulation and support of mass media of communications	0	10	1	21	18	0	50	12.7
26. Labor-management relations	0	0	1	0	0	0	1	0.3
27. Fiscal policy	0	1	0	0	0	1	2	0.5
28. Balance-of-payments stability	0	0	0	0	0	0	0	0.0
29. Domestic monetary policy	0	1	0	1	1	0	3	0.7
30. Movement of goods, services, and other factors of production (not including capital) within the customs union	1	1	1	1	0	0	4	1.1
Subtotal	4	23	15	27	20	6	95	24.0
Percent	8%	34	16	29	43	13		24.0
GRAND TOTAL	49	67	91	91	46	47	391	100.0

support of transportation and the regulation and support of mass media of communications. It also applies to all the political-constitutional functions, as well as all the social-cultural functions except education and research. Many of the external relations issue areas also tended to remain stable: military security; conflict resolution and management among members; diplomatic influence and participation in intra-African affairs; and economic, commercial, scientific and technical relations with minor trading partners. With the exception of diplomatic influence and participation in intra-African affairs, however, the issues that remained stable were the ones that received the least attention as measured by the number of items discussed under each issue area.

The issue areas which showed the greatest fluctuations in terms of numbers of items discussed were: cold war, arms control and disarmament; decolonization and human rights; diplomatic influence and participation in global affairs; global economic, commercial, scientific and technical arrangements; continental economic, commercial, scientific and technical arrangements; regulation and support of transportation; and regulation and support of mass media of communications. With the exception of cold war, arms control and disarmament, these widely fluctuating issue areas accounted for the largest number of items treated by the UAM.

The fluctuations with respect to issue areas falling in the external relations functions category are due to the fact that the UAM was essentially reacting to issues raised in the external environment. As these fluctuated, UAM concern with them also fluctuated. Internal procedures--or more specifically, the tendency of the UAMPT Council of Ministers and the OAMCE Committee for the Coordination of Transport to deal with large numbers of items at each of their sessions (as opposed to spreading these items over several meetings)--account for the fluctuations in the issue areas of transportation and mass communications.

Two issues--economic and technical aid to or from other polities, and economic, commercial, scientific and technical relations with major trading partners--showed a progressive decrease in interest over time. This is because most of the items which fell in these two issue areas arose because of negotiations with the EEC over the renewal of the Convention of Association. By the end of Summer 1962, when the UAM members were no longer involved in formulating basic principles and maximum demands, activity concerning these issues declined.

Only one issue area--education and research--showed a progressive increase in attention received over time. This was a result of two factors: one was the desire of individual members to increase the education and research facilities open to them, and the other was a defensive reaction against external pressures for the creation of continental educational and research institutions, which led to the launching of similar efforts at the UAM level. (This second factor will be discussed in more detail later in the chapter.)

The third feature evident from Table 17 is the uneven distribution of items discussed among the thirty issue areas. This point can best be made with a rank ordering of issue areas for the three-and-a-half year period of the UAM. Table 18 provides such a rank-ordering of issue areas, while Table 19 provides a breakdown of how the categories of issues cluster in the various rank-orders.

Tables 18 and 19 clearly reveal the dominant position of external relations functions in the UAM. Of the five issue areas which fall in the first rank in Table 18, by virtue of their accounting for at least twice as many items discussed as would have been discussed if the 391 items had been evenly distributed among all thirty issue areas, three belong to the external relations functions category. Of the remaining eight external relations functions issue areas, four are in the second rank, which includes issue areas accounting for more items discussed than if there had been a random distribution of items, but less than twice as many more. The other four external relations functions issue areas are in the third rank, which includes issue areas accounting for only slightly less than the mean distribution of items discussed, but greater than one-third of the mean distribution. None of the external relations functions issue areas falls in the fourth rank, which includes those issue areas accounting for less than one-third of the mean distribution of items discussed.

By contrast, three of the four political-constitutional functions issue areas are in the third rank, and the remaining issue area is in the fourth rank. Similarly, only one of the three social-cultural functions issue areas is in the first rank, with the remaining two issue areas in the fourth rank. Finally, one of the twelve economic functions issue areas is in the first rank, one in the second rank, two in the third rank, and the remaining eight in the fourth rank. Ten issue areas accounted for 80.8 percent of the items discussed; of these, seven fall in the external relations functions, one in the social-cultural functions (education and research), and the remaining two in the economic functions (regulation and support of mass media of communications and regulation and support of transportation).

It is interesting to note that of the four external relations functions issue areas which fall below the second rank, one (cold war, arms control and disarmament) just barely fails to qualify for the second rank. The low rank of the issue area of conflict resolution and management among members is explained by the infrequency of conflicts among members--which

Table 18

RANK-ORDERING OF ISSUE AREAS BASED ON NUMBER OF ITEMS TREATED

Rank	Issue Area	Number of Items	Percent of Total
	First Rank - 6.6% and Above	(212)	(54.2)%
1	Diplomatic influence and participation in global affairs	72	18.4
2	Regulation and support of mass media of communications	50	12.7
3	Education and research	36	9.2
4	Economic and technical aid to or from other polities	28	7.2
5	Global economic, commercial, scientific and technical arrangements	26	6.7
	Second Rank - 3.3% to 6.5%	(104)	(26.5)
6	Decolonization and human rights	24	6.1
7	Diplomatic influence and participation in inter-African affairs	23	5.9
7	Economic, commercial, scientific and technical relations with major trading partners (France and the EEC)	23	5.9
9	Regulation and support of transportation	20	5.0
10	Continental economic, commercial, scientific and technical arrangements	14	3.6
	Third Rank - 1.1% to 3.2%	(62)	(16.0)
11	Economic development and planning	11	2.7
12	Cold war, arms control and disarmament	10	2.6
13	Access to legal-normative system	8	2.1
14	Organization and administration of the civil service	7	1.8

Table 18 (continued)

Rank	Issue Area	Number of Items	Percent of Total
14	Conflict resolution and management among members	7	1.8%
16	Military security	6	1.5
17	Economic, commercial, scientific and technical relations with minor trading partners	5	1.3
18	Public health and safety and maintenance of order	4	1.1
18	Movement of goods, services and other factors of production (not including capital) within the customs union	4	1.1
	Fourth Rank - Less than 1.1%	(13)	(3.3)
20	Regulation of economic competition and other government controls on prices and investments	3	0.7
20	Domestic monetary policy	3	0.7
22	Cultural and recreational affairs	2	0.5
22	Fiscal policy	2	0.5
24	Exploitation and protection of natural resources	1	0.3
24	Labor-management relations	1	0.3
24	Social welfare policies	1	0.3
27	Political participation	0	0
27	Counter-cyclical policy	0	0
27	Balance-of-payments stability	0	0
27	Agricultural protection	0	0
	Totals	391	100.0

Table 19

CLUSTERS OF ISSUE AREAS IN VARIOUS RANK-ORDERS

	First Rank		Second Rank		Third Rank		Fourth Rank		Totals	
	Number of Issue Areas	Percent of Total	Number of Issue Areas	Percent of Total	Number of Issue Areas	Percent of Total	Number of Issue Areas	Percent of Total	Number of Issue Areas	Percent of Total
External relations functions (11 issue areas)	3	28%	4	36%	4	36%	0	0%	11	100%
Political-constitutional functions (4 issue areas)	0	0	0	0	3	75	1	25	4	100
Social-cultural functions (3 issue areas)	1	33	0	0	0	0	2	67	3	100
Economic functions (12 issue areas)	1	8	1	8	2	17	8	67	12	100
Total (30 issue areas)	5	17	5	17	9	30	11	36	30	100

should be evaluated as positive rather than negative. The remaining two issues--military security and economic, commercial,
scientific and technical relations with minor trading partners--
fail to rank higher because, as we shall see, the former was
handled mostly in bilateral ties with France (with the exception
of Upper Volta, all the UAM members had signed defense agreements
with France), while in the latter issue area the ties were so
few (the external ties of the UAM members were overwhelmingly
with France) that it is not surprising that little attention was
devoted to them.

Some of the points discussed above will receive more
detailed treatment later in the chapter. The major point that
emerges from an examination of the scope of decision-making in
the UAM is that external relations functions occupied a dominant
position. The three issue areas internal to the region which
received substantial attention were all technical. The contrast
between this situation and the primacy of welfare-laden tasks
involving large masses of people in the EEC is particularly
striking.[9]

The Stage and Locus of Decision-Making

On pages 95-96, we presented Lindberg's range and locus of
decision-making scales. These will now be used to measure the
stage and locus of decision-making attained by the UAM in each
of the thirty issue areas. A summary discussion of each issue
area will be presented to give the reader some idea of what was
attempted and accomplished by the UAM, as well as the reasons
for our scoring these issue areas as we have.

Military Security. Activities in this area ranged from
efforts at determining the nature, source, and intensity of the
external military threat faced by the UAM members to discussions
of the necessity and feasibility of creating joint military
schools. The possibility of designating units of the armed
forces of member states as UAM units which would be kept in
readiness and made available on request to a member facing a
military threat was also discussed. However, none of these
plans were implemented because Senegal and Cameroun disagreed
with the others on the nature of the security problem. Thus a
score of "discussion with no collective problem recognition" is
assigned for the stage of decision-making, and the locus is all
national.

Conflict Resolution and Management among Members. Decision-making in this area was centered around resolving the Congo-

---

[9]Compare with ibid., pp. 70-73.

Gabon conflict of September 1962 and the Niger-Dahomey dispute,
which started in December 1963 but was not settled until January
1965. The Congo-Gabon dispute was settled with the aid of an
ad hoc group of UAM presidents which, together with the presidents of the two disputing countries, worked out the formula for
a settlement of the conflict. The details of the settlement and
their implementation were left in the hands of the parties concerned. Efforts by a similar ad hoc group of UAM leaders to play
a similar role in the Niger-Dahomey dispute failed, and in the
end it was Houphouet-Boigny's personal intervention that terminated the conflict. Plans for formalizing the procedure for
conflict resolution among members failed, as did the attempts at
minimizing the prospects of conflict by instilling a "UAM spirit"
among the wider public. A score of collective definition of
action alternatives is therefore assigned for stage of decision-
making and a score of some collective for locus.

Cold War, Arms Control and Disarmament. Most issues that
fell under this category, particularly those that had to be voted
on in the UN, were discussed at the UAM level. The goal was to
agree on specific policies to be adopted, with implementation
left in the hands of the diplomatic establishment of member
states. On the basis of decisions made (the matter of the degree
of compliance will be taken up subsequently), we assign a score of
detailed collective goal-setting for stage, and the collective
level is dominant for locus.

Decolonization and Human Rights. This issue area was
handled in virtually the same way as the "cold war" issue. In
addition, however, members discussed the feasibility of joint
material support for nationalist movements in the remaining African
colonies, but no decision was ever made on this question. A
score of detailed collective goal-setting is assigned for stage,
and for locus the collective is dominant.

Diplomatic Influence and Participation in Intra-African
Affairs. In comparison to the two preceding issue areas, the
degree of regional involvement in this issue area was less.
Africa-wide diplomatic issues were discussed at the UAM level,
but the bilateral links UAM members had with other African states
were not harmonized in the UAM context. Thus a score of collective decisions on policy guidelines is assigned for stage, and
the locus is substantial activity at the collective level.

Diplomatic Influence and Participation in Global Affairs.
Most of the items treated under this issue area related to efforts
to influence the outcomes of elections in various international
organizations. Members sought to agree on which candidate (member or non-member) would be supported for a particular office or
for a seat in a particular agency or sub-agency. In addition,
attempts were made to work out common positions on substantive

and organizational matters due to come up at various international conferences. As was the case with respect to the preceding issue area, members had full freedom in determining their bilateral ties with third parties. It was once proposed that joint embassies be created in various capitals, but the proposal was rejected. The score assigned for stage is detailed collective goal-setting, and the locus is substantial activity at the collective level.

Economic and Technical Aid to or from Other Polities. Items under this issue area ranged from discussions of the general principles that should govern foreign aid to attempts at providing joint aid to Rwanda and the Democratic Republic of the Congo. Common positions were elaborated on two items relating to French aid to members (increased access to French institutions of higher learning for students from member states and eliminating the responsibility of members to provide free housing for French technical advisors), but efforts at extending this practice to other aspects of French aid failed. The members were able to agree on the general outlines of the foreign aid that should be provided for in the new Convention of Association with the EEC, but proposals for a joint search for sources of aid to finance the development of telecommunications in member states were defeated. Overall, the stage of decision-making merits a score of collective decisions on policy guidelines, while the locus of decision was substantial activity at the collective level.

Global Economic, Commercial, Scientific and Technical Arrangements. As with some of the issue areas treated earlier, efforts in this issue area centered around the formulation of common positions to be adopted at various international conferences. Of particular concern to the UAM members were the timing, strategy, and financial obligations entailed in joining organizations such as the International Monetary Fund (IMF), International Bank for Reconstruction and Development (IBRD), and General Agreement on Trade and Tariffs (GATT). The magnitude of the problem--numerous conferences and large agendas--was such, however, that policy coordination on specific issues was ad hoc. Nevertheless, the principle that UAM delegates to international conferences would meet and try to harmonize their policies was subscribed to by all. On the whole, we assign a score of collective decisions on policy guidelines for stage, and the locus is substantial activity at the collective level.

Continental Economic, Commercial, Scientific and Technical Arrangements. The items under this issue area dealt mostly with various proposals for an African common market, an African development bank, an African payments union, and an African institute of development and planning. The issues were relatively few and simple (because they related to broad principles rather than to specific and highly technical problems), and members were able to agree on specific positions to be adopted. Members' bilateral ties with other African states that fell under this issue area were not treated at the regional level. A score of detailed collective goal-setting is assigned for stage, but the locus is only some activity at the collective level.

Economic, Commercial, Scientific and Technical Relations with Major Trading Partners. As indicated earlier, the UAM members worked out a common general negotiating position with respect to the renewal of the Convention of Association with the EEC. For a few matters dealing with relations with France, such as the establishment of parity between France and the UAM members in the Monetary Committee of the franc zone and moving the seat of certain organizations (e.g., Agence pour la Sécurité de la Navigation Aérienne en Afrique et à Madagascar), common positions were also elaborated. As was the case with respect to French aid, proposals for joint policy formulation on wider aspects of members' relations with France were rejected. Thus a score of collective decisions on policy guidelines is assigned for stage, and the locus is substantial activity at the collective level.

Economic, Commercial, Scientific and Technical Relations with Minor Trading Partners. Activities in this issue area centered on discussions of the need for harmonizing policies and on efforts to establish general principles that would guide individual members in negotiating commercial agreements with the countries of Eastern Europe. The score for stage is collective definition of action alternatives, and the locus is some collective.

Public Health and Safety and Maintenance of Order. In this area, proposals were made for coordinating health policies and for joint purchasing of pharmaceutical products and health equipment. Proposals were also made for cooperation among members in the area of crime prevention and control. None of these proposals was adopted. The score assigned for stage is discussion with no collective problem recognition, and the locus of all decisions remains in national hands.

Access to Legal-Normative System. Items discussed under this issue area dealt with the granting of dual citizenship to citizens of UAM countries, the harmonization of the citizenship laws of member states, and the protection of industrial property rights (inventions, trade markets, etc.) within the UAM. The Office Africaine et Malgache de la Propriété Industrielle (OAMPI) was created to implement an agreement on property rights, but proposals concerning the other two items were still being discussed when the UAM was dissolved. A score of collective definition of alternatives is assigned for stage, and the locus is some action at the collective level.

Organization and Administration of the Civil Service. This issue is assigned a score of collective decisions on policy guidelines for stage of decision-making because several efforts were made to formulate general guidelines for members in organizing their civil service. An attempt was also made to harmonize the salaries of civil servants. The locus of decision-making is only some collective, however, because agreement was reached only on the subcategories to be created in the highest rank of the civil service.

Cultural and Recreational Affairs. At the initiative of the Society for African Culture, the UAM dealt with the nature of a convention to be signed with the Society for African Culture by which the latter would acquire major responsibility for promoting cultural activities in member states. However, each cultural activity sponsored by the Society for African Culture would require an agreement with the state or states affected. Independently of the convention with the Society for African Culture, the UAM members agreed to inform each other of their plans for organizing cultural fairs so that there could be some coordination among these activities. A score of collective problem recognition is assigned for stage, and some collective is the locus.

Education and Research. Issues dealt with under this heading ranged from an exploration of the means of ensuring that students on government scholarships in foreign universities returned home at the completion of their studies to decisions creating joint centers for training and research. Among these centers are the Institut de Développement Appliqué and the Institut des Sciences et Médecine Vétérinaire de Dakar. While the decision-making range achieved varied from issue to issue, our estimation is that this issue area as a whole merits a score of collective decisions of policy guidelines for stage. The fact that each state retained full control over its national educational institutions leads us to assign a score of substantial activity at the collective level for locus of decision.

Social Welfare Policies. During the Libreville conference of September 1962, the question of harmonizing social welfare policies was raised but no decision was taken during the UAM period. Thus a score of collective problem recognition is assigned for stage, but all activity is at the national level.

Regulation of Economic Competition and Other Government Controls on Prices and Investments. Items under this heading dealt with the harmonization of all commercial laws, joint mechanisms for regulating insurance companies, and the creation of a joint insurance company. Only with respect to the latter issue was a definite and positive decision made, whereas the other two items merely elicited a general agreement in principle. On balance, we are led to assign a score of collective definition of alternatives for stage and a score of some collective for locus.

THE UAM IN OPERATION

Economic Development and Planning. Proposals for the
creation of an African Development Bank led to the creation of
the UAM Union of Development Banks and the UAM Association of
Development Banks; both of these bodies were designed to provide
a minimum degree of coordination among the national development
banks of member states. A technical assistance convention among
members was approved, and the principle of coordinating economic
development plans was subscribed to. Along similar lines, agreement in principle was reached with respect to the harmonization
of investment codes and the creation of a joint fund to guarantee
private investments in member states. Since none of these agreements in principle resulted in specific decisions during the UAM
period, we assign a score of collective problem recognition for
stage, and the locus is some activity at the collective level.

Exploitation and Protection of Natural Resources. The
sole item discussed under this heading was Dahomey's proposal for
joint and coordinated mechanisms for the protection of nature.
The outcome was an investigation of means for increasing educational facilities in this area. Thus a score of collective problem recognition is assigned for stage, but the locus of decision-
making is entirely at the national level.

Regulation and Support of Transportation. Clearly the
most important act in this area was the creation of Air Afrique
as the sole international airline of all UAM members, with the
exception of Madagascar. A similar decision was made with respect
to creating a joint maritime navigation company, but it was not
implemented during the UAM period. Decisions were also made
relating to principles for the harmonization of maritime laws
and civil aviation codes, criteria to be used by private airlines
in evaluating the costs of air freight, and the nature and quality
of services to be provided by Air Afrique. Other forms of trans-
portation--both within and between members--were excluded from
decision-making. Thus a score of detailed collective goal-setting
is assigned for stage, and there is a locus of equal activity at
both levels.

Regulation and Support of Mass Media of Communications.
Decisions in this area dealt with almost all aspects of operating
the postal and telecommunications services of members, including
rates, business hours, etc. Management remained in national
hands, however, as did decisions relating to the expansion of
services. Therefore a score of detailed collective goal-setting
is assigned for stage, and the collective level is dominant as
locus.

Labor-Management Relations. In this area agreement was
reached to study the possibilities of harmonizing the labor codes
of members; these studies, however, were not completed before
the dissolution of the UAM. The score for stage is therefore

111

collective problem recognition, but all decisions are in national hands.

Fiscal Policy. After several efforts, the UAM heads of state at Dakar in March 1964 succeeded in adopting a convention on double taxation that had been drawn up two years earlier. Besides this item, no other matter relating to fiscal policies figured in the UAM agenda. Since conventions of this type are characteristic of states not engaged in an effort at regional political integration, we deem it of insufficient importance to warrant a high positive score for the UAM. Hence a score of collective decisions on policy guidelines is assigned for stage, and the locus is some decision-making at the collective level.

Domestic Monetary Policy. The sole effort in this area related to means of increasing deposits in the savings banks of member states; in the end, some kind of publicity campaign was agreed upon. A score of collective problem recognition is assigned for stage; however, the nature of the action agreed upon was so insignificant that it is assumed that all decisions remained in national hands.

Movement of Goods, Services, and Other Factors of Production (Not Including Capital) Within the Customs Union. Table 17 revealed quite clearly that, unlike in the EEC, this issue area occupied a very minimal role in the decision-making activities of the UAM. This becomes very obvious when we examine the issues dealt with and the stage and locus achieved. The question of the movement of persons within the union led to a convention of settlement which provided for individuals to move freely within the union and engage in any gainful employment of their choice. By reason of each country's membership in the Franc Zone, all goods could circulate freely, but customs and fiscal duties decided upon by the members were imposed on these goods. Pressures for the creation of an African Common Market led to an agreement in principle to strengthen the Union Douanière des Etats de l'Afrique de l'Ouest (UDEAO) and what later became the Union Douanière et Economique de l'Afrique Centrale (UDEAC). Thus a score of detailed collective goal-setting is assigned for stage, and the locus is substantial activity at the regional level.

Table 20 summarizes the stage and locus of decision-making attained in each issue area, and makes it possible to compare the rank order of an issue area with its score for stage and locus of decision-making. Not surprisingly, the tendency is for issues with high rank order to have high scores for stage and locus of decision-making. This is particularly true of issues that fall under the external relations category, but other types of issues also reveal the same tendency. A major exception to this tendency is the issue area of economic development and

Table 20

SCOPE, STAGE, AND LOCUS OF DECISION-MAKING IN THE UAM

Issue Area	Number of Issues	Stage	Locus
Diplomatic influence and participation in global affairs	72	Detailed collective goal-setting	Substantive activity at collective level
Regulation and support of mass media of communications	50	Detailed collective goal-setting	Collective is dominant
Education and research	36	Collective decisions on policy guidelines	Substantial activity at collective level
Economic and technical aid to or from other polities	28	Collective decisions on policy guidelines	Substantial activity at collective level
Global economic, commercial, scientific and technical arrangements	26	Collective decisions on policy guidelines	Substantial activity at collective level
Decolonization and human rights	24	Detailed collective goal-setting	Collective is dominant
Diplomatic influence and participation in intra-African affairs	23	Collective decisions on policy guidelines	Substantial activity at collective level
Economic, commercial, scientific and technical relations with major trading partners	23	Collective decisions on policy guidelines	Substantial activity at collective level
Regulation and support of transportation	20	Detailed collective goal-setting	Equal activity at both levels
Continental economic, commercial, scientific and technical arrangements	14	Detailed collective goal-setting	Some collective
Economic development and planning	11	Collective problem recognition	Some collective

Table 20 (continued)

Issue Area	Number of Issues	Stage	Locus
Cold war, arms control and disarmament	10	Detailed collective goal-setting	Collective is dominant
Access to legal-normative system	8	Collective definition of action alternatives	Some collective
Organization and administration of the civil service	7	Collective decisions on policy guidelines	Some collective
Conflict resolution and management among members	7	Collective definition of action alternatives	Some collective
Military security	6	Discussion with no collective problem recognition	All national
Economic, commercial, scientific and technical relations with minor trading partners	5	Collective definition of action alternatives	Some collective
Public health and safety and maintenance of order	4	Discussion with no collective problem recognition	All national
Movement of goods, services and other factors of production (not including capital) within the customs union	4	Detailed collective goal-setting	Substantial activity at collective level
Regulation, economic competition and other governmental controls on prices and investments	3	Collective definition of action alternatives	Some collective

Table 20 (continued)

Issue Area	Number of Issues	Stage	Locus
Domestic monetary policy	3	Collective problem recognition	All national
Cultural and recreational affairs	2	Collective problem recognition	Some collective
Fiscal policy	2	Collective decisions on policy guidelines	Some collective
Exploitation and protection of natural resources	1	Collective problem recognition	All national
Labor-management relations	1	Collective problem recognition	All national
Social welfare policies	1	Collective problem recognition	All national
Political participation	0	No discussion, no collective problem recognition	All national
Balance-of-payments stability	0	No discussion, no collective problem recognition	All national
Agricultural protection	0	No discussion, no collective problem recognition	All national
Counter-cyclical policy	0	No discussion, no collective problem recognition	All national

planning, which barely fails to qualify for the second rank order, but has very low scores for stage and locus. On the other hand, very few items were discussed in the issue area of movement of goods, services, and other factors of production within the customs union, but it obtained a high score for stage and an average score (average as compared with the scores obtained by other issue areas) for locus. The reasons for these discrepancies will be indicated when we deal with the process variables of decision-making norms, bargaining style, and low or exportable visible costs.

A second feature evident from Table 20 is that all issue areas have lower scores for locus than for stage. This suggests that our earlier conclusion with respect to the broad scope of the UAM is somewhat misleading. For, in spite of the fact that practically all issue areas receive at least minimal attention at the UAM level, only a narrow range of topics within each issue area is subject to genuine collective decision-making. Again, the reason for this situation will become obvious when we examine the process variables that emerged--particularly those of decision-making norms and bargaining style. For the present, our concern is with the consequences of the UAM decisions.

The Consequences of Collective Decisions

Three types of decisional consequences are noted by Lindberg. The first is the degree of "penetrativeness" of the decisions as measured by how much behavioral change is implied for how many people. Three possibilities are noted by Lindberg: (a) Decisions are made by governmental negotiators and affect only the future bargaining behavior of the negotiators in the specific issue area in question; (b) collective decisions are made that are binding on national governments, but entail only a commitment to pursue common policy goals; the manner of achieving and implementing these goals remains up to the national governments; (c) collective decisions are made that apply directly to individuals and groups, and are enforced by collective institutions and procedures. The two other types of decisional consequences noted by Lindberg are (1) the degree to which collective decisions are complied with, and (2) the extent to which these decisions change the relative and absolute distribution of rewards and deprivations among and within nations.[10]

---

[10]Lindberg, "Political Integration as a Multidimensional Phenomenon Requiring Multivariate Measurement" in Lindberg and Scheingold, eds., pp. 55-56. For a more extended discussion of these measures, see ibid., pp. 104-113.

THE UAM IN OPERATION

Our findings with respect to the level of collective decision-making in the UAM have indicated that UAM decisions were
generally characterized by only a very marginal degree of penetrativeness. In our view, a high degree of penetrativeness is
dependent on two things--the level of collective decision-making,
and the degree to which the decision-making process is cumulative.
As the level of collective decision-making (particularly the stage
and locus of decision-making) rises, we would expect the degree
of penetrativeness of the decisions made to increase. Further,
as the decision-making process becomes more cumulative (as measured by the degree to which decision-makers abide by earlier
commitments and understandings), the penetrativeness of decisions
will increase. In neither of these ways was the UAM performance
impressive.

As noted earlier, collective decisions in the UAM were
made by the heads of states. However, Table 20 reveals that in
only seven issue areas (cold war, arms control and disarmament;
decolonization and human rights; diplomatic influence and participation in global affairs; continental economic, commercial,
scientific and technical arrangements; regulation and support
of transportation; regulation and support of mass media of communications; and the movement of goods, services, and other factors of production within the customs union) did the decision-
making stage attain that of detailed collective goal-setting with
implementation in the hands of the respective governments. Four
of these fall under the external relations category, and two more
deal with narrow technical issues. These are not the categories
of issues that engender broad and salient domestic interests.
Only official decision-makers tend to be interested in these kinds
of issues. Thus their degree of penetrativeness is very limited.
This conclusion is strengthened by the fact that, as we noted
earlier, collective decision-making in these six issue areas was
confined to a narrow range of topics within each area. In three
of the six issue areas, the community was dominant in decision-
making, and in one area there was equal activity at both the
regional and the national levels. In the remaining two issue
areas, more decision-making occurred at the national than at the
regional level.

The last of the seven issue areas--movement of goods,
services, and other factors of production within the customs
union--has a high potential for penetrating member states. This
potential is, however, dependent on the extent to which decisions
are meaningful as against being merely pro forma. Within the UAM,
trade among members was very small, amounting to no more than 4
percent of total trade in 1961; further, there was hardly any
movement of capital among members. As observed earlier, substantial movements of labor occurred among a few of the UAM members.
We shall see that when conflicts arose among members, the provision for free movement of persons was one of the first to be

117

violated. It should be added that agreements in this area merely preserved arrangements dating back to colonial times, and
entailed no new commitments. For these reasons, we conclude that
decisions in this area were characterized by a low degree of
penetrativeness.

These conclusions with respect to the degree of penetrativeness of UAM decisions characterized by a high level of joint
decision-making apply with even greater force to the remaining
issue areas, in which the level of collective decision-making
was low. The low levels of collective decision-making and the
nature of the issues concerned, as measured by the number and
importance of the societal sectors affected by the decisions,
account for this situation. A more basic explanation, though,
can be found in the nature of the member states themselves. In
all the member states the degree of social mobilization was very
small, voluntary groups were few, weak, and lacked autonomy, and
the political cultures denied the legitimacy of group participation in the decision-making process. Under these circumstances,
regional decisions are unlikely to manifest a high degree of
penetrativeness.

We noted earlier that a second factor that is likely to
determine the degree to which a decision penetrates member states
is the extent to which decision-making is cumulative. This is
part of the larger question of the extent to which members comply
with joint decisions, and the evidence on this score is mixed.

If we utilize UN voting patterns as an indicator of the
extent to which decisions in the external relations area were
implemented, we find that the index of UAM cohesion in the UN
from 1961 to 1965 was 64 percent. In 1961, the index was 78 percent. It rose to 83 percent in 1963, but decreased to 77 percent
in 1965.[11] Compliance was higher in other categories of issue
areas, but the stage and locus of the decisions involved were
for the most part at such low levels as to make compliance in-
consequential. Many of the UAM decisions, as we saw earlier,
entailed no more than broad agreements to certain general principles which were to be implemented after further study and negotiations. Since the planning and studies concerning most of
these were still in process when the UAM was abolished, they
lacked tangible consequences even though they may not have been
violated. In a few instances, however, there were outright
violations. Thus, during the Congo-Gabon dispute of September
1962, each country expelled nationals of the other country residing in its territory. This occurred again during the Niger-

---

[11] I am grateful to Ernst Haas for making these data available
to me.

Dahomey dispute of December 1963. All told, then, the degree of compliance with UAM decisions must be judged as mixed.

Given the low level of collective decision-making, the low degree of penetrativeness of decisions, and the mixed character of compliance with decisions, the redistributive consequences of UAM decisions were virtually nil. The rate of economic development among UAM members varied tremendously, but this was in no way the effect of UAM decisions. The same was true with respect to the international status of the members.

The UAM System: A Summary

The picture we have presented of the UAM thus far is essentially as follows: The UAM was characterized by a very broad scope, but the major preoccupations were external relations functions, mass media, and transportation; decision-making activities were directed mostly at a search for compatible policies to be translated into specific policies by the member states after further study and discussion; overall, there was only the beginning of collective decision-making, with the result that in spite of the degree of compliance, UAM decisions did not penetrate the environments of its members and were lacking in redistributive consequences.

Our next task is to seek explanations for this state of affairs; we will do it in two steps. We will first try to determine the degree to which the nature of the integrative conditions was responsible. Second, we will examine the process conditions that emerged and relate them to the findings concerning the integrative conditions. The result, we hope, will be an understanding not only of why regional political integration failed to take place, but also why the union survived--albeit in a different form.

Impact of Integrative Conditions

Motives, Values, and Expectations. Clearly, these factors played a major role in the poor performance of the UAM. The members' motives were vague, diffuse, and derived from insecurities resulting from the unexpected attainment of independence, combined with a gloomy perception of the African and the international environments. A high value was placed on the sovereignty of members, with joint activity predicated on the free choice of members. Like their motives, the members' expectations were vague and diffuse. Union, it was felt, would enhance the security, prestige, and the rate of economic growth of members, but the rationale and the strategy on which such an outcome was dependent was never articulated.

POLITICAL INTEGRATION IN FRENCH-SPEAKING AFRICA

Under these circumstances, it is not surprising that efforts were directed primarily at securing agreements on very general principles. The very cautious strategy to which the UAM members were committed meant that a great deal of time would elapse before such general agreements could be translated into concrete policies. Later, we shall see that the act of moving from general to specific commitments was hindered by the shortage of skilled personnel to undertake the necessary studies and negotiations.

The prevailing motives, values, and expectations of the members hindered regional political integration by excluding certain areas from joint action. It will be recalled that several countries (the Ivory Coast, Gabon, Mauritania, Madagascar, and Cameroun) expected greater economic rewards from national as opposed to regional economic policies. Thus when Senegal proposed at the Bangui conference in March 1962 that bilateral economic agreements with France be converted into multilateral agreements, these countries opposed such a move. Similarly, when the UAMPT Secretary-General requested at the Ouagadougou conference of March 1963 that he be empowered to investigate the availability of external aid to finance the development of telecommunications in member states, his request was denied on the grounds that it violated the sovereignty of the members.

Vague motives and expectations, combined with values that were opposed to or allowed only minimal commitment to higher levels of political integration, accounted for the low level of collective decision-making and the limited consequences of decisions made by the UAM.

Capacity of Members. By any criteria, the UAM states are very underdeveloped. Yet for regional political integration to succeed--especially one based on functionalist strategy--a great expenditure of time and resources is necessary. The absence of such resources was an important limitation on the UAM.

We have already noted that the UAM lacked the personnel necessary to engage in the studies and negotiations necessary for translating general agreements into specific policies. At several conferences, the various secretariats--particularly those of the UAM and the OAMCE--complained that they lacked the manpower to undertake all the studies they were being asked to conduct. Yet the budgets of the secretariats were not increased because members maintained that they could not afford the added costs.

The functioning of the UAM also increased the manpower burden on member states. Thus as early as February 1962, President Yameogo of Upper Volta made the following complaint:

The government of Upper Volta is becoming more and more preoccupied with the very high number of ministerial and

specialist conferences in which our government has to be
represented. To the ministerial conferences, whether belonging directly to the activity of the UAM or whether belonging
to the activity of the specialized secretariats, are added
the meeting of the technical committees and committees
created ad hoc as needs arise. These increases are costly
and make it more difficult for the heads of ministerial
departments to accomplish the duties for which they are held
responsible in their respective governments.[12]

In 1962, excluding ministerial and expert meetings held during
two heads of state conferences, there were 9 conferences of
experts and 11 of ministers. The comparable figures for 1963
were 11 and 14 respectively. When we add to these the various
other conferences--intra-African, Franc Zone, EEC, international,
UDEAC, UDEAO, Conseil de l'Entente, etc.--to which members had
to send delegates, it is clear that the burdens entailed were
quite substantial. Members reacted to this situation by refrain-
ing from sending delegates to certain UAM conferences. Thus only
four states sent delegates to a meeting of customs experts held
in Paris in November 1962 that was designed to elaborate a common
customs code. Needless to say, such reactions made it impossible
to achieve concrete results.

Another--and more important--manner in which limited
capabilities affected regional political integration was the
impact on the member states' desire for further integration. It
is our contention that government leaders seldom readily engage
in collective decision-making, with all its attendant loss of
autonomy. Rather, they are forced into joint decision-making
because national action is perceived to be inadequate to bring
about the desired results. In other words, integrative behavior
results from increases of burdens over capabilities.

In the case of the UAM states, the external environment
was perceived as threatening around 1960. This resulted in the
creation of the UAM as a defense mechanism. By 1963 the external environment, for most members, was no longer perceived as
threatening. As we shall see in the next chapter, this change
in perception was largely responsible for the change from the
UAM to the UAMCE in 1964.

A situation of stress may emanate not only from the international environment, but also from the domestic environment. One
indicator of the degree of domestic stress is the rate of increase
or decrease in the GDP per capita. A decrease in the GDP per
capita, we hold, is associated with a stress situation, whereas
an increase suggests a non-stress situation. If we are correct,

---

[12]Quoted in Tevoedjre, p. 16.

then states experiencing high growth rates would be opposed to further integration, while states with declining growth rates would favor more integration.

In Chapter 2, Table 16, we saw that between 1960 and 1966 only Mauritania, the Ivory Coast, Gabon, and Cameroun experienced increases in GDP per capita at 1960 prices. Except for Gabon's support of the idea of creating joint embassies at the Bangui conference in March 1962, these countries did not once propose or support measures that would raise the level of political integration. On the other hand, Senegal, which had a decrease in GDP per capita and which was being replaced by the Ivory Coast as the wealthiest state in the region, was very active in pushing for more integration, especially in the economic domain. Another country which pushed for more integration was Madagascar. In the case of Madagascar, though, its efforts were limited to narrow technical areas, particularly the creation of a joint maritime navigation company from which it was expected to gain the most.

Our conclusion is that because of a declining stress situation, as measured by the perceived cogency of the external environment, combined with uneven domestic stress situations, there was little interest among most of the UAM members in enhancing the degree of political integration.

Regional Transactions vs. Extra-Regional Dependence

A high rate of transactions among a group of states implies a high degree of interdependence among them. It means that, given a predisposition to regional cooperation, there are many areas for joint action. On the other hand, a low rate of transactions implies low salience and limited possibilities for joint action even if such a desire exists. We saw in Chapter 2 that transactions among the UAM members were very low and declining. On the other hand, transactions with France were very high, and remained so during the entire period of the UAM. Further, this dependence on France was positively evaluated. Most UAM members preferred the retention of their bilateral ties with France, with the result that little attempt was made to coordinate policies toward France. Since the bulk of the external ties UAM members had were with France, this meant that the issues that were most important to members were excluded from the regional context. Among such issues were monetary policies, fiscal policies, counter-cyclical policies, and balance-of-payments stability, which were handled bilaterally with France. To these may be added education and research, as well as economic development and planning, since France was significantly involved in planning and providing resources for these issue areas. All told, then, the links with France were so numerous and substantial that the possibilities for joint action within the UAM were very few.

However, the impact of external events on African political integration must not be seen in wholly negative terms. Earlier in this chapter, we saw that efforts at creating an African common market, an African development bank, an African payments union, and an African institute for economic research and planning led to the creation of similar agencies, but entailing lower levels of commitment to joint decision-making, at the UAM level. Another beneficial result from the external environment was that, since the external dependencies of the UAM members were identical, disputes resulting from contradictory external ties did not arise in the UAM. Thus it was only after the coup in the Republic of Congo in 1963 that disputes of this kind arose. Congo attempted to reexport goods it had imported from the socialist countries to other UAM members, and the latter were determined to keep the goods out because of their general opposition to the socialist countries. Finally, similar dependence on France meant that the rules, regulations, and policies of the UAM states were substantially alike, because they were patterned after those prevailing in France or were drawn up by French advisers. Currencies were identical or freely convertible because of membership in the Franc Zone. This made the harmonization of policies in such areas as commercial laws easier. The fact that no tangible results followed was due to other factors.

Our conclusion thus far is that regional political integration failed in the UAM because the integrative conditions were unfavorable. Motives, values, and expectations were not conducive to joint activity, and the requisite capacity was either absent or else was of such a nature as to discourage interest in furthering regional political integration. Interdependence among the members was limited, and they preferred handling their substantial ties with France through bilateral means. Yet a full explanation of the failure of the UAM necessitates an examination of the process conditions that developed after the Union was created. We shall see that these were no more functional for regional political integration than were the background conditions.

Process Conditions

Regional Identity. The fact of their having been French colonies and joined together in either the Federation of West Africa or the Federation of Equatorial Africa produced a certain degree of regional identity among the UAM states. In particular, they were highly self-conscious of being Francophones, and thereby different from the Anglophones. But how deep was this feeling of regional identity? How much feeling of mutual identification, trust, and predictability emerged during the process stage? The answer is "Not very much."

POLITICAL INTEGRATION IN FRENCH-SPEAKING AFRICA

One indication of the absence of a high degree of regional identity is the lack of support for movements advocating political union. Whereas such movements existed prior to independence, no such movement emerged after independence. Another indication of the absence of a strong sense of regional identity is that we were unable to find a single case in which a member making a demand appealed to a sense of regional identity. The only context in which such appeals arose was in the context of stressing the need for a united front in various international forums against other African groupings.

Distrust among UAM members was revealed in various ways. One was in discussing the proposal for creating joint embassies at the Bangui conference in March 1962. Several countries insisted that members with substantial interests in the country in which a joint embassy was located should have the right to appoint some members of the embassy staff, implying that the others could not be relied upon to protect their interests.

Two striking demonstrations of the absence of a strong feeling of regional identity were the Gabon-Congo dispute of September 1962 and the Niger-Dahomey dispute of December 1963. The former arose out of charges that Gabonese football players had been mistreated at Brazzaville, whereas the latter was triggered by disputed claims on the small uninhabited island of Lété. Both resulted in domestic violence against the citizens of the other country, and in the Niger-Dahomey dispute, there was actually mobilization of troops. Clearly, a union in which members fight over such issues cannot be said to have a strong sense of regional identity.

Another reason for our conclusion that the degree of regional identity in the UAM was very weak is the responses we got from student leaders, trade union leaders, businessmen, and government officials to the following question: "How significant a loss would (name of country) suffer if it withdrew from the UAM?" Ninety percent of all respondents said "very little or none," and the remaining 10 percent said "little." On the other hand, all respondents said substantial losses would result from withdrawal from the Franc Zone.

Given the low and declining rate of transaction within the UAM, the low level of joint decision-making, and the very limited consequences of UAM decisions, it is understandable that the sense of regional identity would be weak. For while the existence of high scores in these three areas does not guarantee a strong feeling of regional identity, it is difficult to conceive of its existence in their absence.

Bargaining Style. This variable is both cause and effect. To the extent that the integrative conditions in a union score high, we would expect the bargaining style employed by members to reflect this fact. In such situations, the bargaining strategies employed would themselves promote further political integration. On the basis of the degree of autonomy enjoyed by national legislation and the degree of unanimity required for decisions, Schmitter has delineated the following patterns of decision-making:[13]

Degree of Enforced Unanimity

		High	Low
Autonomy of National Representation	Low	Lowest common denominator	Splitting the difference
	High	Package dealing	Upward grading

In the case of the UAM, autonomy of national representatives was nonexistent, while unanimity was required for decisions. In practice, though, less than unanimous decisions were sometimes adopted, but these were only binding on the states supporting the measure. These conditions, combined with the low integrative potential of the union, lead us to expect most decisions to be of the lowest common denominator variety.

Issues falling under the external relations functions often triggered very little debate, largely because the foreign orientations of the UAM members were similar. When disagreements arose, the result was invariably an inability to arrive at decisions. Two examples might be cited. The issue of whether the UAM members would contribute to the cost of the UN operations in the Congo was discussed at both the Bangui and the Libreville conferences. On both occasions, all but Madagascar agreed to pay their assessments for this UN operation. Finally, a resolution stating that these assessments would be paid was adopted, but it was understood that Madagascar would not abide by it. A second example was the dispute over recognition of the Grunitzky government after the assassination of Olympio in January 1963. Disagreements over this issue could not be resolved at the Ouagadougou conference, and the result was no decision.

The only times when the UAM members were able to adopt decisions that went beyond the lowest common denominator in the external relations area were when the costs entailed could be exported to other members. This was the case with respect to presenting UAM candidates for election in various international forums. A form of package dealing was used in which the various

___

[13]Philippe C. Schmitter, "A Revised Theory of Regional Integration" in Lindberg and Scheingold, eds., pp. 248-249.

offices were distributed among the UAM members. However, when a country lacked a qualified person to fill a certain position, and no other office was open for which it could present candidates, this form of package dealing became impossible. This was the case when Upper Volta, Cameroun, Senegal, and Gabon all demanded support for one of the Government seats of the 47th International Labour Organization (ILO) conference. All told, decision-making in this sector was characterized by the lowest common denominator.

In other functional areas, decision-making based on the lowest common denominator was even more pervasive. Proposals to harmonize the salaries of civil servants were rejected, as were proposals to harmonize the monetary value of scholarships given to students for study abroad. The same fate befell plans to co-ordinate the occasions on which commemorative stamps would be issued, as well as the quantities to be issued. In all these cases, failure was due to the fact that the issues entailed un-equal financial costs for the members of the union.

Bargaining within the UAM was thus overwhelmingly of the lowest common denominator variety. Only when an issue was equally salient to all members, entailed no cost, and resulted in equal benefits to all was joint action possible. In our view, this was a result of the low salience members had for each other as mea-sured by the rate of transactions among them, the motives, values, and expectations of the actors, and the weak sense of regional identity present in the UAM.

Politicization. This refers to a process in which the controversiality of issues increases as do the number and variety of actors involved in decision-making at the regional level. Often this is a result of an increase in the level of collective decision-making as well as an increase in the consequences of joint decisions. Politicization enhances political integration by raising the bargaining style characteristic of the union through an increase in the autonomy of the negotiators as well as a relaxation in the degree of enforced unanimity.

At its creation, the UAM was endowed with a very broad scope, and it remained thus during its existence. However, while earlier contacts were initially limited to the heads of state and a few ministries (Foreign Affairs, Economy), meetings had been held among practically all ministries by 1964. The expansion of the number of ministries involved followed the pattern of Nye's "demonstration effect spill-over," in which "less active insti-tutions are stimulated to greater activity by the success of more active institutions. . . ."[14] Thus at the June 1962 ILO

---

[14]Joseph S. Nye, "Central American Regional Integration" in

conference, the UAM labor ministers requested authorization of a
conference among themselves from the UAM heads of state conference
for the purpose of harmonizing the labor code of member states.
They observed that while meetings had been held among most ministers, none had been held among the Ministers of Labor. The result
was a conference of UAM labor ministers in September 1962. An
identical process led to meetings among the Ministers of Information.

However, if there was an increase in the number of governmental actors involved in UAM decision-making, no change occurred
with respect to the nature of the actors. The actors remained
instructed national delegates. Business groups, labor unions,
and other voluntary organizations were conspicuously absent from
UAM activities. The reason for this is simple: the UAM members
lacked well-organized and autonomous voluntary groups. Further,
the political values of the elites opposed regular and institutionalized participation in decision-making by these groups, even
at the national level. It is inconceivable that participation of
these groups in regional decision-making would have been counte-
nanced. Finally, decisional consequences were too low to stir
these groups into seeking participation in regional decision-
making.

The lack of any meaningful degree of politicization meant
that the encounter at the regional level was among individuals
who perceived themselves as embodying the "national will" of
their respective countries. Issues were seen in all-or-nothing
terms rather than in terms of different gains for different groups
at different periods. Under these circumstances, compromise was
difficult, and the result was the inability to arrive at decisions
that we saw earlier.

Regional Reform-Mongering. Given the above conditions,
it is clear that task expansion in the UAM could not result from
any automatic process. The underdeveloped economies of the members and the low rate of transactions among them conspired against
reliance on the functional linkage of tasks. Deliberate action
was required to seek out programs that were likely to elicit
unanimous support. This could be done by one of the members,
by community-type institutions, or by an external actor.

We noted earlier that Senegal consistently tried to play
the role of regional reform-monger. Its motives were far from
altruistic, and resulted from Senegal's economic decline and the
expectation that a higher degree of joint action, particularly

---

J.S. Nye, ed., International Regionalism: Readings (Boston:
Little, Brown and Company, 1968), p. 409.

127

in the economic area, would bring greater rewards. Such efforts, however, proved unsuccessful. The Ivory Coast, Gabon, and other anti-integrationists were always ready to block Senegal's efforts. An even more important factor was that, because of its economic decline, Senegal was in no position to offer material inducements as a way of buying off opposition. The Ivory Coast's position on this score was the opposite. By means of the Solidarity Fund of the Conseil de l'Entente, through which the Ivory Coast subsidized the budgets of Upper Volta, Dahomey, and Niger, these three countries were kept from supporting pro-integrationist measures. Finally, Houphouet-Boigny was clearly the most prestigious individual within the union, and his opposition to a greater degree of integration adversely affected the reform efforts of Senegal. It seems, therefore, that Senegal lacked both the material resources and the prestige necessary for success in its reform-mongering role.

The various UAM secretariats, we observed, were conceived of as administrative agencies lacking autonomous power. To this should be added the fact that the resources available to them were exceedingly limited. The total budget for all four secretariats of the union in 1962 was 153,170,000 CFA francs--or approximately $612,680. Excluding investment expenditures, the total budget for the union in 1963 was 225,224,000 CFA francs-- or approximately $900,900. In 1963, the total number of employees of all four secretariats above the clerical level was 34. These were distributed as follows: UAM--11, OAMCE--8, UAMD--12, UAMT-- 3. With such resources and such broad scope, there was not much the secretariats could do in the nature of reform-mongering.

An additional factor that hindered any reform-mongering by the secretariats was the habit of assigning issues that required further study to one of the members--usually the member making the proposal. Thus Madagascar was responsible for exploring the issue of creating a joint navigation company, Cameroun for harmonizing the citizenship code of members, and Senegal for examining the possibilities of creating a center for veterinary study at Dakar. This practice resulted from the recognition that the secretariats lacked the manpower to undertake all the necessary studies. The consequence, though, was that the secretariats never developed the reputation of being centers of expert and unbiased knowledge, which would have been necessary for them to play a successful reform-mongering role.

Two other factors accounted for the inability of the various secretariats to play the role of reform-monger. One was the disinclination of almost all the Secretaries-General to play the role of activists--either because they did not want to, or because they recognized that such a role would be unacceptable to UAM members. This was particularly the case of the OAMCE Secretary-General, whose proposals for joint action usually entailed very minimal commitments, often necessitating no more than the exchange of information among members. Such was the case with respect to his proposals for harmonizing development plans, cooperation in monetary matters within the union and the Association of Development Banks, and strengthening the UDEAO and the UDE in reaction to pressures for creating an Africa-wide common market.

On the other hand, Albert Tevoedjre, Secretary-General of the UAM from 1961 to 1963, consistently tried to play an activist role. He traveled extensively and tried to establish contacts with other international organizations such as the OAS, as well as with foreign heads of state such as the late President Kennedy. He pushed for meaningful joint actions, such as the creation of joint embassies, joint material support for liberation movements in Africa, and a binding procedure for arbitrating disputes among the UAM members. All these proposals were rejected, and he was dismissed at the Ouagadougou conference. One of the grounds for his dismissal was that he was acting more like a head of state than an administrative Secretary-General. In other words, the regional environment was not conducive to regional institutions playing the role of reform-mongers. Finally, conflicts and rivalries among autonomous secretariats, particularly between the UAM and UAMCE secretariats, prevented a joint approach.

Given its ties with the UAM states, France was clearly in the best position to play a reform-mongering role from the outside. Yet while France was sympathetic to and encouraged cooperation among the UAM states, little concrete aid was given to further this process. France provided technical advisers for the various secretariats and sometimes conducted research for the group. But no financial or other material inducement was offered as a means of furthering the process of political integration. The most plausible explanation seems to be that France was aware of the strength of the anti-integrationist feelings within the union and saw no point in antagonizing an important partner such as the Ivory Coast. It is equally likely that France independently decided that a strong union was not to its advantage and therefore took no strong action in favor of such measures.

On a few occasions, other external actors sought to promote joint activity within the UAM. In 1963, the ILO and the Carnegie Endowment for International Peace offered to create training centers for middle level employees of the Department of Labor and the Department of Foreign Affairs respectively. Both offers were rejected because some countries held they already had national facilities for providing such training and would therefore not participate in these new projects.

It is clear, then, that the UAM environment was hostile to a reform-mongering role by any actor. Task expansion was therefore dependent on the identical or converging goals of national actors. Since the environment was not conducive to the emergence of such goals, encapsulation was the result.

Gains and/or Low or Exportable Visible Costs

Joint decision-making is seldom engaged in for its own sake, but with the hope and expectation of some reward. The reward may be increased security, material gain, and/or prestige for the states or leaders involved. At the same time, joint action invariably entails some cost. To the extent to which costs are low, invisible or exportable to external actors, the prospects for successful regional political integration are enhanced.

We have already seen that in the case of the UAM, neither increased security nor material advantages resulted from membership in the union. On the other hand, several heads of state felt their personal prestige within their countries, and thus their legitimacy, was enhanced by virtue of their role in the UAM. This was particularly true of the new leaders of Upper Volta, the Republic of the Congo, Togo, and the ever-changing leaders of Dahomey, but it was also true of the leaders of Niger, Chad, and the Republic of Central Africa. In other words, the weaker the state, and the less secure the leadership, the greater the likelihood that membership in the UAM would be desired as a means of enhancing personal prestige and thus increasing domestic legitimacy.

Perception of the degree to which the union as a whole and the individual members gained in international prestige because of the existence of the union was mixed. The complaint was frequently made that because of the disunity within the union, the UAM presented a very poor picture of itself at international conferences and thus failed to gain international recognition for itself and its members. It was as a result of this dissatisfaction that the Bangui conference of March 1962 decided to create a permanent secretariat at the UN and to have all UAM ambassadors to the UN attend the UAM heads of state conference preceding each session of the UN General Assembly. Other decisions urged members to make sustained efforts to send representatives or be represented at international conferences, empower their delegates to make political decisions, and generally refrain from issuing rigid instructions to these delegates.

The crowning success of these activities, in the minds of most UAM members, came at the International Civil Aviation Organization conference at Rome in August 1962. At this conference, Madagascar and the Republic of the Congo were elected to the Administrative Council of the ICAO. This was seen as indicative of the prestige the UAM could attain when it presented a

united front. Yet this unity was not to last, and the earlier
lack of unity within the UAM was once more manifested. All told,
we would weigh the gains from integration as mixed, largely
because of the importance of the phenomena of personal prestige
and increased domestic legitimacy for those countries which
needed it.

Two types of costs were entailed in membership in the
UAM. One resulted from the need to send delegates to various
conferences. This, we have seen, was a substantial burden for
the poorer countries. Another cost resulted from the need to
provide personnel for the various secretariats as well as financial resources for these bodies. Since the personnel of these
organizations were few and the budgets small, not much expense
was entailed. Contributions to the budgets of the union were
proportional to the operating budget of each member. Thus in
1962, the largest contribution was made by Senegal (approximately
$105,728) while the lowest contributions were made by Mauritania
and the Central African Republic (approximately $17,376 each).
France provided about one third of the staff for the secretariats,
with most of the other staff members coming from countries like
Senegal, Dahomey, the Ivory Coast, Cameroun, Madagascar, and the
Republic of the Congo. Thus in terms of staffing and operating
the central institutions, the costs entailed were minimal.

A major difficulty, though, was that other costs were
high and highly visible. This was because, as noted earlier, the
participants in the decision-making process were instructed national delegates who perceived themselves as embodying the national wills of their countries. To them, costs were substantial,
immediate, and personal--particularly in the context of the low
capabilities of the member states. Thus when demands were made
on each other, they were resisted. Finally, most costs could not
be exported to external actors, because, as we saw earlier, most
external ties were with France, and members preferred bilateral
to multilateral relations with France. In other words, as long
as the level of joint activity remained low (discussion and harmonization at very general levels), costs were low, somewhat
exportable, but nevertheless highly visible. Attempts at higher
levels of collective decision-making entailed very visible costs
that were high and not exportable. Thus the level of joint decision-making remained low.

Process Conditions: A Summary

In the UAM, process conditions, like integrative conditions, were not conducive to regional political integration.
Regional identity was low and might even have declined during
the process stage. Thus bargaining tended to be of the lowest
common denominator type, and the resulting degree of politicization

was weak. The environmental conditions did not facilitate the emergence of a regional reform-monger. Gains from integration were moderate, whereas the costs of integration were low and somewhat exportable only to the extent that the level of collective decision-making remained low.

Political Integration in the UAM: A Summary

Integrative conditions in the UAM were for the most part not supportive of regional political integration. Capacities of member states were low but varied tremendously, whereas links among members were few. On the other hand, the degree of external dependence was very high. Commitments to political integration were vague and not very strong, whereas opposition to integration was specific and very strong. Only two factors favored the formation of the union: the general value consensus which prevailed among the elites, and the perceived cogency of the external environment. A further factor might have been the fact of identical external dependence.

The union scored very low in most of the process conditions discussed: regional identity, bargaining style, politicization, and regional reform-mongering. Only with respect to the gains from integration did the union secure a mixed score. The costs of integration also received a mixed score, but only at low levels of joint decision-making.

Given the above conditions, it is not surprising that the moment the perceived cogency of the external environment declined, pressure was exerted for the abolition or the restructuring of the union with the hope of reducing costs and increasing economic gains. This suggests to us that the continued existence of the UAM was largely a function of the degree to which the external environment was perceived as threatening. The debate over the restructuring of the UAM is our concern in the next chapter.

Chapter 5

FROM THE UNION AFRICAINE ET MALGACHE TO
THE ORGANISATION COMMUNE AFRICAINE ET MALGACHE

As early as March 1962, less than a year after the creation of the UAM, demands were being made for its transformation.
These demands were triggered by the Lagos conference of January
1962, at which Liberia presented a charter for a new organization
that would encompass all independent African states and thus eli-
minate the conflicts among rival African groups. It was in this
context that Senghor made the following observation to the UAM
heads of state conference at Bangui in March 1962:

Certainly, the UAM does not include all of Africa even though
it includes all of Madagascar; it is only a part, though a
not insignificant one, of Africa south of the Sahara and of
the states of the Monrovia group. We must keep this truth
in mind, and the fact that, however large we may be, we are
only a regional organization of the continent. The goal still
remains that of jointly organizing the entire continent. It
follows from this fundamental option that we must endeavor,
year after year, and by successive advances, to insert the
Union into the Organisation Africaine et Malgache whose main
lines were traced at Lagos. In this perspective, we will
maintain in the UAM that which must be maintained, we will
modify what must be modified, we will suppress what must be
suppressed.[1]

These comments by Senghor created the climate in which
the proposed Lagos charter was discussed at the Bangui UAM heads
of state conference. The central concern was whether adoption
of the Lagos charter implied the dismantling of the UAM. The
unanimous conclusion was that it did not. Following Senghor's
logic, it was held that the new African group was itself only a
regional organization when compared with the United Nations.
While participation in the new African group was recommended,
the retention of the UAM, with some unstated modifications in
its structure and functioning, was strongly advocated.[2]

---

[1] Union Africaine et Malgache, Compte-rendu de la Conférence de
Bangui, 25-27 March 1962, p. 7. [Emphasis in original.]

[2] Ibid., p. 96.

133

Collapse of the efforts at reconciling the rival African groups resulted in a temporary shelving of proposals for the restructuring of the UAM, and it was not until after the Addis Ababa conference of May 1963 that attention was once more directed at these proposals. At the UAM heads of state conference at Ouagadougou in March 1963, the UAM leaders decided to meet soon after the Addis Ababa conference. The main agenda of the conference was to be an assessment of the results of the Addis Ababa conference; it was held at Cotonou in July 1963.

Two opposing recommendations concerning the future of the UAM in light of the creation of the OAU were presented at the opening session of the Cotonou conference. In his welcoming address, President Hubert Maga of Dahomey made the following observation:

> The UAM, with its cohesion, its experience, and its well-tested technical organizations has a more important role to play. Far from being overtaken by the charter of the OAU as some people believe, it is one of the best guarantors of the OAU. The more a group is split up, the less solid it is. Thus an Africa made up of fifty different parts will be less strong than an Africa structured in a few harmoniously counterbalanced groups. With the Maghreb and the Federation of East Africa, the UAM will therefore constitute the structure of the new Africa.[3]

An opposing view was presented by President Yameogo of Upper Volta in his speech opening the conference. He urged that the UAM must not put itself in a position of being accused some day of having "torpedoed" African unity, noting that "besides, Francophones or Anglophones, the children of our mother Africa all speak the same language, that of solidarity, of justice, of love, and of liberty." Yameogo added that "we do not have the right to remain marginal with respect to African history" and "we must persuade ourselves that there will no longer ever be two Africas but a single one." Specifically, Yameogo proposed that Air Afrique and the OAMCE be turned over to the OAU.[4]

Debates on the question of the future of the UAM revealed a general consensus on the need for modifications in the UAM. Specifically, it was agreed that the frequency of UAM conferences should be reduced and that several autonomous secretariats were unnecessary. These points, however, had little to do with the

---

[3] Union Africaine et Malgache, Compte-rendu des travaux de la Conférence de Cotonou, 27-30 July 1963, p. 2.

[4] Ibid., pp. 6-9.

creation of the OAU. As noted in the preceding chapter, the multiplicity of UAM conferences entailed significant burdens. The existence of several autonomous secretariats had led to a substantial degree of duplication, lack of coordination, and rivalries among the secretariats. Earlier efforts to correct this situation had failed, and the consensus at the Cotonou conference was that all but one secretariat should be abolished.

However, this consensus could not be translated into specific decisions for two basic reasons. First, no agreement could be reached on the future of the UAM. Upper Volta, Cameroun, and Senegal advocated the abolition of the UAM, while Dahomey, the Ivory Coast, Madagascar, Niger, and Gabon were in favor of retaining the UAM in some form. Second, two of the leading UAM figures--Houphouet-Boigny and Senghor--were not present at the conference.

Given this situation, it was decided that the future of the UAM would be determined at the next UAM heads of state conference in Dakar. In the interim, the only concrete decision taken was one which abolished the UAM group and permanent secretariat at the United Nations. It was widely felt that the creation of the OAU entailed at least a commitment to harmonize foreign policies, particularly UN policies, at the regional rather than at the subregional level. Countries like the Ivory Coast and Madagascar, which did not share this view, felt that a UAM group at the UN was unnecessary, since the harmonization of foreign policies was executed through direct contacts among the heads of state.

A striking feature of the UAM heads of state conference at Dakar in March 1964 was the large number of heads of state who were absent. Of the 14 countries, only seven (Cameroun, Senegal, Madagascar, Mauritania, Dahomey, Upper Volta, and Niger) sent delegations headed by their respective heads of state. Of the other seven heads of state, four were represented by ministers, while the heads of state of Central Africa and Rwanda failed to send even representatives to the conference. Given the fact that the main item on the agenda was the future of the UAM, these absences indicated that the UAM members were deeply split on the future of the union.

Yameogo's opening address to the Dakar conference revealed a complete change in the position he had taken at Cotonou six months earlier. At Dakar he said that considerations of realism and effectiveness required that certain conditions be met before primacy was given to the OAU. Among these conditions were agreement on the following principles: interdependence is effective and irreversible; economic and political interests have become complementary. He concluded that until these conditions were met, "We have the duty to continue to think 'UAM'; for, even in the context of a complete fusion into the OAU, regional economic solidarity will remain a reality which it will not be wise to lose sight of."[5] The main reason for this shift in position seems to have been an increase in border conflicts between Upper Volta and Ghana, a development which resulted in Upper Volta turning once more to the Conseil de l'Entente and the Ivory Coast.

On the other hand, Senghor observed in his welcome address that "the major problem is that of our economic independence, which could only be solved by the reinforcement of our horizontal solidarity within the UAM and, beyond the UAM, within the OAU." According to Senghor, "It is indeed at Geneva, at the World Conference on Trade and Development, that these solidarities must be ultimately aimed for in order that they may be extended to all the nations of the Third World. At Geneva . . . the proletarian nations in which we are included must conquer or die."[6] Implicit in these statements was a demand for changing the UAM into an organization primarily concerned with economic matters-- a clear reflection of the worsening economic position of Senegal (see Chapter 3 above).

Debates about the future of the UAM at the Dakar conference centered on the proposals of Madagascar, Senegal, and Cameroun. Madagascar proposed that the number of UAM conferences be reduced to one a year, that the meetings of the UAM Council of Foreign Ministers be institutionalized, that the Supreme Council of the UAM Defense Pact be replaced by a specialized Consultative Commission which would serve as an advisory body to the Council of Foreign Ministers in matters of defense, and that the Secretariat of the UAM Defense Pact be replaced by a defense division within the UAM Secretariat. More far-reaching were the proposals of Senegal and Cameroun, both of which called for the alteration of the UAM into an organization devoted entirely to economic and technical matters. Specifically, Cameroun proposed that the new organization be renamed the Union Africaine et Malgache de Coopération Economique et Technique, and that the political and military concerns of the UAM be eliminated from the new organization.

The major point of controversy at the Dakar conference was whether the UAM or any new organization would be concerned with political matters or be limited strictly to economic and technical issues. With the exception of Dahomey, all the Conseil de l'Entente states, together with Madagascar and Gabon, were in favor of the union's retaining its political tasks. Opposed were

---

[5]Union Africaine et Malgache, Compte-rendu des travaux de la Conférence de Dakar, 6-10 March 1964, p. 6.

[6]Ibid., p. 2.

Senegal, Cameroun, Mauritania, Dahomey, and the Republic of the Congo, who were motivated largely by a desire to improve their relations with non-UAM African states.

For Senegal, besides the economic factor noted earlier, transformation of the UAM into a nonpolitical organization was seen as a necessity if relations with Guinea were to be improved. During the colonial period, Guinea had been one of Senegal's major African trading partners. Reestablishment of these links, combined with cooperation with Guinea, Mali, and Mauritania, was perceived as a prerequisite for the economic resurgence of Senegal. Finally, Senghor had never been comfortable with the Francophone-Anglophone split. Mauritania, as noted in an earlier chapter, was more oriented to North Africa than to the UAM states, and had been forced to join the UAM because of a conflict with Morocco which resulted in its diplomatic isolation. The elimination of the UAM as a political group would provide a way out of an alliance that was no longer necessary, given the settlement of the conflict with Morocco. Cameroun had initially been reluctant to join the UAM for fear it would lead to French colonization or too close an identification with France. As a country bordering on an English-speaking country (Nigeria) and made up of both English- and French-speaking sections, Cameroun could not reconcile itself to membership in a purely French-speaking political union.

Changes in the positions of Dahomey and the Republic of the Congo with respect to the future of the UAM were the result of leadership changes. Souroy Apithy, a former member of Senghor's IOM, replaced Maga as President of Dahomey after a coup in October 1963. Apithy favored a less pro-Western foreign policy orientation than did the other members of the Conseil de l'Entente. Thus during 1964, he proposed an exchange of embassies with the Soviet Union and the People's Republic of China. Further, Apithy spent much of 1964 trying to persuade Ghana to join a union composed of Nigeria, Ghana, Togo, and Dahomey. Membership in a political UAM, given its conservative foreign policy orientation, was perceived as incompatible with Dahomey's new foreign policy orientation. Similarly, the government of Massamba-Débat, which took over in the Republic of the Congo after a coup in August 1963, had grown increasingly unhappy with the pro-Western foreign policy of the UAM, and thus favored the idea of a nonpolitical UAM.

These attitudes favoring the transformation of the UAM were fostered by an African environment that was perceived as less threatening than was the case in 1960. The creation of the OAU had, for many, symbolized the end of conflicts among the African states. This view was, however, not universally shared. The coup in Dahomey of August 1963 increased the fear of subversion in Niger, and in late 1963 and early 1964 there were increasing border conflicts between Upper Volta and Ghana. Thus the Ivory Coast, which perceived the UAM as a necessary base for facilitating its leadership role in African affairs, had no difficulties in persuading the latter two states to oppose major alterations of the UAM. Mba of Gabon, saved from a coup in February 1964 by French military intervention, also favored a political UAM for reasons of security, particularly from a perceived potential threat from the Republic of the Congo. Finally, with respect to Madagascar, it was primarily because of its political functions that the UAM was important, since Madagascar had few economic links with the other UAM states.

With the support of Togo and the Central African Republic, the proposal for changing the UAM into a strictly economic and technical union obtained a bare majority of votes. Togo supported the proposal because its President--Nicolas Grunitzky--had been a member of Senghor's IOM, whereas Central Africa supported the change because President Dacko had since 1963 decided to adopt a less pro-Western foreign policy orientation and had established ties with the Soviet Union and the People's Republic of China.

It was thus decided that the UAM was to be changed to the Union Africaine et Malgache de Coopération Economique (UAMCE). The tasks of the union were to be limited to economic, technical, and cultural matters, and all the previous specialized secretariats were to be grouped into a single administrative secretariat. The UAMD was to be abolished immediately. To signify the change from the UAM to the UAMCE, and to further consolidate the victory of the UAMCE supporters, the UAMCE Secretariat was to be located in Yaoundé and the power to nominate the Secretary-General was to be given to Senegal.[7] Clearly, these decisions represented an attempt on the part of the majority to impose its will on the minority rather than an effort to arrive at a general consensus. Little respect was shown for the concerns of the minority. Understandably, the Ivory Coast, Niger, and Upper Volta refused to sign the resolutions, which augured ill for the future of the UAMCE.

Only the general nature of the UAMCE was decided at the Dakar conference. The treaty of the new union was to be drawn up at a foreign ministers' conference at Nouakchott in the latter half of April. Members were urged not to give binding instructions to their delegates so that unanimous agreement could be reached, and the ministers were to be empowered to sign the charter.

Soon after the Dakar conference, the Ivory Coast Minister of Finance, Raphaël Saller, told a meeting of the Association of

---

[7]See ibid., pp. 48-49 and 52. The resolution on the UAMD was treated as "Confidential."

Overseas Journalists in Paris that the dissolution of the UAM and its replacement by the UAMCE was a profound mistake. Instead, he said, the UAM should have been kept and the OAMCE abolished. He noted that "the idea of an African Common Market is fantastic. There is no African country which could buy the products of Ivory Coast." On the other hand (he continued) among the Francophone African states, "there are obvious political ties among them . . ., for the ancient attachments and the more recent ones since independence correspond to real affinities and not to ideas which are more or less foreign."[8] This was a clear signal that the Ivory Coast would have nothing to do with the UAMCE. Thus it is not surprising that the Ivory Coast, together with Upper Volta and Niger, refused to send delegates to the April 1964 foreign ministers' conference at Nouakchott.

Given the absence of these states, the foreign ministers at Nouakchott agreed to only initial the UAMCE charter. This stratagem was designed to allow those absent to be present at the actual signing of the charter, which was to occur at a heads of state conference at Tananarive in December. The hope was that during the interim period, the Conseil de l'Entente states could be persuaded to accept the change from the UAM to the UAMCE.

Ould Daddah, the President of Mauritania, spent much of the rest of 1964 trying to develop a consensus on the nature of the UAMCE. At the same time, Houphouet was busy trying to regroup his forces in order to reverse the decision of the 1964 Dakar conference. In this he was greatly assisted by marked changes in the African environment. One of these changes was a deterioration in the relationship between Ghana and Togo as a result of Nkrumah's failure to reopen the border between the two countries. This and other conflicts between the two countries, particularly the killing of a Togolese customs officer within Togolese territory by Ghanaian guards in January 1965, led to a rapprochement between the Ivory Coast and Togo.[9] In addition, alleged Ghanaian support for an attempt by dissident elements resident in Ghana to overthrow the government of Niger in September 1964 increased the salience of the issue of subversion in Africa. Houphouet was able once more to raise the specter of Communist subversion through countries like Ghana. Increased fighting and internal disorder within the Democratic Republic of the Congo, combined with charges of intervention by radicals and Communists, provided Houphouet with further ammunition. Houphouet decided to make sure that his base in the Conseil de

---

[8] Marchés Tropicaux et Méditerranéens, 13 June 1964, p. 15005.

[9] See W. Scott Thompson, Ghana's Foreign Policy: 1957-1966 (Princeton: Princeton University Press, 1969), pp. 367-369.

l'Entente was secure. He did so by proposing the creation of a "dual nationality" within the Entente countries, which would ensure equal rights to all citizens of the member states of the Entente. This measure was particularly attractive to Togo and Dahomey, with their surpluses of educated individuals who could then seek employment in the Ivory Coast and elsewhere.

It was in this context that the next heads of state conference was held at Nouakchott in February 1965. At this conference, only Rwanda was not represented, and the only President absent was Massamba-Débat of the Republic of the Congo. The major item on the agenda was the nature of the union to be created. Linked to this issue was the problem of subversion in Africa and the renewed conflict in the Congo.

The argument of the Conseil de l'Entente states at the Nouakchott conference was a simple one. They held that with the creation of the OAU, it was assumed that African states would respect each other's sovereignty and refrain from interfering in each other's internal affairs. Recent events had shown that this assumption was false. As long as others failed to respect the charter of the OAU, a political union was necessary. This was the position taken by the Ivory Coast, Niger, Upper Volta, Togo, Gabon, and Madagascar, with a certain degree of support from Dahomey. Senegal, Cameroun, and the Republic of the Congo continued to insist that the creation of the OAU precluded the retention of regional political groups. Chad and Central Africa were sympathetic to this position, largely because they felt that a political union would be dominated by the states of West Africa.[10] In an attempt to achieve a compromise, Ould Daddah proposed that the new union should be "a kind of intermediary step between the OAU and the regional economic groups to which several of our countries belong."[11]

The outcome of the debate was a victory for those who favored a political union. Thus the final communique stated: "The new organization, called the Organisation Commune Africaine et Malgache (OCAM), is an African group whose goal is to strengthen the cooperation and solidarity of the states of Africa and Madagascar, within the framework of the OAU, in order to accelerate their development in the political, economic, social, technical and cultural domains."[12] However, in a spirit of compromise, it was agreed that the earlier decisions to create only one

---

[10] See Le Monde, February 10, 1965, p. 10.

[11] Combat, February 11, 1965.

[12] La Documentation Francaise, No. 01658, 18 March 1965.

Secretariat, to locate it at Yaoundé, and to empower Senegal to nominate the Secretary-General, would be retained. The charter of the OCAM was to be approved at a heads of state conference at Tananarive in January 1966 after it had been drawn up at a preceding conference of foreign ministers.

Included among the many declarations supporting the shift from the UAMCE to the OCAM was one from the French government. Thus, after a meeting of the French Council of Ministers on February 17, 1965, it was announced that "the Council felt that the cohesion manifested by the states participating at the Nouakchott conference is of a kind that will consolidate the links between these countries and France and justifies the pursuit of the policy of cooperation." De Gaulle added that "France could only congratulate itself for the creation of this organization. We feel that the African Francophone countries have the greatest mutual interest in reinforcing the ties and cooperation among them. The OCAM is sufficiently adaptable to reconcile national independence and common interests."[13] These statements clearly suggest that efforts by France had something to do with the shift from the UAMCE to the OCAM.

The developments from 1963 to 1965 indicate that external events continued to play a major role in determining the nature of the union among the French-speaking states of West and Equatorial Africa. A decrease in the perceived compellingness of the external environment was largely responsible for the changeover from the UAM to the UAMCE. This was combined with two other factors treated in the preceding chapter: the failure of the UAM to yield positive results (particularly those of an economic nature) and the increasing manpower burden entailed in participation in the UAM. The UAMCE, because of its simpler structure, would reduce such burdens. At the same time, since the UAMCE was to concentrate on economic and technical issues, it was anticipated that there would be more positive economic rewards. These calculations were altered by what was perceived as an increasingly threatening environment by some members in the second half of 1964. The result was the creation of the OCAM which, it was understood, would be empowered to deal with political questions. The commitment to a "political" OCAM was, however, neither unanimous nor equally salient to all members. In other words, the February 1965 decision did not resolve the basic differences over the nature of the union to be created. In the next chapter, we shall show the impact of these differences on the negotiations that led to the adoption of the OCAM charter as well as their impact on the OCAM charter itself.

---

[13]Le Monde, February 18, 1965.

Membership Changes

The shift from the UAMCE to the OCAM, as noted above, was the result of a counteroffensive launched by the states of the Conseil de l'Entente--notably the Ivory Coast. Renewed conflicts in the Democratic Republic of the Congo and allegations about subversive activities by Ghana had provided the fuel for this counteroffensive. Thus the final communique of the February 1965 heads of state conference at Nouakchott "energetically condemn[ed] the action of certain states, notably Ghana, which harbor agents of subversion and organize training camps on their national territory." The communique stressed the need for restoring peace in the Democratic Republic of the Congo by aiding the legal government.[14] This meant supporting Moïse Tshombe, who had been appointed Prime Minister in July 1964. On both positions, the leaders of Cameroun, Mauritania, and the Republic of the Congo held views that were opposed by the majority of the OCAM members. Nevertheless, the Conseil de l'Entente states, jubilant over their victory at Nouakchott in February 1965, pressed forward with measures designed to isolate Ghana and to support Tshombe. The climax of these efforts came at the OCAM conference at Abidjan in May 1965.

Between February and May 1965, two events occurred which had a significant impact on the Abidjan conference of May 1965. The most important of these was the attempted assassination of Hamani Diori in April by an agent who had presumably been trained in China and Ghana. Ghana was accused of having instigated the attack, and the result was an increase in the efforts of the Conseil de l'Entente states to isolate Ghana. Specifically, these efforts took the form of sending high level diplomatic missions to several African countries to win support for a boycott of the OAU summit conference at Accra in September 1965. Outside the OCAM, these efforts proved to be fruitless, and this made Houphouet more determined to rally his followers within the OCAM. Another factor which affected the May 1965 Abidjan conference was the victory of Tshombe's party in the April 1965 elections in the Democratic Republic of the Congo. This gave the government of Tshombe greater legitimacy and encouraged the Conseil de l'Entente states in their determination to support his government.

It was in this context that Yameogo, on behalf of the Conseil de l'Entente states, called for an OCAM summit conference in Abidjan, at which the Congo problem and the OAU summit conference at Accra would be discussed. This meeting was agreed to, but confusion soon arose as to the date on which it would be held. Thus on May 21, it was announced by Ould Daddah, the OCAM

---

[14]Combat, February 13, 1965.

President, that the conference would be held on June 17. But on the very same day, the Ivory Coast Minister of Information announced that the conference would be held on May 25. He refused to comment on Ould Daddah's statement.[15] This was a clear indication that there were strong disagreements over the questions to be discussed at the conference.

When the OCAM conference opened at Abidjan on May 25, only eight heads of state were present. Those absent were Ould Daddah, Ahidjo, Massamba-Débat, Dacko, Apithy, and Grégoire Kayibanda, President of Rwanda. The absences of the first three were due to their opposition to the direction in which the OCAM seemed to be moving, but the latter three were absent for other reasons. Nevertheless, the conference proceeded to deal with the two main items on its agenda.

On the Congo question, the main issue before the conference was the application for membership in the OCAM by the Democratic Republic of the Congo. Strong support for granting membership came from the Conseil de l'Entente states, as well as from Madagascar and Gabon; Senegal, Chad, and the Central African Republic expressed a willingness to go along. Support for admission was based on the feeling that it would put an end to the diplomatic isolation of the Democratic Republic of the Congo, and thus strengthen the central government vis-à-vis subversive groups. The major problem, however, was the person of Tshombe and the negative attitudes toward him held by many African leaders. On this point, Houphouet noted as follows: "The Democratic Republic of the Congo has requested admission to the OCAM. On this important question, we do not have to pass judgment on individuals. We simply have to reply to the request of a country belonging to the OAU."[16]

For the leaders of Cameroun, the Republic of the Congo, and Mauritania, the request of the Democratic Republic of the Congo could not be separated from the person of Tshombe. The leaders of these three countries had very negative feelings toward Tshombe because of his role in the Katanga secession and his use of white mercenaries against the rebels in the Democratic Republic of the Congo. Beyond their opposition to the person of Tshombe, they were also of the opinion that the way to bring about peace and stability in the Democratic Republic of the Congo was to mediate the conflict between the central and the rebel governments. Support for the central government, they felt, would make it more intransigent and less willing to negotiate.

---

[15] A.F.P. Bulletin d'Afrique, No. 5685, 22 May 1965.

[16] A.F.P. Bulletin d'Afrique, No. 5688, 26 May 1965.

Finally, they argued that the issue should be handled at the OAU level in order not to precipitate a breach in African unity.

In spite of the opposition of these leaders, the Abidjan conference decided to admit the Democratic Republic of the Congo into the OCAM. Other African countries were asked not to support the Congolese rebels, and Ghana was once more denounced for its subversive activities. With respect to the second main item on the agenda--the OAU summit conference at Accra--it was decided that members would boycott the conference. However, they agreed to take part in a foreign ministers' conference at Lagos proposed by Nigeria in order to seek a way of saving the OAU conference. For the Conseil de l'Entente leaders, the results of the conference constituted a significant victory in their campaign against Ghana. For the OCAM, however, it seemed as if the conference would result in a gain of one new member at the cost of the loss of three old members.

Soon after the Abidjan conference, the decision to admit the Democratic Republic of the Congo was criticized in Brazzaville, Yaoundé, and Nouakchott. Thus Massamba-Débat said in a radio interview at Conakry that the Abidjan decision compromised African unity and the fraternity of the African people. He added that "if the OCAM turns in the direction of conspiracy, disunity, intrigue, and cynicism, there could be no place for Congo-Brazzaville in the OCAM."[17] Along similar lines, Ahidjo observed that Cameroun was dissatisfied with developments in the OCAM and that it might reconsider its membership. He added: "For the moment, we are in the OCAM. We hope that things will improve and that this organization will function normally. If not, we will start wondering why we should remain in the OCAM."[18] Similar comments were made by the leaders of Mauritania.

In the end, the only state which withdrew from the OCAM was Mauritania. This decision was taken on June 24 and announced officially on July 7, 1965. The official reason given was that Mauritania could not form an integral part of a group of states which might be a possible rival of the OAU or which might harm the authority of the OAU. The real reason, however, was aptly stated as follows:

Mauritania has made its choice! . . . The Moroccan pretensions have been blunted, and there is no longer any immediate danger menacing its frontiers. . . . The culture and organization of the Mauritanian state are oriented more toward

---

[17] L'Horoya, 2 June 1965.

[18] A.F.P. Bulletin d'Afrique, No. 5734, 22 July 1965.

Africa north of the Sahara. . . . Between Africa south of
the Sahara and Africa north of the Sahara, President Mocktar
has chosen the North. . . .[19]

Prior to the announcement of the withdrawal of Mauritania,
its President paid a visit to Ahidjo at Garoua. The reason for
the visit was to persuade Cameroun to also withdraw from the
OCAM. In this respect, the visit was a failure. The main reason
for Cameroun remaining in the OCAM related to the efforts of
Senghor, who took on the role of conciliator after the Abidjan
conference. As noted earlier, the ties between Senghor and
Ahidjo were strong and intimate, and it was the former who persuaded the latter to stay in the OCAM. Expectations of economic
gain from the OCAM were another factor which influenced the decision of Cameroun. Thus in September, Ahidjo stated that he would
attend the OCAM conference scheduled for Tananarive in January
1966. He added:

Certainly, we have recently had some disagreements with certain of our partners. But I think that if both sides show
proof of good will and understanding, the OCAM will become
a reality and could be able to play a constructive role in
Africa, particularly in the economic and technical domains.[20]

Three factors were responsible for the decision of the
Republic of the Congo to stay in the OCAM. One was the expectation of economic gain from the OCAM. The creation of a common
market for sugar within the OCAM was being discussed. The Republic of the Congo stood to gain from such an agreement, and it
did not want to jeopardize these gains. Second, serious conflicts
existed between the two Congos, largely as a result of the civil
war in the Democratic Republic of the Congo, and withdrawal from
the OCAM, it was felt, would make it more difficult to solve
these conflicts. Finally, the dismissal of Tshombe by Kasavubu
in October 1965 removed the main grounds on which the Republic
of the Congo had objected to the membership of the Democratic
Republic of the Congo in the OCAM.

By October 1965, all was set for the January 1966 OCAM
summit conference. The OCAM had gained one member and lost one
member. The consequences of this change in membership for the
degree of homogeneity of the union will concern us in later sections of this study.

---

[19] Afrique Nouvelle, 15 July 1965.

[20] L'Effort Camerounais, 29 September 1965.

POLITICAL INTEGRATION IN FRENCH-SPEAKING AFRICA

Negotiating the OCAM Treaty

On October 13, 1965, Diakha Dieng, the OCAM Secretary-General, announced at Tananarive that the OCAM summit conference would begin at Tananarive on January 15, 1966. Plans for the conference progressed until about a week before it was scheduled to commence, when it was revealed in Dakar that the summit conference would be postponed but that the foreign ministers' conference would be held on schedule. Request for postponement of the summit conference came from several heads of state, including Houphouet. These heads of state felt that the time was inappropriate for them to leave their countries. This feeling was a result of a series of military coups in Africa--in the Democratic Republic of the Congo in November 1965, in Dahomey in December 1965, and in Upper Volta and the Republic of Central Africa in January 1966.

At the foreign ministers' conference held at Tananarive from January 12-18, 1966, the main item on the agenda was the treaty of the OCAM. Two draft proposals were presented. Togo's draft proposal was more in the spirit of the UAMCE, and provided for cooperation essentially in the economic and technical areas. On the other hand, Madagascar's draft treaty was more in keeping with the decision to create the OCAM, and called for cooperation not only in the economic and technical areas but also in political or foreign policy matters. It was therefore decided to use Madagascar's draft treaty as the working document of the conference.

The main issues of disagreement relating to the charter of the OCAM were as follows: (1) whether harmonization of foreign policies was to be one of the tasks of the union, (2) the frequency with which the Council of Ministers was to meet, (3) the need to create an Assistant Secretary-General, (4) the necessity of creating specialized commissions, and (5) limitations on the principle of qualified majority voting in the heads of state conferences. A sixth issue, which arose outside the context of the nature of the OCAM treaty, was one which dealt with the fate of the conventions adopted during the UAM period.

Among other tasks, Madagascar's draft proposal called for the harmonization of foreign policies. Strong objection was raised to this by the Republic of the Congo on the grounds that the goal was unrealistic, since there were significant differences in the foreign policies of the member states. Others pointed out that failure to include foreign policy as one of the tasks of the union would indicate a return to the UAMCE and thus be a violation of the understanding that led to the creation of the OCAM, but this had no effect on the position of the Republic of the Congo. Two compromise amendments were offered, both designed to reduce the level of commitment entailed. Thus an amendment

146

offered by Dahomey stated that "while respecting the sovereignty and the fundamental options of the member states, the Organization will strive to harmonize the activities of the members" in the areas of foreign, economic, and social policies and also to co-ordinate the development programs of the members. Along similar lines, the Democratic Republic of the Congo proposed that the members agree to harmonize their economic, technical, and cultural policies, coordinate their development programs, and "facilitate consultation in foreign policy matters among themselves." Neither of these amendments was acceptable to the Republic of the Congo, which continued to demand that the tasks of the union be stated as follows: "[T]he Organization will strive to harmonize the activity of the member states in the economic, social, technical and cultural areas, and to coordinate their development programs."21

Discussion of this matter extended over a period of two days, and agreement could not be reached even after the delegate of the Republic of the Congo contacted his government for further instructions. A compromise solution was proposed, which was a fusion of the amendments of Dahomey and the Democratic Republic of the Congo. It provided that "the Organization will strive to harmonize the activity of member states in the economic, social, technical, and cultural areas, coordinate their development programs and, while respecting the sovereignty and the fundamental options of each member-state, facilitate consultation in foreign policy matters among them."22 In other words, what was proposed as a "compromise" was in reality no compromise at all. Rather, the existing differences were merely to be swept under the rug. Though the Republic of the Congo still refused to accept the proposal, the others adopted it. As a result, the Congo refused to initial the charter.

Madagascar's draft treaty called for semiannual meetings of the Council of Ministers. Since the heads of state would be meeting only once a year, it was hoped that the Council of Ministers would become an instrument for coordinating the activities of the union. However, for reasons of economy, and because of the large number of other international conferences, it was decided that the Council of Ministers would also meet only once a year. For similar reasons of economy, a proposal for the creation of specialized commissions in the OCAM was rejected.

21Secrétariat-Général de l'OCAM, Conseil des Ministres de l'Organisation Commune Africaine et Malgache: Tananarive, 12-18 Janvier 1966, p. 6.

22Ibid.

A provision for an Assistant Secretary-General was also rejected. This provision had been included in Madagascar's treaty because, during the UAM period, some members had begun to criticize the fact that Dahomey had a monopoly on the post of Secretary-General. During the discussion of the provision, however, it became clear that creating such a new position would result in confusion and administrative difficulties. Recollections of the conflicts and inefficiencies resulting from several Secretaries-General during the UAM period finally persuaded members to agree on a single Secretary-General.

The final issue of controversy relating to the OCAM charter dealt with the voting formula in the heads of state conferences. Madagascar proposed that all decisions at the heads of state conferences require a two-thirds majority. Senegal held that this was unworkable, and would lead either to the failure to implement decisions or to the breakup of the union. On major matters, Senegal held that the emphasis should be on consensus rather than on a specified majority. A compromise was agreed upon in which unanimity would be required for "recommendations of a political nature."

On the question of the validity of treaties adopted during the UAM period, the Democratic Republic of the Congo insisted that it had not been a party to those negotiations, that the OCAM was a new organization, and that it [the Congo] could not automatically subscribe to such treaties. Some members (notably Cameroun) urged the complexity of the problem, and proposed that decision on the matter be referred to the heads of state. This proposal was adopted, and the OCAM Secretary-General was asked to send copies of the various conventions and agreements to the member states.

When the heads of state met at Tananarive in June 1966, the Democratic Republic of the Congo still refused to accept the validity of the UAM conventions. It had the support of Cameroun, Upper Volta, and Central Africa. They pointed out that the agreements in question were deficient, largely ignored, and had been precipitously adopted during the euphoria of independence. Specifically, they pointed to the deficiencies in the Convention on General Diplomatic Representation, the Convention of Settlement, the conventions dealing with technical cooperation, and the Convention on Cooperation in Judicial Matters. They proposed the modification of all these agreements. To break the deadlock, the Ivory Coast and Dahomey proposed that the previous agreements be considered still valid, providing "bilateral links" among the signatories. Those who had not signed the treaties would be "invited" to sign them. Clearly, this proposal (which was adopted) merely avoided rather than solved the issue. It is therefore not surprising that the Democratic Republic of the Congo never associated itself with any of the earlier agreements.

Several features stand out in the negotiating process that led to the adoption of the OCAM treaty. These negotiations revealed substantial disagreements over the nature of the union that was being created, as well as the absence of any cumulative decision-making pattern. When disagreements existed, they were solved on the basis of the lowest common denominator, or they were obscured by the adoption of essentially meaningless decisions. Clearly, these features did not augur well for the ability of the OCAM to engage in joint decision-making.

The Treaties of the OCAM

At the OCAM heads of state conference at Tananarive in June 1966, the OCAM treaty elaborated by the foreign ministers in January was adopted and signed without amendments. The basic texts of the union consisted of the OCAM charter, the Internal Rules of the Conference of Heads of State and Government, the Internal Rules of the Council of Ministers, and the Convention Regulating the Personnel of the OCAM.[23]

Article 1 of the OCAM charter described the organization as open to all independent and sovereign African states. The admission of a new member was to be by unanimous vote. The goal of the union, according to Article 2, was "to reinforce the cooperation and solidarity among the states of Africa and Madagascar in order to accelerate their economic, social, technical and cultural development." Article 3 described the tasks of the OCAM as that of harmonizing activities in the economic, technical, social, and cultural domains, coordinating development programs, and facilitating consultations in foreign policy matters while respecting the sovereignty and the fundamental options of each member. The three institutions of the union were a Conference of Heads of State and Government (referred to hereafter as the Conference), the Council of Ministers (referred to hereafter as the Council), and the Administrative General Secretariat.

The OCAM Conference was to be constituted by the heads of state and heads of government or their representatives. Meeting once a year, it was to be the supreme organ of the union. At the request of one member, and with the approval of two-thirds of the members, emergency sessions of the Conference could be held. Article 6 stipulated that the tasks of the Conference were to "study questions of common interest and make decisions. . . ."

---

[23]These four documents are to be found in Secrétariat-Général de l'OCAM, Textes constitutifs de l'Organisation Commune Africaine et Malgache: Tananarive, 28 Juin 1966. Subsequent citations are from this publication.

Article 9 provided that all decisions made in the presence of a quorum (two-thirds of the members) and with the required majority were binding on all members. (According to Article 24 of the Internal Rules of the Conference, resolutions required a two-thirds majority for adoption; however, recommendations of a political nature required unanimity. Procedural questions were to be decided by simple majority, while the question of whether an issue was substantive or procedural was to be decided by a two-thirds majority.) A final provision worth noting is in Article 8 of the Internal Rules of the Conference. This provided for the election of a President of the union at each ordinary session of the Conference. It was the duty of the President to coordinate and harmonize the points of view of the members, in consultation with the members of the Conference, to give the organization the stimulus necessary for the realization of its objectives.

According to Article 10 of the OCAM charter, the Council was to be made up of foreign ministers or any other ministers designated by the member states. It was to hold one ordinary session yearly, a few days before the meeting of the Conference, and in the same city. Request for an emergency session of the Council required the support of two-thirds of the members. It was the responsibility of the Council to prepare the Conference of heads of state, inform itself on all questions referred to it, and oversee the implementation of decisions made by the Conference. The Council was to implement the goal of cooperation among the members according to the directives of the Conference. Sessions of the Council required a quorum of two-thirds of the members, and before a recommendation could be sent to the Conference, it had to receive the support of two-thirds of the members.

Article 15 of the charter provided that the OCAM Secretariat was to be in Yaoundé. It was to be headed by an "Administrative Secretary-General" appointed for renewable periods of two years by the Conference on the recommendation of the Council. The duty of the Secretary-General was to assure the administrative working of the organs of the union, under the authority of the President of the OCAM. He was also empowered to follow the activities of the joint enterprises, specifically Air Afrique and the UAMPT. Finally, the Secretary-General was to serve as the secretary of both the Conference and the Council.

In a basic sense, there was little difference between the UAM treaties and those of the OCAM with respect to the level of commitment entailed and the nature of the tasks and structures. Like the UAM, the OCAM charter provided for cooperation over a wide scope of issue areas. Commitments contained in the OCAM charter were very general and vague; nothing specific was agreed to, and rather than political integration being built into the treaty, the provision was for its negotiation over an indefinite period of time. The central institutions created were self-consciously of an intergovernmental nature, with decision-making authority exclusively in the hands of the heads of state. Neither the OCAM President, the Council of Ministers, or the Secretary-General had autonomous powers of decision. While the voting provisions made it possible for less than unanimous decisions to be taken in certain areas, developments during the UAM period suggest that it is highly unlikely that states opposed to particular decisions would feel themselves bound by them. Given the low level of commitment, the broad but vague tasks, and the weak central institutions, success in political integration would require particularly favorable integrative and process conditions. We shall now examine the integrative and process conditions existing between 1966 and 1970 and the level of political integration achieved during this period.

Chapter 6

THE OCAM SYSTEM

Integrative Conditions

In the previous chapters, we noted that integrative conditions had been only marginally favorable for political integration under the UAM system. Factors which seemed to favor integration were the similarity in the political systems of the UAM members, the similarity in elite values, the congenial nature of the relationships among the elites, and the perceived existence of a compelling external environment. On the other hand, there was a substantial degree of inequality in the economic capabilities of the UAM members, and transactions among them were limited and unbalanced. The uniform dependence of the member states on France was rated as ambiguous in terms of its impact on political integration within the UAM. In this section, we shall review these integrative conditions to determine what changes may have occurred in them under the OCAM system between 1966 and 1970.

When the UAM was created in 1961, all its member states had authoritarian political systems. This uniformity in the nature of the political systems of the member states ended with the rebellion in the Republic of the Congo in August 1963. Since then, the Republic of the Congo has been in the category of a "mobilization" system, despite the military coup which overthrew the government of Massemba-Débat in August-September 1968. The new government of the Republic of the Congo proclaimed itself the People's Republic of the Congo in January 1970, becoming the first African country to declare itself a people's republic.

The political changes in the Republic of the Congo were the most far-reaching of those that occurred during this period, but there were several other changes that should be noted. As indicated in the preceding chapter, the government of the Democratic Republic of the Congo was overthrown by a military coup headed by General Joseph Mobutu in November 1965. Two months later, the governments of Upper Volta and the Central African Republic were overthrown by military coups, and in January 1967 a similar situation developed in Togo. In Dahomey, which first experienced a military coup in October 1963, civilian and military rule alternated until December 1965, when General Soglo staged his third coup; another military coup occurred in December 1967, followed by a short period of civilian rule and a sixth military coup in December 1969.[1] In short, Dahomey was experiencing a significant degree of political instability from 1963 to 1970.

Thus, of the fourteen OCAM members, eight were authoritarian political systems, four were military oligarchies, one was a mobilization system, and the other exemplified what Samuel Huntington calls a "praetorian" political system.[2] This made the OCAM a great deal more heterogeneous than the UAM in terms of the political systems of the member states. Obviously, however, it is necessary to look beyond the changes in domestic political systems to determine to what degree the policies of the OCAM states became divergent. The evidence suggests that, with the exception of the People's Republic of the Congo, no basic changes in policies resulted from the changes in political systems.

Immediately upon assuming power, the military leaders of Dahomey, Upper Volta, Togo, and the Republic of Central Africa announced their attachment to France and their desire to stay in the OCAM. The domestic economic policies of these states continued to be a gradual approach to economic development, with heavy reliance on private foreign investments. This was also the orientation of the Democratic Republic of the Congo under Mobutu. In the Republic of the Congo, however, there were significant policy changes. There was a commitment to the nationalization of all the means of production, but the realization of this goal was postponed until some unspecified time in the future. More immediately, close relationships were established with the Communist countries. Relations with France were strained, but both sides made determined efforts to prevent a complete break in ties.

Thus, in spite of the differences in political systems, thirteen of the fourteen OCAM members opted for the gradualist path to political and economic development. These thirteen states showed little desire to play an activist role in international affairs. Their external ties were mostly with the West, which meant France or Belgium in the case of Rwanda and the

---

[1] For the histories of the coups in Upper Volta, Dahomey, and the Central African Republic, see Victor T. Le Vine, "The Coups in Upper Volta, Dahomey, and the Central African Republic" in Robert I. Rotberg and Ali A. Mazrui, eds., Protest and Power in Black Africa (New York: Oxford University Press, 1970). Treatment of the coups in Dahomey, Upper Volta, and Togo can also be found in Virginia Thompson, West Africa's Council of the Entente (Ithaca: Cornell University Press, 1972).

[2] See Samuel Huntington, Political Order in Changing Societies (New Haven: Yale University Press, 1968), pp. 78-83, for a discussion of praetorian polities.

Democratic Republic of the Congo. Therefore, whereas the OCAM scored low with respect to similarity in the political systems of its members, its score for complementarity of elite values was high.

One important consequence of the governmental changes was a change in the top leadership of the OCAM states. Of the eleven heads of state who signed the UAM charter in September 1961 (we are disregarding Mauritania since it is not a member of the OCAM), four had been overthrown by the time of the signing of the OCAM treaty in June 1966. A fifth, Mba of Gabon, died in November 1967. Further, Togo's President at the time it was admitted to the UAM in July 1963 was overthrown in January 1967, and Tshombe, who had engineered the admission of the Democratic Republic of the Congo into the OCAM, was dismissed from office in October 1965. Thus, of the fourteen OCAM heads of state, only six had been participants in the regional political integration effort since 1961; a seventh, the President of Rwanda, had joined this effort in 1963.

As a result of these changes in leadership, there was a sharp decline in the congeniality of the relationships among the elites in the OCAM. Two of the OCAM heads of state had never participated in the trans-territorial political institutions and movements of French West or Equatorial Africa because their countries had been under Belgian rather than French rule. In five other cases, the background of the new leaders was in the military, which meant that they also had not participated in these institutions and movements. Such was also true of Albert Bongo of Gabon, who worked his way to the presidency by way of the bureaucracy rather than through electoral politics. All this meant that strong personal ties among the political elites, which were a strong factor in the creation and the survival of the UAM, were absent in the OCAM situation.

A further consequence of the leadership changes was a reinforcement of the degree of elitism within the OCAM. As we shall show in subsequent sections, partly because of the inexperience, insecurity, and lack of prestige of the new leaders, initiative within the OCAM tended to be mainly in the hands of Houphouet-Boigny, Senghor, Ahidjo, and Tsiranana. The insecurity of the new leaders created a situation in which the potential negative impact of the decline in congeniality among the elites was greatly reduced. For the present, however, we must assign a low score for the elite ties in the OCAM.

An integrative condition which had received a high score during the UAM period was the perceived cogency of the external environment. We have already seen that from mid-1964 to early 1966 the score for this variable was high, and accounted largely for the shift from the UAMCE to the OCAM. With the overthrow of the Nkrumah regime in February 1966, there was a sharp decline in the perceived cogency of the external environment as the new government of Ghana strove to establish amicable relations with neighboring states. Guinea threatened to invade Ghana by way of Liberia and the Ivory Coast in order to restore Nkrumah, but these threats were not taken seriously. Some time earlier, in June 1965, Ben Bella's government in Algeria had been overthrown by Houari Boumedienne. While this coup did not alter the radical nature of Algerian policies, it resulted in a weakening of the radical African bloc, since the new government of Algeria displayed less interest than its predecessor in developments south of the Sahara. Further, in November 1968, Modibo-Keita of Mali was overthrown by a military coup. Finally, the increased tensions in the Middle East and the resulting war there in June 1967 meant that the U.A.R., another of the radical African states, was largely a non-actor in the African subsystem between 1966 and 1970.

All told, then, the history of the OCAM during this period has been coterminous with the disintegration of the radical African bloc. For much of this period, Nigeria has been only a marginal actor in the African scene because of its civil war. Developments in southern Africa, such as Rhodesia's unilateral declaration of independence in November 1965, have not been perceived as threatening by the OCAM states. The only salient external threat that has emerged in recent years is that faced by Chad as the result of Sudanese aid for guerrilla movements in northern Chad. However, this threat is perceived as one directed at a particular member rather than at the OCAM members in general. In sum, there has been a significant decrease in the perceived cogency of the external political environment.

With respect to the perception of the external economic environment, there were significant variations among the OCAM states. Senghor had spoken of the deteriorating global economic position of the UAM members, and the perceived cogency of the external economic environment by some members was one of the reasons for the change from the UAM to the UAMCE. For these members, this perception remained the same during the 1966-70 period. Poor economic performance was a major factor in all the military coups. For some OCAM members, however, such as the Ivory Coast, Gabon, and Cameroun, the 1966-70 period was one of significant economic growth, and they did not perceive the external economic environment as threatening. In sum, the perceived cogency of the external political environment decreased between 1966 and 1970 for all OCAM member states, while the perceived cogency of the external economic environment during the same period was high for some, but not all, members. We therefore assign a mixed score to this variable.

During the UAM period, the economies of the member states showed a high degree of disparity in size and growth. Further, this disparity increased during the life of the UAM. Table 21 provides a summary of developments in the economic sphere during the OCAM period.

In each of the measures of economic performance included in Table 21, there was a wide range of difference among the OCAM states. The ratio between the lowest and highest GDP per capita at 1960 prices in 1965 was 1 to 9, and for 1968, 1 to 11. Comparative ratios for per capita exports and per capita governmental expenditures in 1968 were 1 to 66 and 1 to 28 respectively. The share of manufacturing in the GDP of member states in 1965 varied from a low of 5.1 percent to a high of 12.6 percent; in 1968, the respective figures were 2.9 and 17.1 percent. Finally, the extent to which exports paid for imports varied from a low of 40.5 percent to a high of 152.4 percent in 1965, and 48.9 to 190.8 percent in 1968.

Growth rates among the OCAM members between 1965 and 1968 also varied widely. The countries which experienced high growth rates in all three measures of growth (GDP per capita at constant prices, output of manufactured goods, and exports) were Togo, the Ivory Coast, Cameroun, Gabon, and Upper Volta. Republic of the Congo enjoyed moderately high growth rates with respect to per capita GDP and the output of manufactured goods, but its performance in the area of exports was very poor. Dahomey did very well in the area of exports, fairly well with respect to per capita GDP, and its output of manufactured goods is reported to have increased rapidly.[3] Senegal and Madagascar did poorly in all three areas, and the Democratic Republic of the Congo did poorly except with respect to exports. Both Chad and the Republic of Central Africa reportedly experienced slow industrial growth rates between 1965 and 1968;[4] these countries fall in the category of states with poor economic performance (except for exports in the Republic of Central Africa). Both Rwanda and Niger (except for output of manufactured goods) also fall in the category of poorly performing economies.

Allowing for the size of the territories involved, the 1965-1968 period saw the continued economic ascendancy of the Ivory Coast, Cameroun, and to some extent the Republic of the Congo, and the continued economic decline of Senegal and Madagascar. The Democratic Republic of the Congo was among the economic

---

[3] United Nations Economic Commission for Africa, A Survey of Economic Conditions in Africa, 1969 (New York: United Nations, 1971) [E/CN.14/480/Rev. 1 (Part 1)], p. 48.

[4] Ibid., p. 49.

Table 21

OCAM: BASIC ECONOMIC INDICATORS

| Country | GDP Per Capita at Constant 1960 Prices | | | Share of Manufacturing in GDP at Current Factor Prices | | | Total Exports | | | Import Coverage by Exports: Percent | | Per Capita Exports: 1968 | Per Capita Government Expenditures (Ordinary Budget): 1968 |
| | Value in U$S | | Average Annual Growth Rate: | Percent | | Average Annual Growth Rate: | Value in U$S Millions | | Average Annual Growth Rate: | | | | |
	1965	1968	Percent	1965	1968	Percent	1965	1968	Percent	1965	1968	(in U$S)	1968 (in U$S)
Cameroun	107	132	7.8%	8.3%	8.6%	12.8%	139.1	189.3	10.8%	92.0%	100.5%	34	26
Central Africa	84	90	2.4	n.a.	8.9	n.a.	26.3	35.7	10.8	92.9	90.0	24	29
Chad	56	51	-3.0	n.a.	5.3	n.a.	27.2	27.6	0.3	87.1	73.7	11	13
Congo (Democratic Republic)	85	89	1.6	16.6	17.2	4.7[b]	336.0	570.0	19.3	105.0	142.5	26[d]	25[d]
Congo (Republic)	127	145	4.7	n.a.	10.6	6.3	46.6	49.3	2.0	72.3	58.3	56	56
Dahomey	67	73	3.0	5.0[a]	6.9	n.a.	13.6	21.8	17.0	41.2	48.9	8	13
Gabon	337	373	3.6	5.1	6.6	12.3	95.9	124.0	8.9	152.4	190.8	257	112
Ivory Coast	228	268	5.8	10.4	12.3	15.3	277.1	424.8	15.2	117.4	135.3	102	45
Madagascar	95	96	0.4	n.a.	4.6	1.9	91.6	115.8	8.0	66.7	68.2	16	16

Table 21 (continued)

Country	GDP Per Capita at Constant 1960 Prices			Share of Manufacturing in GDP at Current Factor Prices			Total Exports			Import Coverage by Exports: Percent		Per Capita Exports: 1968 (in US$)	Per Capita Government Expenditures (Ordinary Budget): 1968 (in US$)
	Value in US$		Average Annual Growth Rate: Percent	Percent		Average Annual Growth Rate: Percent	Value in US$ Millions		Average Annual Growth Rate: Percent				
	1965	1968		1965	1968		1965	1968		1965	1968		
Niger	76	74	-0.9%	5.6%	6.7%	9.0%	25.3	28.0[c]	3.5%	65.8%	62.2%	10	10
Rwanda	37	34	2.7	n.a.	2.9	n.a.	14.0	14.8	1.9	66.7	68.2	4	4
Senegal	184	180	-0.7	12.6	13.7	5.4	129.0	151.1	5.4	80.6	83.4	42	40
Togo	97	132	12.4	5.5	17.1	42.0	27.0	38.6	12.7	60.0	83.0	21	13
Upper Volta	36	41	4.6	5.3	8.9	9.0	15.0	21.4	12.7	40.5	51.2	4	6

[a] 1966.
[b] At 1960 factor cost.
[c] Provisional estimates.
[d] 1967.

Sources: United Nations Economic Commission for Africa--A Survey of Economic Conditions in Africa, 1969 (New York: United Nations, 1971) [E/CN.14/480/Rev. 1 (Part 1)]; Summaries of Economic Data: Possible Economic Out-turn for 1971 for 43 Countries in Africa (November 1971); Statistical Yearbook, 1970 (Part 1). Secretariat-Général de l'OCAM--OCAM 1968.

leaders of the OCAM, largely because of its size.[5] In sum, the score assigned for degree of economic equality in the OCAM is therefore low.

Do the political inequalities among the OCAM members follow the same pattern as the economic inequalities? Given the personalization of power in Africa, the indicator of political ranking is the personal prestige of the head of state. The UAM period was characterized by a competition for leadership between Houphouet-Boigny (Ivory Coast) and Senghor (Senegal), with other influential leaders being Ahidjo (Cameroun) and Tsiranana (Madagascar). These leaders continued to play a dominant role in OCAM affairs; in newspaper accounts Houphouet, Senghor, Ahidjo, and Tsiranana have been described as "Les doyens de l'OCAM--les 'vieux.'"[6] One leader whose prestige increased during this period was Diori (Niger), but this was largely because he remained a faithful ally of Houphouet. Because of Houphouet, Diori was reelected to an unprecedented second term as President of the OCAM in January 1968.[7] Mobutu (Republic of the Congo) resented the nature of the leadership in the union, but made little effort to challenge this leadership.

Mobutu was an uncertain quantity in the OCAM. He had none of the personal prestige of a Senghor or a Houphouet, but as head of the largest and most developed state in the OCAM, he had leadership ambitions. Thus in 1968, he sought to destroy UDEAC and create the Union des Etats de l'Afrique Centrale with Chad and the Republic of Central Africa. He was also anxious to extend his influence over Rwanda and Burundi. Finally, his lack of personal ties with the OCAM leadership made him uncomfortable

---

[5]Its population in 1970 was estimated at 21,638,000; the next largest member of the union (Madagascar) had a population of only 6,750,000. The GDP at current market prices in 1970 for the Democratic Republic of the Congo was $1.9 billion, while the figure for the Ivory Coast (which had the next highest GDP in 1970) was about $1.5 billion. The DRC contributed 4.9 percent of all manufactured goods produced in Africa in 1968; the contributions of the Ivory Coast, Senegal, and Cameroun were 3.0, 2.2, and 1.7 percent respectively. Finally, the total exports of the DRC were $796 million in 1970, while for the Ivory Coast the figure was $470 million. (Sources: United Nations Economic Commission for Africa, Summaries of Economic Data: Possible Economic Outturn for 1971 for 43 Countries in Africa [November 1971], and A Survey of Economic Conditions in Africa, 1969.)

[6]Le Monde, January 23, 1968.

[7]See Afrique Contemporaine, No. 35, January-February 1968.

with the hierarchy in the union and, as we shall see, was a factor in his withdrawal from the OCAM in April 1972.

One factor which changed under the OCAM was the rivalry between Senghor and Houphouet. With the change from the UAMCE to the OCAM, Senghor conceded the dominant role to Houphouet. At the Niamey conference of January 1968, a "sacred union" between the two leaders was officially confirmed, and Senghor started referring to himself as the "vice-doyen" and to Houphouet as the "doyen" of OCAM. According to one observer, one of the consequences of the Niamey conference was the confirmation of the authority of the Conseil de l'Entente, particularly that of Houphouet, within the OCAM.[8] Thus not only did political inequalities reinforce economic inequalities, but political leadership was in the hands of the individual least interested in promoting political integration. This clearly did not bode well for political integration in the OCAM.

The last of the integrative conditions to be considered here has to do with regional interdependence as compared with the interdependence between OCAM members and third parties. Under the UAM, extra-regional dependence, mostly with France, was very high, while regional interdependence was very low. Table 22 provides measures of these two forms of interdependence in terms of trade figures.

From Table 22 it is clear that interdependence between the OCAM states and France is still high. Ten of the fourteen OCAM members sent more than a third of their exports to France in both 1966 and 1968. The four countries which did not have such a relationship with France were Upper Volta, the Republic of the Congo, the Democratic Republic of the Congo, and Rwanda. In the case of the latter two countries, low exports to France are explained by the fact that they were colonies of Belgium and thus tended to trade more with Belgium. The exports of these two countries to Belgium were 24.8 and 33.1 percent in 1966 and 34.9 and 23.6 percent in 1968 respectively. Most of the exports of the Republic of the Congo went to West Germany, the Netherlands, and Britain, while those of Upper Volta went mainly to the Ivory Coast.

Altogether, France received 34.8 percent of the exports of the OCAM states in 1966 and 29.6 percent in 1968, indicating that exports to France have been on the decline. There was a decrease in the exports of nine OCAM states to France between

---

[8]Philippe Decraene, "La Conférence de l'OCAM a confirmé l'influence politique du Conseil de l'Entente au sein de l'Afrique francophone," Le Monde, January 25, 1968.

Table 22

DIRECTION OF OCAM EXPORTS BY PERCENTAGES: 1966 AND 1968

FROM:	1966			1968		
TO:	France	Other EEC	OCAM	France	Other EEC	OCAM
Cameroun	37.6%	29.2%	2.7%	33.7%	36.5%	8.0%
Central Africa	37.4	12.0	--[a]	38.0	7.4	--[a]
Chad	48.8	6.5	--[a]	63.5	12.1	6.6
Congo (Democratic Republic)	7.5	38.9	n.a.	5.7	47.4	n.a.
Congo (Republic)	10.3	50.5	0.6	10.6	53.0	3.3
Dahomey	52.8	14.6	12.1	36.9	14.6	9.4
Gabon	43.2	17.3	4.3	33.7	15.5	5.9
Ivory Coast	38.8	22.4	3.7	34.5	28.5	5.1
Madagascar	45.8	7.4	3.0	33.5	6.0	4.9
Niger	54.9	12.4	5.8	63.1	13.2	6.5
Rwanda	--[a]	34.4	n.a.	2.5	27.0	n.a.
Senegal	73.8	7.8	4.4	66.3	9.3	8.0
Togo	40.3	37.1	2.3	38.5	43.7	3.0
Upper Volta	18.0	1.5	51.9	14.3	4.7	55.2

[a]Less than 0.1 percent.

Sources: Secrétariat-Général de l'OCAM, Annuaire OCAM, 1968, and Bulletin Statistique de l'OCAM, No. 15 (Juin 1970).

1966 and 1968. The percentage of exports to France during this period remained about the same for the Republic of Congo and the Republic of Central Africa, while in Niger, Chad, and Rwanda there were increases in the exports to France. Exports to other EEC members during the period increased for nine OCAM members, decreased for four members, and remained the same for one member. Nevertheless, France remained the dominant export partner for most of the OCAM states.

Table 22 reveals that regional trade among the OCAM members was very low. In 1966, only three members (Upper Volta, Dahomey, and Niger) sent more than 5 percent of their exports to other members of the union. However, in 1968, eight members sold 5 percent or more of their exports within the region.

Regional exports as a percentage of total exports increased for ten members between 1966 and 1968, decreased for one member (Dahomey), and remained about the same for the Republic of Central Africa. While figures are not available for the regional exports of the Democratic Republic of the Congo and Rwanda, it is estimated that the figure is very small.

In spite of the increases in regional transactions between 1966 and 1968, regional trade--as noted--remained very limited. The only exceptions were Upper Volta and, to a much lesser extent, Dahomey. The high regional exports for these two countries, however, are indicative of their dependence on neighboring states. Thus 50.4 percent of the 1966 exports of Upper Volta went to the Ivory Coast, while the figure for 1968 was 53.0 percent--made up mainly of animals and animal products. In the case of Dahomey, 8.1 percent of its 1966 exports went to Togo; in 1968 the figure was 5.9 percent. For the countries for which complete figures are available, regional exports in 1966 constituted 4.1 percent of total trade, while in 1968 the percentage was 7.2. The value of regional trade between 1966 and 1968 increased by 98.3 percent. Clearly, then, regional interdependence has been increasing under the OCAM, but it is still relatively low and falls far short of the interdependence with France. We therefore assign a mixed score to this variable.

In sum, integrative conditions during the OCAM seem to be less conducive to regional political integration than during the UAM. The domestic political systems are more heterogeneous under the OCAM than they were under the UAM, the degree of congeniality among the elites is less, the inequalities among the member states are greater, and the external political environment is less compelling. Further, extra-regional dependence remains high; regional interdependence has been increasing, but it remains low.

The expectation, therefore, is that integration under the OCAM will be less than it was under the UAM. Specifically, the scope of decision-making under the OCAM will be narrower. Given the leadership and political changes that have occurred, we expect less success with respect to joint decision-making in the external relations functions area. On the other hand, given the increased trade dependence and the poor economic performance of many states, we expect greater efforts at joint decision-making in the social, cultural, and economic functions areas. However, even in these areas, the inequalities among the member states and the differential results of national strategies toward economic development, combined with the low level of economic development of all members (which makes them less inclined to postpone demands for immediate payoffs and more concerned with the equal distribution of rewards), will make it difficult for agreements to be reached or implemented. In the remainder of this chapter our concern is with the level of integration attained up to 1970 and the process conditions which emerged between 1966 and 1970.

The Level of Political Integration in the OCAM

In seeking to determine the level of political integration achieved by the OCAM, we will follow the pattern used for the UAM. We will first survey the distribution of issues discussed at OCAM heads of state conferences, and then measure the locus and range of decision-making in the OCAM. Finally, we will assess the consequences of decision-making in the OCAM.

Before treating the distribution of issues discussed under the OCAM, we should point out that decision-making under the OCAM was identical to the pattern which prevailed during the UAM period. Most issues originate with the national governments, but in some cases issues are raised by the Secretariat. Matters are first discussed among experts before being forwarded to the Council of Ministers. All decisions, recommendations, and non-decisions of the Council of Ministers are ultimately sent to the heads of state for ratification or decision. Since delegates at the expert and ministerial levels are given binding instructions, there are very few occasions for decisions made or positions taken at lower levels to be overturned at the higher levels. In spite of the voting provisions of the OCAM charter, the tendency is for member states to seek consensus. Members who are opposed to a decision refrain from preventing it from being made as long as it is understood that they will not be bound by the decision. In all this, nongovernmental actors are conspicuously absent.

Tables 23, 24, and 25 indicate the distribution of issues discussed at each of the OCAM heads of state conferences among the thirty issue areas specified in Chapter 4 above in our analysis of the operations of the UAM, the rank ordering of these issue areas, and the manner in which these issue areas cluster around four rank orders. We are interested not only in what these tables tell us about decision-making in the OCAM, but also in how the pattern differed from that which prevailed during the UAM period. Thus the findings from these tables should be compared with those from Tables 17, 18, and 19.

The first thing that strikes one in comparing Tables 17 and 23 is the smaller number of items discussed under the OCAM. Three-hundred-and-ninety-one topics were discussed at six UAM conferences, for an average of 65 topics per conference; in the case of the OCAM, 177 topics were discussed at four conferences, for an average of 44 topics per conference. Thus there was a reduction of 32 percent in the number of subjects treated under the OCAM. While four issue areas were never discussed under the UAM, _eight_ issue areas were completely neglected under the OCAM.

Table 23

NUMBERS OF ISSUES DISCUSSED AT THE OCAM HEADS OF STATE CONFERENCES

Issue Area	Tananarive (June 1966)	Niamey (January 1968)	Kinshasa (January 1969)	Yaoundé (January 1970)	Total Number	Total Percent
External Relations Functions						
1. Military security	2	1	0	0	3	1.7%
2. Conflict resolution and management among members	0	1	1	2	4	2.3
3. Cold war, arms control and disarmament	0	0	0	0	0	0.0
4. Decolonization and human rights	0	2	0	0	2	1.1
5. Diplomatic influence and participation in intra-African affairs	1	3	1	7	12	6.8
6. Diplomatic influence and participation in global affairs	4	5	2	5	16	9.0
7. Economic and technical aid to or from other polities	2	3	3	2	10	5.7
8. Global economic, commercial, scientific, and technical arrangements	0	5	3	7	15	8.5
9. Continental economic, commercial, scientific,						

Table 23 (continued)

Issue Area	Tananarive (June 1966)	Niamey (January 1968)	Kinshasa (January 1969)	Yaoundé (January 1970)	Total	
					Number	Percent
External Relations Functions (continued)						
scientific, and technical arrangements	3	2	1	1	7	3.9%
10. Economic, commercial, scientific, and technical relations with major trading partners (France, the EEC)	1	3	1	2	7	3.9
11. Economic, commercial, scientific, and technical relations with minor trading partners	0	0	0	0	0	0.0
Subtotal	13	25	12	26	76	42.9
Percent	43%	41	40	46		
Political-Constitutional Functions						
12. Public health and safety and maintenance of order	0	0	1	1	2	1.1
13. Political participation	0	0	0	0	0	0.0
14. Access to legal-normative system	0	0	0	1	1	0.6

Table 23 (continued)

Issue Area	Tananarive (June 1966)	Niamey (January 1968)	Kinshasa (January 1969)	Yaoundé (January 1970)	Total	
					Number	Percent
Political-Constitutional Functions (continued)						
15. Organization and administration of the civil service	0	0	0	0	0	0.0%
Subtotal	0	0	1	2	3	1.7
Percent	0%					
Social-Cultural Functions						
16. Cultural and recreational affairs	2	3	1	1	7	3.9
17. Education and research	4	10	6	8	28	15.8
18. Social welfare policies	0	0	0	1	1	0.6
Subtotal	6	13	7	10	36	20.3
Percent	20%	21	23	18		
Economic Functions						
19. Counter-cyclical policy	0	0	0	0	0	0.0
20. Regulation of economic competition and other government controls on prices and investments	1	1	0	1	3	1.7

Table 23 (continued)

Issue Area	Tananarive (June 1966)	Niamey (January 1968)	Kinshasa (January 1969)	Yaoundé (January 1970)	Total Number	Total Percent
Economic Functions (continued)						
21. Agricultural protection	0	1	0	2	3	1.7%
22. Economic development and planning	5	6	4	5	20	11.3
23. Exploitation and protection of natural resources	0	4	0	0	4	2.3
24. Regulation and support of transportation	3	4	1	3	11	6.2
25. Regulation and support of mass media of communications	1	3	1	0	5	2.8
26. Labor-management relations	0	0	0	0	0	0.0
27. Fiscal policy	0	1	1	2	4	2.3
28. Balance-of-payments stability	0	0	0	0	0	0.0
29. Domestic monetary policy	0	0	0	0	0	0.0
30. Movement of goods, services, and other factors of production (not including capital) within the customs union	1	3	3	5	12	6.8
Subtotal	11	23	10	18	62	35.1
Percent	37%	38	34	32		
GRAND TOTAL	30	61	30	56	177	

Table 24

RANK-ORDERING OF ISSUE AREAS BASED ON
NUMBER OF ITEMS TREATED

Rank	Issue Area	Number	Percent of Total
	First Rank--6.6% and Above	(103)	(58.2)%
1	Education and research	28	15.8
2	Economic development and planning	20	11.3
3	Diplomatic influence and participation in global affairs	16	9.0
4	Global economic, commercial, scientific, and technical arrangements	15	8.5
5	Movement of goods, services, and other factors of production (not including capital) within the customs union	12	6.8
5	Diplomatic influence and participation in intra-African affairs	12	6.8
	Second Rank--3.3% to 6.5%	(42)	(23.6)
7	Regulation and support of transportation	11	6.2
8	Economic and technical aid to or from other polities	10	5.7
9	Cultural and recreational affairs	7	3.9
9	Continental economic, commercial, scientific, and technical arrangements	7	3.9
9	Economic, commercial, scientific, and technical relations with major trading partners (France and the EEC)	7	3.9
	Third Rank--1.1% to 3.2%	(30)	(17.0)
12	Regulation and support of mass media of communications	5	2.8
13	Fiscal policy	4	2.3

Table 24 (continued)

Rank	Issue Area	Number	Percent of Total
13	Exploitation and protection of natural resources	4	2.3%
13	Conflict resolution and management among members	4	2.3
16	Agricultural protection	3	1.7
16	Regulation of economic competition and other government controls on prices and investments	3	1.7
16	Military security	3	1.7
19	Decolonization and human rights	2	1.1
19	Public health and safety and maintenance of order	2	1.1
	Fourth Rank--Less than 1.1%	(2)	(1.2)
21	Access to legal-normative system	1	0.6
21	Social welfare policies	1	0.6
23	Cold war, arms control and disarmament	0	0.0
23	Economic, commercial, scientific, and technical relations with minor trading partners	0	0.0
23	Political participation	0	0.0
23	Organization and administration of the civil service	0	0.0
23	Counter-cyclical policy	0	0.0
23	Labor-management relations	0	0.0
23	Balance-of-payments stability	0	0.0
23	Domestic monetary policy	0	0.0
	Total	177	100.0

Table 25

CLUSTERS OF ISSUE AREAS IN VARIOUS RANK-ORDERS

Category of Issue	First Rank		Second Rank		Third Rank		Fourth Rank		Total	
	Number of Issue Areas	Percent of Total	Number of Issue Areas	Percent of Total	Number of Issue Areas	Percent of Total	Number of Issue Areas	Percent of Total	Number of Issue Areas	Percent of Total
External Relations Functions (11 issue areas)	3	27%	3	27%	3	27%	2	18%	11	99[a]
Political-Constitutional Functions (4 issue areas)	0	0	0	0	1	25	3	75	4	100
Social-Cultural Functions (3 issue areas)	1	33	1	33	0	0	1	33	3	99[a]
Economic Functions (12 issue areas)	2	17	1	8	5	42	4	33	12	100
Total (30 issue areas)	6	20	5	17	9	30	10	33	30	100

[a]Does not add up to 100% because of rounding.

170

In other words, the scope of joint decision-making decreased by 13 percent under the OCAM.

Three of the four issue areas not discussed during the UAM period were not discussed during the OCAM period either. The fourth of these issue areas (agricultural protection), however, advanced in rank order from 27 during the UAM to 16 during the OCAM. Of the five additional issue areas not discussed under the OCAM, three (cold war, arms control and disarmament; organization and administration of the civil service; and economic, commercial, scientific, and technical relations with minor trading partners) were in the third rank order during the UAM, while the remaining two (domestic monetary policy and labor-management relations) were in the fourth rank order. Under the OCAM, there were declines in the rank order of two issue areas in the external relations functions category, one in the political-constitutional functions category, and two in the economic functions category.

The issue areas that were never discussed at OCAM conferences fell into the following classifications: external relations functions = 2 of 11, or 18 percent; political-constitutional functions = 2 of 4, or 50 percent; and economic functions = 4 of 12, or 33 percent. The comparable classifications for the UAM were as follows: political-constitutional functions = 1 of 4, or 25 percent; and economic functions = 3 of 12, or 25 percent. Thus in the OCAM there was 25 percent less discussion of political-constitutional functions, 18 percent less of external relations functions, and 8 percent less of economic functions. Of the 11 external relations issue areas, 6 (55 percent) declined in rank order, one remained the same, and 4 (36 percent) advanced in rank order status. Of the 4 political-constitutional issue areas, 3 (75 percent) declined in rank order, and one remained the same. All 3 social-cultural issue areas advanced in rank order status, as did 7 of the 12 (58 percent) economic issue areas. Two of the economic issue areas remained in the same rank order, while the remaining 3 (25 percent) declined in rank order. What these figures indicate is that the decrease in scope of discussions occurred mostly in the political-constitutional functions and external relations functions areas. The categories which received increased attention were the social-cultural functions and economic functions. (These data are summarized in Table 26.)

Tables 19 and 25 also show that the attention given to the external relations functions by the OCAM decreased in comparison to the UAM, while that given to social-cultural and economic functions increased. Thus, whereas 7 (64 percent) of the external relations issue areas were in the top two rank orders during the UAM period, the figure for OCAM was 6 (55 percent). In contrast, the figure for the social-cultural issue areas was 1 (33 percent) for the UAM compared to 2 (67 percent)

Table 26

COMPARISON OF THE RANK-ORDER POSITIONS OF ISSUE AREAS
BETWEEN THE UAM AND THE OCAM PERIODS

Issue Area Category	Rose in Rank Order		Remained Same		Declined in Rank Order		Total	
	Number	Per-cent	Number	Per-cent	Number	Per-cent	Number	Per-cent
External Relations	4	36%	1	9%	6	55%	11	100%
Political-Constitu-tional	0	0	1	25	3	75	4	100
Social-Cultural	3	100	0	0	0	0	3	100
Economic	7	58	2	17	3	25	12	100
Total	14	47	4	13	12	40	30	99[a]

[a]Does not add up to 100% because of rounding.

for the OCAM. The figures for economic functions increased from 2 (16 percent) under the UAM to 3 (25 percent) under the OCAM. In neither period did any of the political-constitutional issue areas fall in the first two rank orders.

Table 23 shows that of the total items discussed at OCAM conferences, most dealt with external relations functions. Thus, of the 177 items discussed at the four conferences, 76 (42.9 percent) dealt with external relations functions, 3 (1.7 percent) with political-constitutional functions, 36 (20.3 percent) with social-cultural functions, and 62 (35.1 percent) with economic functions. The comparable figures for the UAM were 61 percent, 5 percent, 10 percent, and 24 percent respectively. Thus while every measure suggests a decline in the importance of external relations functions and a rise in the importance of economic and social-cultural functions, external relations functions still head the list, followed by economic functions, social-cultural functions, and political-constitutional functions--in that order.

Of the four external relations issue areas which rose in rank order, three did so by only one step, and the fourth by only 2. Education and research increased its rank order by 2 steps, social welfare by 3, and culture by a huge 13. Of the 7 economic issue areas that rose in rank order, 5 made huge advances. Specifically, the changes were as follows: regulation

of transportation = 2 steps; regulation of economic competition
and other government controls on prices and investments = 4;
fiscal policy = 9; economic development and planning = 9; agricultural protection = 11; protection of natural resources = 11;
and movement of goods, services, and other factors of production
within the customs union = 13.

What these figures suggest is that with the shift from
the UAM to the OCAM, attention was shifted from policies directed
at third parties toward coordinating policies within the region.
Increases in the discussion of topics relating to the movement
of goods, services, and other factors of production within the
union, combined with those dealing with economic development and
planning, are particularly suggestive of this trend. Such a
trend implies a greater concern with economic, as contrasted
with political, issues; this is confirmed by the nature of the
11 issue areas falling in the first two rank orders (see Table
24). Of these 11 issue areas, one deals with culture and recrea-
tion, one with diplomatic participation at the African level,
and one with diplomatic participation at the global level. The
remaining 8 issue areas deal with economic, technical, and educational links among the members, participation in continental and
global economic, commercial, scientific, and technical arrangements, foreign aid policies, and relations with France and the
EEC.

Another indication of a greater concern with economic,
educational, and technical coordination of policies within the
OCAM is that there is less fluctuation in the number of items
treated under specific issue areas at the various conferences.
Under the UAM, the number of topics treated fluctuated widely
for 7 issue areas. In the case of OCAM, however, the only issues
which seem to fluctuate widely are (1) diplomatic influence and
participation in intra-African affairs and (2) global economic,
commercial, scientific, and technical arrangements. Three other
issues (compared with 2 for the UAM)--continental economic, commercial, scientific, and technical arrangements, military security, and regulation and support of mass media of communications--
show a gradual decrease over time.

In 3 issue areas--decolonization and human rights, access
to legal-normative system, and exploitation and protection of
natural resources--topics were discussed at only one conference.
This, as we shall see, was the result of a desire to stay away
from issue areas on which meaningful joint decision-making was
for some reason impossible. Four issue areas--diplomatic influence and participation in global affairs, education and research,
economic development and planning, and regulation and support
of transportation--remained roughly stable. In contrast to the
situation which existed during the UAM, these issue areas are
high in the rank order. Finally, the movement of goods, services,

and other factors of production within the customs union received increased attention between 1966 and 1970, as did global economic, commercial, scientific, and technical arrangements.

In general, the picture that emerges is that the OCAM has been more concerned with intra-union matters than was the UAM, and that the OCAM has devoted more of its attention to economic than to political matters. These trends make sense in terms of our earlier findings that economic transactions among the OCAM members increased between 1966 and 1968, and that the economic situation of several members deteriorated. It is understandable that intra-union matters would take precedence over extra-regional activities, and that economic questions would take precedence over political questions. The extent to which these shifts in concerns resulted in higher levels of political integration as measured by the stage and locus of joint decision-making is our next concern.

Stage and Locus of Decision-Making

Military Security. At the Tananarive conference in June 1966, Rwanda asked for a discussion of strategies to be used in the fight against subversion in Africa. The Council of Ministers refused to discuss the topic on the grounds that the UAMD, which they maintained was still in force, adequately dealt with the problem. At the same time, it was noted that Upper Volta was preparing proposals for a new defense organization, and that all discussions should be postponed until these proposals were submitted. At the heads of state level, this problem was linked to that of the continued validity of the UAMD. No agreement was reached because the earlier differences over the nature and source of the security problems faced by members continued.

During the Niamey conference, the focus of attention was on the recent series of military coups in Africa--particularly those that had occurred in Dahomey. This discussion took place among the four top leaders of the OCAM--Houphouet, Senghor, Ahidjo, and Tsiranana--and they concluded that the military coups were largely desperate efforts to solve intractable economic problems. They decided to urge France to resume its aid to Dahomey, which had been halted after the December 1967 coup. This decision was, however, never ratified by the formal OCAM heads of state conference. Further, no proposals for revising the UAMD were submitted by Upper Volta, while the existence of the UAMD itself became a mystery. Several members kept insisting that the UAMD treaty was still valid even though there was no organizational structure. There was no collective definition of the problem of military security, and all decision-making remained in national hands.

THE OCAM SYSTEM

Conflict Resolution and Management among Members. The
OCAM has had to deal with three conflicts among its members.
The first was between Rwanda and the Democratic Republic of the
Congo over the former's refusal to repatriate white mercenaries
to the latter for trial. The second was between the two Congos
over the "affaire Mulelé," in which Pierre Mulelé, head of a
rebel group in the Democratic Republic of the Congo, was persuaded by the Foreign Minister of the Democratic Republic of
the Congo to return from Brazzaville on the basis of Mobutu's
declared policy of national reconciliation. On his arrival,
Mulelé was arrested, summarily tried, and executed. The result
was a break in diplomatic relations between the two Congos.
Finally, there was the conflict between the Democratic Republic
of the Congo, Central Africa, and Chad as a result of Central
Africa's decision to withdraw from the Union des Etats de l'Afrique Centrale and rejoin UDEAC. The first two conflicts were
handled by the four major leaders, and the third conflict by
Diori. In all cases, efforts at mediation and conciliation were
ad hoc. The proposal for binding arbitration of disputes which
had emerged during the UAM period was never taken up. In no case
was the OCAM successful in its mediatory efforts, and the Yaoundé
conference decided to leave the solution of the conflict between
the two Congos to the two countries involved. The only concrete
decision by the OCAM heads of state was one made at Yaoundé to
sponsor sporting events, competition for prizes in arts, letters,
and research, and similar activities among the general public as
a way of "associating the masses with the efforts of the heads
of state to promote African unity." Thus the decision-making
stage attained was that of collective problem recognition, and
there were only the beginnings of collective decision-making.

Decolonization and Human Rights. The issues of apartheid
and the future of the nonindependent African countries were discussed at Niamey. The usual resolution condemning apartheid and
calling for the independence of all African countries was adopted,
but the Republic of the Congo's proposal that concrete material
assistance be jointly provided for rebel and nationalist movements
in Africa was rejected; each member was left free to undertake
such measures independently, however. One issue noticeably absent
from the discussion in this issue area was the manner of dealing
with the unilateral declaration of independence by Southern
Rhodesia. Nor was there any discussion of the increased fighting
in the Portuguese colonies in Africa. Thus the concern in this
area was much narrower than under the UAM. The decision-making
stage attained was collective definition of specific action alternatives, and there was only a small degree of regional involvement in decision-making, with the role of national governments
being preponderant.

Diplomatic Influence and Participation in Intra-African
Affairs. Topics under this heading ranged from proposals to

coordinate positions on the Pan-African festival at Algeria, to joint efforts at getting a national of the OCAM appointed president of the African development bank, to joint elaborations of proposals for altering the structure of the OAU and changing its general secretary, to joint attempts at mediating the civil war in Nigeria--for which purpose Diori and Mobutu were selected. However, bilateral matters remained in the hands of the national governments. In each instance, specific policy decisions were made, and in this issue area a decision-making stage of detailed collective goal-setting was achieved. The breadth of the issues covered meant that there was roughly equal activity at both regional and national levels.

Diplomatic Influence and Participation in Global Affairs. Topics discussed under this issue area were not nearly as broad as was the case for the preceding issue area. Thus when the Middle East situation was raised at the Yaoundé conference, it was removed from the agenda on the grounds that it was too controversial an issue, and that members had taken different policy positions on the question. The tendency was for members to concentrate their efforts on influencing the outcomes of elections in various international bodies, and on seeking to harmonize their positions on issues such as the peaceful uses of the seabed. The decision-making stage attained was that of detailed collective goal-setting, and while there was substantial activity at the collective level, the national level was still dominant.

Economic and Technical Aid to or from Other Polities. Aid among the OCAM states fared very badly. It was decided that the idea of a technical assistance program among the member states, as approved during the UAM days, was unrealistic. At the same time, the idea of multilateral cultural cooperation was altered in the direction of bilateral arrangements to be elaborated by the states interested. However, the principle of providing Rwanda with technical assistance was retained. Further, members agreed to ask France and other countries and interested organizations for technical assistance for the OCAM Secretariat. Agreement in principle was reached to harmonize fiscal policies on aid from the Fonds d'Aide et de Coopération, and Senghor's proposal for a Francophone technical cooperation program was also approved in principle. Aid from the European Development Fund for the training of statisticians was approved; bilateral foreign aid matters, however, were never discussed. Decisions in some instances entailed only agreements to broad guidelines, but specific decisions were also sometimes made. In sum, a score of collective decisions on policy guidelines is assigned for stage, and a score of substantial activity at the collective level for locus.

Global Economic, Commercial, Scientific, and Technical Arrangements. At the suggestion of the OCAM Secretary-General, members agreed to the principle of collaboration between the OCAM

Secretariat and organizations such as UNESCO and the United Nations Industrial Development Organization. There was further agreement on the principle of pursuing coordinated policies at the New Delhi UNCTAD conference and in the elaboration of the program of the UN Second Development Decade. Also agreed to in principle was the harmonization of commercial laws and regular consultations on the problems faced by cotton in the world market. Finally, at the suggestion of the Republic of Central Africa, the principle of creating a joint export organization was agreed to. Most of these decisions entailed only agreements in principle, with specific policies to be elaborated subsequently. Such specific policy decisions were forthcoming with respect to the UNCTAD conference and the UN Second Development Decade, but the idea of creating a joint export organization was never implemented, and multilateral discussions on the problem of cotton never took place. Thus, the decision-making stage was collective decisions on policy guidelines, and the locus was substantial activity at the regional level, with the national level still dominant.

Continental Economic, Commercial, Scientific, and Technical Arrangements. Senegal's proposal for a regional group that would include all states--English- and French-speaking--from Mauritania to the Democratic Republic of the Congo was merely noted, as was the report on the creation of the Economic Community of West Africa. Further, Senegal's proposal for creating an African institute for civil protection was indefinitely postponed. However, approval was given to the idea of creating an African commission for civil aviation. Finally, the OCAM states made determined efforts to coordinate their policies in the ECA and the African Development Bank. A score of detailed collective goal-setting is assigned for stage, and the collective level seems to be dominant with respect to locus.

Economic, Commercial, Scientific, and Technical Relations with Major Trading Partners. It will be recalled that the UAM states had agreed to coordinate their policies in the EEC. During the negotiations in 1968 and 1969 for the renewal of the Yaoundé convention, the OCAM played a dominant role in coordinating negotiating positions. The Secretariat conducted a good deal of the research for the negotiations. As President of the OCAM, Diori was very active in pressing the needs and demands of the member states, and it was because of his activities in this area that he was reelected President of the OCAM in January 1968. Senghor first presented his idea of creating a Francophone commonwealth to the OCAM, and won support for it before the matter was formally raised with France; in spite of this, relations with France were mostly conducted bilaterally. Thus the score for stage is detailed collective goal-setting, and while substantial activities occurred at the regional level, the fact that there were almost no joint policies vis-à-vis France indicates that the national level remained dominant.

Public Health and Safety and Maintenance of Order. The two topics treated under this issue area dealt with ways and means of preventing labor accidents and professional sickness. A conference on these topics was held at Libreville in September 1969, at which several resolutions were drawn up. These were adopted by the heads of state at Yaoundé in January 1970, but implementation was left in national hands. Thus the score for stage is detailed collective goal-setting, but since the topic treated was so narrow, there was only the beginning of collective decision-making in this issue area.

Access to Legal-Normative System. At the Yaoundé conference in January 1970, the Secretary-General reported that at each international meeting of African jurists, uneasiness was expressed over the fact that, since independence, the laws of the member states were evolving in isolation from each other. He therefore proposed that members agree "to harmonize our laws in areas where this is possible." The response of the Council of Ministers was that the proposal was premature since "within our states, the organization of our activities is not regulated by specific laws in all areas." However, the Secretary-General was asked to undertake studies to determine in which areas harmonization was urgent and possible. The Secretary-General's task was made difficult by the fact that his request for creating a division on judicial matters within the Secretariat was rejected on the grounds of the costs entailed. Few results have therefore been forthcoming. Thus while there was collective problem recognition, all activity remained at the national level.

Cultural and Recreational Affairs. Many of the issues in this area that were treated during the UAM period continued to receive attention during the OCAM period. Among these were collaboration with the Society for African Culture for the promotion of cultural activities in member states and the creation of national African cultural centers which would be linked with an Institute of African Culture. To further examine these matters, which were agreed to in principle, a conference was held at Fort Lamy in December 1969. Among the decisions of the Fort Lamy conference were that members should devote at least one percent of their national budgets for promoting cultural activities and that laws be passed to protect the cultural heritage of member states. A further conference was scheduled for some time in 1970 among the ministers of national culture to elaborate the statutes of the cultural center and the Institute of African Culture. Thus decision-making took the form of collective decisions on policy guidelines; nevertheless, the content of the cultural programs to be pursued remained in national hands. In sum, while substantial activity occurred at the regional level, the national level was dominant.

Education and Research. Topics discussed under this issue area were wide-ranging. They included proposals for the coordination of research activities in geology and petroleum products, the creation of a regional center for research in agronomy and zootechnique, and the establishment of a development research center for applied research and training. However, the only agreement reached was on the coordination of research activities by the exchange of documents through the Secretariat. Decisions were made to create the Institut des Sciences et Médecine Vétérinaire at Dakar and the Ecole Inter-Etats d'Ingenieurs de l'Equipment Rural at Ouagadougou; both of these decisions, which date back to the UAM period, were ultimately implemented. Another institution whose creation was agreed to was the Ecole Inter-Etats d'Informatique, which was to be located at Libreville. Members also agreed to jointly elaborate a common program with professional unions and associations in Africa for training Africans for management positions in the private sector.

At a meeting of educational ministers at Yaoundé in December 1969, members elaborated a common doctrine for teaching African history at the primary school level and agreed to periodic meetings for the exchange of pedagogical experiences among educators. Members also agreed to the reform of African universities, the harmonization of diplomas, and the elaboration of a common statute for African researchers. The question of student participation in university governance was discussed, but no decision was made. We assign a score of detailed collective goal-setting for stage since, even with respect to the regional schools to be created, the states in which they are to be located played a dominant role in seeking external financing. With respect to locus, considering the wide range of activity which remained in national hands (investments in education, foreign training for nationals, the management of national educational institutions, etc.), though substantial activity occurred at the regional level, the national level was still dominant.

Social Welfare Policies. At the Yaoundé conference in January 1970, Dahomey proposed that in light of the agreement on the free movement of labor, members should harmonize their social security laws to ensure that workers who migrate within the union do not lose their social security benefits. This was agreed to in principle--except for Gabon, which registered certain reservations. The conference empowered the Secretary-General to undertake studies designed to facilitate the harmonization of the social security systems of member states and organize a conference among the directors of social security for the purpose of elaborating a convention designed to guarantee the interests and rights of workers who migrate. Negotiations and studies are still being conducted on these points. Thus the decision-making stage is still that of collective problem recognition, and there is only the beginning of collective decision-making in this area.

Regulation of Economic Competition and Other Government
Controls on Prices and Investments. The sole topic in this issue
area was the creation of a joint insurance company. An ad hoc
meeting of experts at Yaoundé in November 1967, in light of the
agreement to create this company dating back to the UAM days,
proceeded to work out the details of the project. The company
was to have a capital of about $2 million, and all private in-
surance companies were to cease their operations and be integrated
into the joint company. France objected to this requirement, and
the Council of Ministers noted at Niamey in January 1969 that
they were now faced with a political problem. With the exception
of the ministers of Senegal, Chad, and Madagascar, they suggested
that the heads of state take up the matter with France. It is
not known whether this was ever done, but French opposition seems
to have killed the project. Nevertheless, a decision was taken
at the OCAM level which would have resulted in an autonomous
regional body. The decision-making stage therefore was that of
detailed collective goal-setting. Since the regulation of other
economic activities remained in national hands, there was only
the beginning of collective decision-making in this area.

Agricultural Protection. Decisions in this area took
the form of organizing a conference at Fort Lamy in December 1969
to discuss problems relating to animal breeding and illness prevention. At the Yaoundé conference in January 1970, a similar
conference on the improvement and protection of food production
was agreed to. The purpose of these conferences was to exchange
experiences and seek common solutions to problems. Thus the
decision-making stage seems to be that of collective definition
of specific action alternatives; there were only the beginnings
of collective action.

Economic Development and Planning. Several types of activities were included in this issue area. One was the organization of a series of conferences on planning and on popular participation in national development efforts. These conferences
resulted in specific recommendations that were ratified by the
OCAM and then submitted to the heads of state for ratification.
At another level, members agreed to harmonize their bookkeeping
procedures as well as their statistical methods. Both of these
decisions led to meetings among experts in this field at Yaoundé
in October 1968. Again, specific recommendations were made,
ratified by the OCAM, and then turned over to the states for
implementation. At a third level, members discussed but rejected
the idea of including business and labor leaders in decision-
making in the area of economic development.

The ideas of jointly creating a guarantee fund for private
investments and elaborating a charter for regulating differences
between member states and foreign investors were agreed to in
principle, but they have not yet been implemented. At the request

of Senegal, an EEC study on industrial development in Africa was discussed from the point of view of coordinating industrial development in Africa and then referred to the Secretariat for further study. The same fate befell a proposal for regional coordination of industrial development proposed by Mauritius at the Yaoundé conference in January 1970. (Mauritius became a member of the OCAM in January 1970.) Finally, Chad's proposal that the development of electrical energy in Africa be coordinated was approved by the Council of Ministers but removed from the Yaoundé conference agenda by the heads of state. Thus, issues entailing the coordination of industrial development were either rejected or referred for further study. The latter approach was often designed to avoid joint decision-making when this did not seem possible. Thus while the decision-making stage attained was that of detailed collective goal-setting when it was possible to arrive at decisions, there were only the beginnings of collective decision-making.

Exploitation and Protection of Natural Resources. At the recommendation of Madagascar, the members agreed to the principle of joint action to protect their mineral, petroleum, and water resources. This agreement was mostly of a pro forma nature, however, with further discussion being postponed until further studies were conducted. Needless to say, nothing resulted from these decisions. On the other hand, a conference on the fertilization and protection of soils was held at Tananarive. Thus the decision-making stage was that of collective problem recognition, and there was only the beginning of collective action in this area.

Regulation and Support of Transportation. Issues relating to Air Afrique dominated this category. The most important topic was the fiscal regime to be applied to Air Afrique. After four years of discussion, a decision on the matter was finally made in January 1970. Other matters relating to Air Afrique were coordinating the activities of Air Afrique with those of Air Cameroun, Air Madagascar, and the national airlines of the Democratic Republic of the Congo. It was agreed that Air Afrique would establish air links between Mauritius and Europe by way of West Africa. A final item treated was Upper Volta's call for the improvement of land and road transportation among members. The importance of this proposal was recognized, and members agreed to increase their efforts in this area. The decision-making stage was therefore that of detailed collective goal-setting. Since only matters relating to Air Afrique were collectively decided, national decision-making was still dominant in this area.

Regulation and Support of Mass Media of Communications. This issue area had occupied an important position during the UAM period. The decrease in its importance represents a case of task fulfillment. As a result of the substantial degree of harmonization of policies in the area of post and telecommunications during the UAM, there was little left to be done. Instead, attention shifted to the creation of a joint press agency. After this had been agreed to in principle, experts met at Abidjan in July 1967 to work out the necessary details. The capital of the agency was to be about $1.2 million. The OCAM states were to provide half of the capital, and it was hoped the rest would come from private press agencies. However, delegates to the Niamey conference concluded that the financial costs entailed had been minimized, and called for an ad hoc committee to study the matter further. This ad hoc committee never met, and it was therefore decided to limit action in this area to an exchange of information and programs among national radio networks. Thus little that was new occurred in this area. However, since decisions made during the UAM period continued to be implemented under the OCAM, we will assign scores of detailed collective goal-setting for stage, with equal decision-making at both collective and national levels for locus.

Fiscal Policy. At the Niamey conference in January 1968, Niger called for the elaboration of joint policies dealing with the taxation of companies operating in more than one member state. Subsequently, questions relating to the avoidance of double taxation among members and mutual assistance in collecting taxes from multinational companies were raised. All these matters were referred to the Secretary-General for further study, but at the Yaoundé conference these topics were removed from the agenda. Thus while there was collective problem recognition, all decisions remained in national hands.

Movement of Goods, Services and Other Factors of Production (Not Including Capital) within the Customs Union. The most important issues in this area dealt with the creation of a common market for sugar and meat. The first was agreed to at a conference of experts at Tananarive in May 1966 and ratified by the Tananarive heads of state conference in June 1966. By the Niamey conference in January 1968 problems had arisen largely because of the increased cost of sugar. Thus Togo refused to apply the agreement on the grounds that it resulted in an increase of 30 CFA francs per kilogram for sugar. Other problems such as the repayment of debts by importing states subsequently arose. All in all, the implementation of this agreement was plagued with continuous difficulties.

At Niamey in January 1968, a decision to create a common market on meat that would include Mali and Mauritania was made. An ad hoc committee of experts met at Yaoundé in September 1969 and elaborated most of the details except those dealing with the headquarters of the organization, the basis for contributing to its budget, the voting formula in the organization, and the naming of the director of the organization. The Yaoundé conference referred the matter to an ad hoc committee and thus buried it.

Other concerns in this area were ways of ensuring the application of the Convention d'Etablissement and the agreement on the free movement of workers within the union. The idea of abolishing visa requirements among the member states was discussed. In none of these areas was success achieved.

Thus the only meaningful decision taken in this area was the one dealing with a common market for sugar. This merits a score of detailed collective goal-setting for decision-making stage. Considering the nondecisions and lack of decisions on all the other items falling under this issue area, we conclude that there were only the beginnings of collective decision-making in this area.

The scores assigned to each issue area in our discussion of the stage and locus of decision-making in the OCAM are summarized in Table 27. From Table 27 it is clear that the UAM pattern was largely repeated under the OCAM. The scores for decision-making stage are consistently higher than those for locus of decision-making, which means that actors isolate items within each issue area for more intensive decision-making. Further, there is a tendency for the scores for both stage and locus to increase as an issue area rises in rank order. This is less true of issue areas under the external relations category--no doubt a result of the fact that in these issue areas the member states are forced to pursue coordinated policies if they are to have any influence at all, since very few of the OCAM members could individually exert much leverage.

A comparison between Tables 27 and Table 20, which summarized the stage and locus of decision-making in the UAM, enables us to ascertain which of the two organizations attained a higher level of integration. The scores of these two tables are summarized for comparison in Tables 28 and 29.

Table 28 indicates that while under the OCAM many more items fell in the category of discussions not resulting in collective problem definition, there has been a definite shift since the UAM toward more intensive decision-making. Thus while only three issue areas reached the stage of detailed collective goal-setting during the UAM period, eleven issues attained that stage during the OCAM period. Decision-making in the UAM was concentrated on the low slopes of the hill, while in the OCAM it is to be found on the first leg of the downward climb on the other side of the hill.

This shift toward more intensive decision-making in the OCAM is particularly noticeable with respect to economic functions.

Table 27

SCOPE, STAGE, AND LOCUS OF DECISION-MAKING IN THE OCAM

Issue Area	Number of Issues	Stage	Locus
Education and research	28	Detailed collective goal-setting	Substantial activity at collective level
Economic development and planning	20	Detailed collective goal-setting	Some collective
Diplomatic influence and participation in global affairs	16	Detailed collective goal-setting	Substantial activity at collective level
Global economic, commercial, scientific and technical arrangements	15	Collective decision on policy guidelines	Substantial activity at collective level
Movement of goods, services and other factors of production (not including capital) within the customs union	12	Detailed collective goal-setting	Some collective
Diplomatic influence and participation in intra-African affairs	12	Detailed collective goal-setting	Equal activity at both levels
Regulation and support of transportation	11	Detailed collective goal-setting	Substantial activity at collective level
Economic aid to or from other polities	10	Collective decision on policy guidelines	Substantial activity at collective level
Cultural and recreational affairs	7	Collective decision on policy guidelines	Substantial activity at collective level

Table 27 (continued)

Issue Area	Number of Issues	Stage	Locus
Continental economic, commercial, sci-entific and technical arrangements	7	Detailed collective goal-setting	Collective is dominant
Economic, commercial, scientific and technical relations with major trad-ing partners (France and the EEC)	7	Detailed collective goal-setting	Substantial activity at collective level
Regulation and support of mass media of communications	5	Detailed collective goal-setting	Collective is dominant
Fiscal policy	4	Collective problem recognition	All national
Exploitation and protection of national resources	4	Collective problem recognition	Some collective
Conflict resolution and management among members	4	Collective problem recognition	Some collective
Agricultural protection	3	Collective definition of action alternatives	Some collective
Regulation of economic competition and other government controls in prices and investments	3	Detailed collective goal-setting	Some collective
Military security	3	Discussion with no collec-tive problem definition	All national
Decolonization and human rights	2	Collective definition of action alternatives	Some collective

Table 27 (continued)

Issue Area	Number of Issues	Stage	Locus
Public health and safety and maintenance of order	2	Detailed collective goal-setting	Some collective
Access to legal-normative system	1	Collective problem recognition	All national
Social welfare policies	1	Collective problem recognition	Some collective
Cold war, arms control and disarmament	0	No discussion, no collective problem recognition	All national
Economic, commercial, scientific and technical relations with minor trading partners	0	No discussion, no collective problem recognition	All national
Political participation	0	No discussion, no collective problem recognition	All national
Organization and administration of the civil service	0	No discussion, no collective problem recognition	All national
Counter-cyclical policy	0	No discussion, no collective problem recognition	All national
Labor-management relations	0	No discussion, no collective problem recognition	All national
Balance-of-payments stability	0	No discussion, no collective problem recognition	All national
Domestic monetary policy	0	No discussion, no collective problem recognition	All national

Table 28

COMPARISON OF DECISION-MAKING STAGES IN THE UAM AND THE OCAM

Decision-Making Stage	Issue Areas: UAM					Issue Areas: OCAM				
	External Relations Functions	Political-Constitutional Functions	Social-Cultural Functions	Economic Functions	TOTAL	External Relations Functions	Political-Constitutional Functions	Social-Cultural Functions	Economic Functions	TOTAL
Discussion but no collective problem definition	1	2	0	3	6	3	2	0	4	9
Collective problem recognition	2	0	2	4	8	1	1	1	2	5
Collective definition with specific action alternatives	4	1	0	1	6	1	0	0	1	2
Collective decision on policy guidelines	4	1	1	1	7	2	0	1	0	3
Detailed collective goal-setting; implementation by national rules	0	0	0	3	3	4	1	1	5	11
Decision on policies and rules directly binding on individuals	0	0	0	0	0	0	0	0	0	0
Collective implementation and enforcement	0	0	0	0	0	0	0	0	0	0
TOTAL	11	4	3	12	30	11	4	3	12	30

Table 29

COMPARISON OF LOCI OF DECISION-MAKING IN THE UAM AND THE OCAM

Decision-Making Locus	Issue Areas: UAM					Issue Areas: OCAM				
	External Relations Functions	Political-Constitutional Functions	Social-Cultural Functions	Economic Functions	TOTAL	External Relations Functions	Political-Constitutional Functions	Social-Cultural Functions	Economic Functions	TOTAL
All activities at national level	1	2	1	6	10	3	3	0	5	11
Preponderance at national level, some collective	3	2	1	3	9	2	1	1	4	8
Substantial activity at collective but national is dominant	5	0	1	1	7	4	0	2	2	8
Roughly equal activity at collective and national levels	0	0	0	1	1	1	0	2	2	8
Collective is dominant, but substantial national	2	0	0	1	3	1	0	0	1	2
Preponderance at collective, small national role	0	0	0	0	0	0	0	0	1	1
All activity at collective level	0	0	0	0	0	0	0	0	0	0
TOTAL	11	4	3	12	30	11	4	3	12	30

Though four of the issue areas in this category reached only the stage of discussion with no collective problem definition, five reached the stage of detailed collective goal-setting. The corresponding figures for the UAM are 3 and 3 respectively. A similar shift can be seen in the external relations functions area. In the other two functions areas, the shift is very marginal.

On the other hand, Table 29 shows a slight decrease in the extent to which decision-making in the OCAM takes place at the regional level in comparison to under the UAM. This decrease seems to be true not only of the OCAM as a whole, but in each functional category as well.

These findings suggest that the shift from the UAM to the OCAM was a case of retrenchment. According to Schmitter, retrenchment means that the scope of decision-making is reduced while the level of joint decision-making in the areas remaining is increased.[9] What were the consequences of this new pattern of joint decision-making?

The Consequences of the New Pattern of Decision-Making

It is not surprising that, given the more intensive joint decision-making in the OCAM and the shift in concern from external to intra-regional issues, the consequences of decision-making increased. Compliance with regional decisions rose sharply, and there were few complaints that members were systematically violating such decisions. The increased compliance was almost certainly a result of the reduction in scope of decision-making and the concentration on issues on which meaningful decisions could be reached. Further, the strategy of killing issues by referring them for further study reduced the tendency for decisions to be made which would not be implemented.

At the same time that compliance increased, the penetrativeness of decisions increased. The reason for this lay in the nature of the decision-making areas involved as well as in the decision-making stage attained. Decisions like the one creating a common market on sugar could not help but affect large numbers of individuals--at least in the sugar-producing countries. This also held true for decisions in the area of education and research, though to a much lesser degree.

Finally, as a result of the decision to create a common market on sugar, the redistributive consequences of decisions

---

[9]See Schmitter, "A Revised Theory of Regional Integration." [IIS Reprint No. 425]

increased--but only very slightly. The redistributive nature of this decision led to significant difficulties in its implementation which were never fully resolved. In other areas, there were no redistributive consequences because no member was asked to give up anything. This was true even with respect to the creation of regional educational centers. The establishment of such centers was pushed by the state or states most directly affected, and they were presented as regional educational centers to increase the chances of securing foreign economic assistance for them.

The general picture presented by the OCAM between 1966 and 1970 was that of an organization with a narrower scope but with more intensive decision-making than the UAM had. We have already suggested that changed integrative conditions--notably the increased transactions among member states and the increased compellingness of the external economic environment for several member states--were partially responsible for these differences between the UAM and the OCAM. We shall now examine changes in the process conditions to determine their role.

Process Conditions

There is no evidence that feelings of regional identity have increased during the OCAM. The conflicts between the Democratic Republic of the Congo and its neighbors suggest that the tensions, animosities, and rivalries of the UAM period continue to be present in the OCAM. A decision was made to organize various competitions and sporting events among the general public to increase feelings of regional identity, but little resulted from this decision. Finally, there is the fact that resort has never been made to appeals based on regional identity at bargaining sessions.

Politicization also has remained at the level it attained during the UAM. The number and variety of governmental actors participating in regional conferences has increased, but private actors still have no role in these activities. A slight exception to this was the Abidjan conference of April 1969, at which the program for Africanizing management positions in the private sector was elaborated.

Bargaining style, on the other hand, seems to have improved slightly. There have been fewer threats and ultimatums and more determined efforts to arrive at agreements that will be acceptable to all. On the other hand, members have learned not to press issues where there is strong opposition. Thus the proposals for regional coordination of investment programs were never pressed by Senegal, Chad, or Mauritius. The result is a bargaining style that takes the form of splitting the difference. There was even a tentative move in the direction of package-dealing in the form of a decision to create a common market on meat. This would have compensated some members who did not benefit from the agreement on a common market for sugar. Difficulties encountered in implementing the sugar agreement terminated this effort, however. It should be borne in mind that the brighter picture in the realm of bargaining is in large part a reflection of the avoidance of controversial issues rather than an indication of increased abilities to cope with such issues.

Regional reform-mongering activities on the part of the Secretariat have increased slightly, but the strategy has remained cautious. No attempt has been made to play the role that Tevoedjre tried to play. Instead, the emphasis has been on calling the attention of members to problems that need to be solved and urging them to take action. One focus of attention has been on getting members to remove restrictions on the movement of factors of production within the union. While the success of the Secretariat has been minimal, it has succeeded in winning the respect of member states for the care with which it has carried out research activities assigned to it.

Perhaps one reason for the enhanced role of the Secretariat has been a slight increase in its resources. Thus the 1968 OCAM budget was approximately $1 million, or about 11 percent higher than the 1963 budget. Two years later, the budget was $1.2 million--an increase of 20 percent. Further, the Secretariat had a staff of only 40 above the clerical level in 1966; this increased to 48 in 1970. While these increases have been small, they have enabled the Secretariat to accomplish more than was possible under the UAM.

The states that have been active in pressing for more joint action are Senegal, Madagascar, Chad, and Upper Volta, while states like the Ivory Coast, Gabon, and Togo have frequently objected to task expansion. For the most part, Cameroun, the Democratic Republic of the Congo, and the Republic of the Congo have played a marginal role. The fact that the views of the larger members of the union have not been in harmony undoubtedly has made successful reform-mongering is more difficult.

Finally, we should note that no external actor has actively tried to encourage the process of integration. France has continued to give its aid largely in a bilateral manner while expressing general sympathy and support for the OCAM. On a few occasions, French intervention has been more forceful and direct, but these were designed mainly to prevent a split in the OCAM. Thus in January 1969, at the height of the conflict between the Democratic Republic of the Congo and her neighbors, the Secretary of State in the French Foreign Ministry, Yvon Bourges, paid a visit to Kinshasa, reportedly with a special message from de Gaulle to Mobutu, and with an official invitation for the latter to visit France. The interpretation given to this visit was that France attached particular importance to Franco-Congolese cooperation and did not want anything to jeopardize the Democratic Republic of the Congo's membership in the OCAM.[10]

Similarly, it was reportedly because of French intervention that Tombalbaye was elected President of the OCAM at Yaoundé in January 1970. Tombalbaye aspired to this office in January 1969, and apparently was very disappointed when Diori was re-elected. In January 1970, Houphouet apparently favored Mobutu for the presidency, but France was apparently concerned that this might lead to Chad's withdrawal from the OCAM. While efforts of this nature have no doubt been useful in keeping the OCAM together, they have not done much to promote integration.

Finally, with respect to the last of the process conditions--that dealing with the exportability or amount of the visible cost of integration--there might have been a slight decrease as a result of the reduction in the frequency of OCAM conferences. While the Secretariat staff and budget have increased, the increase has not been large enough to be a substantial burden on any state. In 1970, for example, the largest contribution to the OCAM budget came from the Ivory Coast: about $140,000. Rwanda made the lowest contribution: about $24,000. However, while contributions have remained low, they have also been highly visible and nonexportable.

In sum, then, two process conditions have remained the same, and the remaining three have improved slightly. The process variables which have gained slightly further confirm the shift to greater pragmatism by the OCAM. They are indicative of the fact that concrete material interests and interdependencies provide the fuel for the integration process within the OCAM.

The OCAM: A Summary

The OCAM, we have concluded, represents a case of retrenchment from the level of political integration achieved under the UAM. This retrenchment has been in part the result of a learning process. Members have learned that it is a waste of time to press issues which cannot be agreed upon or implemented. The result of this has been a decrease in the scope of decision-making. Another factor which has played a part in the decrease in scope is the decline in the perceived compellingness of the external environment. At the same time, however, the external

---

[10] Le Monde, January 28, 1969.

economic environment has become more compelling, and regional transactions have increased. The result has been an increased concentration on intra-regional economic and social-cultural affairs. Integrative conditions, previous learning, and the issue areas themselves have permitted a higher level of bargaining, coupled with increased reform-mongering activities. The impact of these factors on the rate of integration, however, has been limited by the inequalities among the member states, the differences in their previous experiences, and the divergences in the lessons they have drawn from their earlier strategies. As long as these differences endure, it is difficult to see how the OCAM can make much progress toward political integration.

Chapter 7

THE FUTURE OF THE OCAM

In the preceding chapter, we indicated the level of
political integration achieved by the OCAM up to 1970, and contrasted it with the level of political integration attained
under the UAM. The differences in the levels of integration of
the two organizations--in our judgment--are not great enough for
us to describe in terms of systemic changes. To clarify this
point, we must go beyond measures of scope, stage, and locus,
and analyze the two organizations in systemic terms.

Three possible outcomes of the integrative process have
been specified by Ernst Haas.[1] These differ from each other
according to how legitimate authority is diffused. The most
integrated of the three is the "regional state," in which political authority is concentrated at the center. The regional center
extracts and distributes resources and has legitimacy in the eyes
of individuals, groups, and subordinate structures. Next in
degree of integration achieved is the "asymmetrical regional
overlap." In this system, authority has been withdrawn from the
sub-units and distributed asymmetrically among several centers,
none of which is dominant. While the sytem as a whole has
legitimacy, there is no clear focus for this legitimacy. Finally,
there is the "regional commune":

It is an anarchoid image of a myriad of units which are so
highly differentiated in function as to be forced into interdependence. Authority is involved primarily in the sense of
having been taken away from previous centers without having
found a new single locus. Legitimacy, however it can be
imagined, would not take the form of a loyalty akin to
nationalism.[2]

It is our view that the UAM and the OCAM systems did not
attain and have not attained even the level of political integration to be found in the regional commune. The regional commune
involves at least a moderate degree of interdependence among the

---

[1]Ernst B. Haas, "The Study of Regional Integration . . .,"
pp. 30-31. [IIS Reprint No. 363]

[2]Ibid., p. 31.

units as a result of a high degree of functional differentiation
of these units. Further, though the regional commune lacks a
single center of authority, the authority lost by the member
states is assumed to be floating around within the system. None
of these conditions has prevailed with respect to the UAM or the
OCAM. Rather than highly differentiated units, there have been
units with very low levels of economic development and pluralism.
Further, the degree of interdependence among the units has been
very limited, and to the extent to which the units have lost
their authority, authority has been found mostly outside the
system.

We therefore propose a fourth possible outcome of the
integrative process, in which the degree of political integration is even less than in the regional commune. Following the
terminology used to describe traditional political systems, this
system might be called "segmental."[3] Such a system is differentiated from other systems on the basis of the degree of interdependence among the units, the nature of the authority structure,
the extent of mutual identification among the units, and the
presence of a sense of security-community.

In segmental systems, the degree of interdependence among
the units is very low and tends to be ad hoc and sporadic. This
is largely the result of (1) a dearth of communications networks,
(2) the simple nature of the economies of the units, which tends
to make them self-sufficient, and (3) a similarity in the goods
produced by the units, which limits the potential for economic
transactions among them. The strongest link among units in this
type of system takes the form of joint action against external
threats, but only when the threats are perceived as salient by
all members.

The loss of authority by the sub-units within a segmental
system is virtually nil. What exists is a commitment to joint
discussion of a broad range of issue areas. Such discussions,
it is hoped, will lead to similar policies and joint action.
However, no unit is expected to sacrifice significant interests.
Thus, bargaining style invariably takes the form of seeking the
lowest common denominator, predicated on common perceptions,
common interests, and equal rewards. Occasionally, decision-
making based on splitting the difference may take place, where
the stakes involved are minimal and there is a desire to avoid
the stigma of continuous opposition to joint policy-making. Only

---

[3]For a description of this type of system in the context of
traditional political systems, see David E. Apter, The Politics
of Modernization (Chicago: University of Chicago Press, 1965),
pp. 89-90.

when the system as a whole is threatened does decision-making based on advancing the common interest occur.

Mutual identification among the units is very weak and diffuse, and is largely a result of a perceived common ancestry. However, the bilateral links between each unit and the "ancestor" are far more important than the multilateral links among the units resulting from the common ancestor. The members are conscious of important differences among themselves, but they also perceive that they constitute a group vis-à-vis third parties. This does not prevent individual members from establishing profitable ties with third parties, even when they are detrimental to other members of the system. However, such links with third parties are not maintained if they pose major threats to the system or one of the units.

The main difference between a segmental system and the "essential nature" of international systems is the presence of a security-community in the former and its absence in the latter. There is a security-community in a segmental system in the sense that war is not an instrument of state policy in the interaction among the units. This does not mean that violent conflicts do not occur, but when they occur, they are the result of temperamental outbursts. Such conflicts are of a short duration, involve low levels of violence, and take place mostly among citizens (with the active or passive encouragement of their respective governments) rather than among armed forces. Thus the destruction that results from these conflicts is minimal.

This model of a segmental system closely approximates the UAM and the OCAM systems. Interdependence among the units has been very limited, and has been induced primarily by a compelling external environment. In neither case has the level of commitment to join policy-making been high. Rather, the only agreement has been to try to seek agreement, with no member being required to make major sacrifices. The sense of mutual identification among the members has been largely a result of their having been French colonies, and bilateral links with France have been far more important than links with each other. On the other hand, there has been a consciousness of being Francophones, and thus different from the Anglophones. Finally, while several conflicts have occurred among the members, they have mostly taken the form of anomic violence rather than being expressions of state policy.

Alternative Futures

Of the several alternative futures open to the segmental system, one is more of the same, with very marginal and incremental changes which might result in system transformation over a long period of time. The OCAM may very well follow this alternative. Individual units might withdraw from the organization, but the union would persist. The units most likely to withdraw are those that are marginal with respect to the degree of mutual identification. Thus the Democratic Republic of the Congo, which has a different "ancestor" from the other member states, withdrew from the OCAM in April 1972. Mobutu's withdrawal from the OCAM seems to have been motivated largely by conflicts with France over convertibility between the franc and the zaïre, plus his resentment of the leadership position of Houphouet in the OCAM. The Democratic Republic of the Congo, it will be recalled, joined the OCAM under the aegis of Tshombe, who was seeking legitimacy and acceptance in the African diplomatic scene. Mobutu has less of a stigma attached to him, because of his earlier role in the internal conflicts in the Democratic Republic of the Congo, and thus did not need the OCAM as much to ensure his acceptance.

Further, Mobutu has tried to identify himself with the main currents of African nationalism. As early as 1969, he resurrected the name of Lumumba, changed the evaluation of Lumumba to that of a national hero, and tried to wear Lumumba's mantle. More recently, he has changed names of places and asked all citizens to change their names from Western to African names. Thus the Democratic Republic of the Congo is now called the Republic of Zaïre, and Mobutu has added the names Sese Seko to his former name. All this has increased his status and prestige both within his country and in Africa as a whole. In fact, Mobutu felt strong enough to bypass a chance of becoming President of the OCAM in January 1969 and let the office go to Tombalbaye, even though he had the support of Houphouet for the position.

Mobutu's increased prestige, combined with indications of higher economic growth rates in the last two years, has led him to desire a leadership role in Africa. Already in 1968, he attempted to establish a position of preeminence in Equatorial Africa by breaking up the UDEAC and establishing close ties with Chad and Central Africa within the framework of the Union des Etats de l'Afrique Centrale. While he succeeded with Chad, he failed with respect to the Central African Republic. At the present time, he is attempting to establish his leadership over Rwanda and Burundi.

Within the OCAM, Mobutu had been relegated to a secondary position and had never been included in the councils of the four top leaders. This was a position it was hard for him to tolerate--not only for the reasons mentioned above, but also because his not having been a part of the pre-independence movements in French West Africa meant that he had fewer obligations and no feelings of deference to Houphouet. Mobutu would never refer to Houphouet as "notre chef à nous," as Yameogo once did. Yet being a member of the OCAM entailed acceptance of Houphouet as at least the "primus inter pares." Given this situation, and given the lack of any concrete gains from membership in the OCAM, the Democratic Republic of the Congo withdrew. Mobutu's present position is that bilateral relations among African states are more important than multilateral ones.

Another member that might withdraw is Cameroun. Cameroun, as we observed in Chapter 1, was never as attached to France as the other UAM members. Further, the disputes over the admission of the Democratic Republic of the Congo into the OCAM indicated that Cameroun's continued membership in the OCAM is far from automatic. Recently, there have been rumors that Ahidjo is quite dissatisfied with the OCAM because of Houphouet's dominant position, as well as disagreements over Houphouet's call for a dialogue with South Africa. Thus Cameroun's departure from the OCAM would hardly be surprising.

Another type of member that might withdraw from the OCAM is one that has experienced major domestic economic and/or political changes. At the present, this means the Republic of the Congo. The continued membership of the Republic of the Congo has always been a puzzle. It seems that it decided to remain in the OCAM in 1966 because the common market on sugar was in the process of being elaborated. With all signs pointing to the collapse of this scheme, the Republic of the Congo may very well leave the OCAM. Except for Gabon, the Equatorial African states are also unhappy with the OCAM because of the dominant position of the West African states.

In the final analysis, the decision to stay or leave the OCAM will be dependent largely on the effect of such a decision on bilateral relations with France. To the extent to which France continues to find it in her interest to maintain the OCAM, departures will be few. The foreign policies of other states will also influence developments in the OCAM. Since the end of the Nigerian civil war, Nigeria has apparently been courting Niger and Dahomey. Given its size, Nigeria might be able to detach these countries from the OCAM in the absence of countervailing pressures from France. The question, then, is the degree of leadership that Nigeria may aspire to and the extent to which it is willing to expend its resources to achieve its aims. The same holds true for the Democratic Republic of the Congo, which has been courting Rwanda and Chad.[4]

---

[4]A few weeks before the OCAM heads of state conference was to be held at Lomé in January 1970, Tombalbaye resigned as President of the OCAM because of his dissatisfaction with developments in the OCAM. He attributed the shortcomings of the OCAM to the fact

These predictions of departures from the OCAM are predicated on the fact that dissatisfaction with the OCAM is widespread. There has not been as much coordination of economic activities as some members had hoped for, and there has been practically no gain, particularly of an economic nature, from the OCAM. The only exception to this is the countries which have succeeded in securing external aid for creating new educational institutions as a result of their presenting these institutions as regional centers. The gains here, however, have been quite marginal. It is doubtful that even the Ivory Coast is fully satisfied with the OCAM, given the deemphasis of foreign policy coordination and the lack of substantial support within the OCAM for Houphouet's policy of dialogue with South Africa. Thus the availability of external alternatives may easily entice members away from the OCAM.

Irrespective of which members leave or stay, decision-making patterns will remain the same. Tasks will be added and subtracted depending on the combination of interests prevailing at any particular time. But there will be nothing cumulative in this. Already, with the withdrawal of Senegal from the sugar agreement, the whole scheme seems about to collapse. Air Afrique, which members had considered to be their major achievement, also seems to be on the verge of collapse because of the financial difficulties it is experiencing due to the failure of member states to pay their debts to the company, and because of claims that Air Afrique provides unequal services for members. It is for these reasons that both Chad and Cameroun have withdrawn from Air Afrique.

Another path to disintegration of the OCAM might be de facto if not de jure nationalization (such as the new veterinary center at Dakar), as individual members create national centers in important areas. Such disintegration would be slow and gradual, however, and would occur at the same time that common services and policy coordination are developing in other areas. Thus integration and disintegration in different sectors might cancel each other out.

A final factor likely to affect the future of the OCAM would be a decrease in the need for membership in the OCAM as a

---

that positions in the Secretariat were not equally distributed among members. This, he said, meant that "since it is not possible to cut the umbilical cord which links them [the members of the Secretariat] with their respective states, projects advance and are completed more or less quickly depending on whether it concerns this or that region" (see Jeune Afrique, May 6, 1972, p. 15).

means of enhancing domestic legitimacy. For the military leaders who came to power in 1965 and 1966, the main motivation for OCAM membership was to increase their domestic legitimacy. Over time, this need may disappear. Already, there are signs that this is occurring in some situations. Thus Colonel Etienne Eyadéma, who led the second Togo coup in January 1967 to the intense displeasure of France and the Ivory Coast, was sufficiently secure domestically by 1972 to reject the presidency of the OCAM. It might be added that the OCAM conference in January 1972 had great difficulty finding someone who would accept the presidency. After Eyadéma's rejection of the offer, the presidency was offered to Ahidjo, who also rejected it. Finally, Senghor was persuaded to accept it. Thus there has been a substantial devaluation in the prestige emanating from the OCAM, and this will undoubtedly have negative consequences for political integration.

The picture we have sketched above of one of the possible future alternatives of the OCAM is one of slow disintegration. The policies of external actors play a crucial role in this process. It is possible, however, that the policies of external actors might be of such a nature as to enhance political integration. Thus Nigeria may decide to play a leadership role in Africa for which purpose it may desire to dismantle the OCAM. France may conclude that it is in her vital interests that the OCAM survive, and may therefore exert greater leverage for regional political integration. There may very well be a French form of the Marshall Plan for the OCAM states; this would undoubtedly have major positive consequences for political integration.

In much of the discussion above, we have assumed that domestic socio-economic changes will not occur or will occur to only a very limited degree. This is a very questionable assumption, at least for OCAM members like the Ivory Coast and Cameroun. Further, even very small socio-economic changes will have a long-range impact on developments within the OCAM. We must therefore examine the possible socio-economic changes and their consequences for regional political integration.

A very likely possibility is that countries like the Ivory Coast and Cameroun will continue to grow at a rapid pace. In particular, they will reach higher levels of industrial development. It may therefore become important for them to gain access to the markets of the less industrial OCAM members. Thus a form of customs union for several or all products might be created. Given the inequalities among the member states, the results of such a customs union would be unbalanced trade and rates of industrial growth. The less industrial members are very likely, therefore, to press for coordinated industrial

200

development. Experiences in East Africa and Central America suggest that agreement on a regional industrial development program would be very difficult--if not impossible--to negotiate and implement. Failure in this area would most likely lead to a spill-back from the customs union, unless an external actor stepped in and provided the necessary resources to correct the imbalances in the gains from integration.

Creation of a customs union, combined with even small rises in the levels of economic development, might very well result in increased transactions among the member states. The level of this interdependence might be sufficiently high for the losses entailed in a complete breakdown in the arrangement to be too costly for it to be permitted. This seems to have occurred in East Africa and may very well occur in the OCAM. The end result in these circumstances is likely to be a hybrid organization that is part free trade, part customs union, and part economic union taking the form of the harmonization of some economic policies. Such an organization would closely approximate the regional commune. For this alternative to occur, external alternatives must be nonexistent, or members would be tempted to pursue these external alternatives at the cost of the breakup of the union. This was what happened in the UDEAC in 1968 when Chad (Central Africa initially made a move in the same direction) decided to withdraw from the UDEAC and pursue the alternative offered by the Democratic Republic of the Congo.

In sum, the prospects for regional political integration in the OCAM are not very good. The most likely outcome is a continuation of the segmental system. Domestic political changes are likely to increase the domestic legitimacy of member states and thus reduce the attraction of membership in the OCAM. As domestic political leaders change, elite ties will weaken. Further, new political leaders may be less attached to France (even if their dependence on France remains high), and thus the degree of mutual identification in the OCAM may decrease. Domestic economic changes, while they may initially increase the level of political integration, will in the long run lead to disputes over the distribution of rewards, and the end result will be a decrease in the level of political integration. Finally, actors may well emerge in Africa that provide alternatives to continued membership in the OCAM. Only a determined effort on the part of France or some other external actor will succeed in increasing the degree of political integration in the OCAM to any substantial extent. Such an effort may well usher in an asymmetrical regional overlap. Whether such an effort will be made is an open question.

BIBLIOGRAPHY

BOOKS

Africanus, Leo. L'Afrique noire devant l'indépendance. Paris: Librairie Plan, 1958.

Ambassade de France, Service de Presse et d'Information. French Africa: A Decade of Progress, 1948-1958. New York, 1958.

Apter, David E. The Politics of Modernization. Chicago: University of Chicago Press, 1965.

Berg, Elliot J. "The Economic Basis of Political Choice in French West Africa," American Political Science Review, Vol. LIV, No. 2 (June 1960).

_____, and Butler, Jeffrey. "Trade Unions" in James S. Coleman and Carl G. Rosberg, Jr., eds., Political Parties and National Integration in Tropical Africa. Berkeley: University of Callifornia Press, 1964.

Buell, Raymond D. The Native Problem in Africa. New York: Macmillan, 1928.

Coquery-Vidrovitch, Catherine. "French Colonization in Africa to 1920: Administration and Economic Development" in L.H. Gann and Peter Duignan, eds., Colonialism in Africa, 1870-1960. Cambridge: Cambridge University Press, 1969.

Crowder, Michael. "Independence as a Goal in French West African Politics: 1944-60" in William H. Lewis, ed., French-Speaking Africa: The Search for Identity. New York: Walker and Company, 1965. [IIS Reprint Series, No. 205]

Dahomey, Ministère de l'Economie et du Plan. Annuaire Statistique du Dahomey, Vol. 3.

De Lusignan, Guy. French-Speaking Africa Since Independence. New York: Frederick A. Praeger, 1969.

Deutsch, Karl W. et al. Political Community and the North Atlantic Area. Princeton: Princeton University Press, 1957.

Dévezé, Michèle. La France d'outre-mer, de l'empire colonial à l'Union Francaise 1938-1948. Paris: Hachette, 1948.

La Documentation Francaise. Documentation UAM. Paris: Imprimerie d'Haussy et Cie., 1963.

Dumon, Frédéric. La Communauté Franco-Afro-Malgache. Brussels: Université Libre de Bruxelles, 1960.

203

BIBLIOGRAPHY

Etzioni, Amitai. "European Unification: A Strategy of Change" in International Political Communities. New York: Doubleday, 1966.

Foltz, William J. From French West Africa to the Mali Federation. New Haven: Yale University Press, 1965.

France, Ministère de la Coopération. Cinq ans de fonds d'aide et de coopération.

_____. Perspectives de population dans les pays africains et malgache d'expression francaise.

_____. Planification en Afrique, Vols. IV and V, January 1963.

_____. République Centrafricaine: Economie et plan de développement, July 1969.

_____. République du Gabon: Economie et plan de développement, March 1962.

_____. République islamique de Mauritanie: Economie et plan de développement, December 1963.

France, Secrétariat-Général du Comité Monétaire de la Zone Franc. La Zone Franc en 1957, . . . 1959, . . . 1960, . . . 1962, . . . 1964.

France, Service des Statistiques d'Outre-Mer. Outre-Mer, 1958.

Haas, Ernst B. "International Integration: The European and the Universal Process" in International Political Communities. New York: Doubleday, 1966.

_____. "The Study of Regional Integration: Reflections on the Joy and Anguish of Pretheorizing" in Lindberg and Scheingold, eds. See Lindberg and Scheingold. [IIS Reprint Series, No. 363]

_____, and Schmitter, Philippe C. "Economics and Differential Patterns of Political Integration: Projections about Unity in Latin America" in International Political Communities. New York: Doubleday, 1966.

Hailey, Baron William Malcolm [Lord Hailey]. An African Survey. London: Oxford University Press, 1957.

Hayter, Teresa. French Aid. London: The Overseas Development Institute, Ltd., 1966.

Huntington, Samuel. Political Order in Changing Societies. New Haven: Yale University Press, 1968.

International Monetary Fund. Surveys of African Economies, Vols. 1 and 3. Washington, D.C., 1968 and 1970.

International Political Communities. New York: Doubleday, 1966.

Jalloh, Abdul A. "The Politics and Economics of Regional Political Integration in Equatorial Africa." Unpublished dissertation, University of California, Berkeley, 1969.

BIBLIOGRAPHY

Leduc, Michel. Les Institutions monétaires africaines: Pays francophones. Paris: Editions A. Pedone, 1965.

Le Vine, Victor T. "The Coups in Upper Volta, Dahomey, and the Central African Republic" in Robert I. Rotberg and Ali A. Mazrui, eds., Protest and Power in Black Africa. New York: Oxford University Press, 1970.

Ligot, Maurice. Les Accords de Coopération entre la France et les états africains et malgache d'expression francaise. Paris: La Documentation Francaise, 1964.

Lindberg, Leon N. "Political Integration as a Multidimensional Phenomenon Requiring Multivariate Measurement" in Lindberg and Scheingold, eds. See Lindberg and Scheingold.

Lindberg, Leon N., and Scheingold, Stuart A., eds. Regional Integration: Theory and Research. Cambridge: Harvard University Press, 1971.

Malgache, Ministère des Finances et du Commerce. Inventaire Socio-Economique de Madagascar, 1960-1965.

Morgenthau, Ruth Schachter. Political Parties in French-Speaking West Africa. Oxford: Oxford University Press, 1964.

Mortimer, Edward. France and the Africans, 1944-1960. New York: Walker and Company, 1969.

Nye, Joseph S. "Central American Regional Integration" in J.S. Nye, ed., International Regionalism: Readings. Boston: Little, Brown and Co., 1968.

OCAM, Secrétariat-Général. Annuaire OCAM, 1968.

_____. Conseil des Ministres de l'Organisation Commune Africaine et Malgache: Tananarive, 12-18 Janvier 1966.

_____. Textes constitutifs de l'Organisation Commune Africaine et Malgache: Tananarive, 28 Juin 1966.

Rivkin, Arnold. The African Presence in World Affairs: National Development and Its Role in Foreign Policy. New York: The Free Press of Glencoe, 1963.

Schmitter, Philippe C. "A Revised Theory of Regional Integration" in Lindberg and Scheingold, eds. See Lindberg and Scheingold. [IIS Reprint Series, No. 425]

Sénégal. Comptes Economiques: Années 1959-1960-1961-1962, 1963.

Sousatte, René Paul. L'AEF, berceau de l'Union Francaise. Paris: Chez Brodard et Taupin, 1953.

Tevoedjre, Albert. Pan-Africanism in Action. Cambridge: Harvard Center for International Affairs, Occasional Papers in International Affairs, No. 11, November 1965.

Thompson, Virginia. "The Ivory Coast" in Gwendolen Carter, ed.,

BIBLIOGRAPHY

African One-Party Systems. Ithaca: Cornell University Press, 1962.

_____. West Africa's Council of the Entente. Ithaca: Cornell University Press, 1972.

_____, and Adloff, Richard. The Emerging States of French Equatorial Africa. Stanford: Stanford University Press, 1960.

_____, and _____. French West Africa. Stanford: Stanford University Press, 1958.

Thompson, W. Scott. Ghana's Foreign Policy, 1957-1966. Princeton: Princeton University Press, 1969.

Union Africaine et Malgache, Secrétariat-Général. Compte-rendu de la Conférence de Bangui: 25-27 Mars 1962.

_____. Compte-rendu des travaux de la Conférence de Cotonou: 27-30 Juillet 1963.

_____. Compte-rendu des travaux de la Conférence de Dakar: 6-10 Mars 1964.

_____. Compte-rendu des travaux de la Conférence de Libreville: 10-13 Septembre 1962.

United Nations, Department of Economic and Social Affairs. Economic Developments in Africa, 1956-1957 [CE/3117/5T/ECA/56].

United Nations, Economic Commission for Africa. African Economic Indicators, 1968.

_____. Economic Cooperation and Integration in Africa: Three Case Studies [ST/ECA/109]. New York, 1969.

_____. Economic Survey of Africa [E/CN/14/370], Vol. 1. 1966.

_____. Statistical Yearbook, 1970, Part 1.

_____. Summaries of Economic Data: Possible Economic Outturn for 1971 for 43 Countries in Africa. November 1971.

_____. A Survey of Economic Conditions in Africa, 1969 [E/CN.14/480/Rev. 1], Part 1.

Wallerstein, Immanuel. Africa: The Politics of Unity. New York: Random House, 1967.

Zartman, I. William. International Relations in the New Africa. Englewood Cliffs: Prentice-Hall, 1966.

Ziéglé, Henri. Afrique Equatoriale Francaise. Paris: Editions Berger-Levrault, 1952.

Zolberg, Aristide R. One-Party Government in the Ivory Coast. Princeton: Princeton University Press, 1969.

PERIODICALS AND NEWSLETTERS

A.F.P. Bulletin d'Afrique, various issues.

_____. Spécial Outre-Mer, January 27, 1961, and April 12, 1961.

Afrique Contemporaine (Paris), No. 35, January-February 1968.

Afrique Nouvelle (Dakar), December 21, 1960, and July 15, 1965.

Ahidjo, Ahmadou. "Le But ultime de la Conférence de Yaoundé," Communauté France-Eurafrique, April 1961.

Bulletin de l'Afrique Noire (Paris). Memento Statistique de l'Economie Africaine, No. 413 (1966), No. 509 (1968), and No. 557 (1969).

_____. Memento de l'Industrie Africaine, 1966, Numéro Spécial, No. 413.

Combat (Paris), various issues.

D'Arboussier, Gabriel. "L'UAM," Revue Politique et Parlementaire, May 1962.

Decraene, Philippe. "La Conférence de l'OCAM a confirmé l'influence politique du Conseil de l'Entente au sein de l'Afrique francophone," Le Monde, January 25, 1968.

La Documentation Francaise (Paris), January 19, 1961, and March 18, 1965.

L'Effort Camerounais, September 29, 1965.

Le Figaro (Paris), various issues.

France, Bureau Central de la Statistique et de la Mécanographie. Etudes Economiques (Brazzaville), No. 7, 1958.

Hodgkin, Thomas, and Schachter, Ruth. "French-Speaking West Africa in Transition," International Conciliation, No. 528 (May 1960).

L'Horoya (Conakry), June 2, 1965.

Houphouet-Boigny, Félix. "Avant cinq ans," Afrique Nouvelle, March 22, 1961.

_____. "Une Politique d'unité, d'essor et de paix," Communautés et Continents, April-June 1962.

Jeune Afrique (Paris), May 6, 1972.

Marchés Tropicaux et Méditerranéens, June 13, 1964.

Le Monde (Paris), various issues.

Nye, Joseph S. "Comparative Regional Integration: Concept and Measurement," International Organization, Vol. XX, No. 4 (Autumn 1968).

Organisation Commune Africaine et Malgache, Secrétariat-Général. <u>Bulletin Statistique de l'OCAM</u>, No. 7 (September 1967), No. 8 (March 1968), and No. 15 (June 1970).

Peureux, G. "La Création de l'Union Africaine et Malgache et les conférences des chefs d'état d'expression francaise," <u>Revue Juridique et Politique d'Outre-Mer</u>, No. 4 (October-December 1961).

Robinson, Kenneth E. "The Public Law of Overseas France since the War," <u>Journal of Comparative Legislation</u>, Vol. XXXII (1950).

Terray, Emmanuel. "Les Révolutions congolaise et dahoméenne," <u>Revue Francaise de Science Politique</u>, October 1964.

"L'Union Africaine et Malgache: Une Année d'existence," <u>Revue Juridique et Politique d'Outre-Mer</u>, No. 3 (July-September 1962).